WHEN *TISH* HAPPENS

WHEN

Frank
DAVEY

The Unlikely Story of

Canada's "Most Influential

Literary Magazine"

TISH

HAPPENS

ECW PRESS

TORONTO

Copyright © Frank Davey, 2011

Published by ECW Press
2120 Queen Street East, Suite 200, Toronto, Ontario, Canada M4E 1E2
416.694.3348 / info@ecwpress.com

LIBRARY AND ARCHIVES CANADA CATALOGUING IN PUBLICATION

Davey, Frank, 1940–
When Tish happens : the unlikely story of Canada's
most influential literary magazine / Frank Davey.

ISBN 978-1-55022-958-5
ALSO ISSUED AS 978-1-55490-958-2 (PDF); 978-1-55490-944-5 (EPUB)

1. Tish. 2. Canadian poetry (English)—20th
century—History and criticism. 1. Title.

PS8141.D38 2011   C811'.5409   C2010-906831-9

Cover and text design: Gordon Robertson
Cover photo: © Pearl Bowering

Printing: Transcontinental   1   2   3   4   5

The publication of *When Tish Happens* has been generously supported by the Canada Council
for the Arts which last year invested $20.1 million in writing and publishing throughout Canada,
by the Ontario Arts Council, by the Government of Ontario through Ontario Book Publishing
Tax Credit, by the OMDC Book Fund, an initiative of the Ontario Media Development
Corporation, and by the Government of Canada through the Canada Book Fund.

PRINTED AND BOUND IN CANADA

Mixed Sources
Product group from well-managed forests,
controlled sources and recycled wood or fiber
www.fsc.org Cert no. SW-COC-000952
© 1996 Forest Stewardship Council

FSC

ECW PRESS
ecwpress.com

for Daphne, Glady, George, Fred, Jamie, Lionel

and my other Tish companions

Acknowledgements

I am especially grateful to Maria Hindmarch, Lionel Kearns and Jamie Reid for their suggestions and reminders, and to Maria, Daphne Marlatt, George Bowering and Fred Wah for their permission to quote from their unpublished letters. I also thank Eric Swanick, Head of the Special Collections and Rare Books department of Simon Fraser University's W.A.C. Bennett Library, for helping me find my way through the various fonds of its Contemporary Literature Collection, the Ontario Arts Council for enabling me to travel to those textual remains of my distant past, and Jack David for urging me to go. All unpublished letters cited here are from the SFU Contemporary Literature Collection.

Somewhat more gratitude follows. FD

eventually all other stories
will appear untrue beside this one.

bpNichol

CONTENTS

WHEN *TISH* HAPPENS

PART 1 THE TIGER ON THE MOUNTAIN

World War 2, Postwar, Pre-Tish (1942–1957)

1942 . . .

There's a broad low mountain just south of Abbotsford in British Columbia that in winter displays on its north side a snowfall pattern shaped like a prowling animal. Only people in Abbotsford can see it. Some think it might be a lamb, and others that it is a tiger. Some even call the mountain "Tiger Mountain," although it is in the U.S., and mapped there as Sumas Mountain, just northwest of a Black Mountain, and a bit more northwest of Mount Baker, which, at 11,340 feet, towers its white volcanic glamour over Abbotsford and much of the surrounding Fraser Valley. In 1942 I have seen Mount Baker and seen the tiger but I have never thought about the U.S. or maps or about the real names of mountains . . .

December 1942 . . .

A war is going on somewhere to the east, and also somewhere to the west. My bath toys are all small grey plastic warships. For Christmas I have got a colouring book. It is blue, with a close-up of the prow of a battleship on its cover. Each of its 100 pages has the outline of a different tank, jeep, ship or airplane. Sometimes the guns are firing. When I start colouring, I imagine I am helping to win the wars.

May 1943 . . .

Each Friday night on his walk home from work my father buys a "brick" of Palm ice cream and a copy of the *Star Weekly*. It's the weekly magazine of the *Toronto Star*, although I don't know this. I haven't yet heard of Toronto. Each issue of the *Star Weekly* contains a full novel on tabloid newsprint, which my maternal grandmother, who lives with us, reads and saves to mail, once the war is over, to one of her sisters in England. If it's a Zane Grey or Erle Stanley Gardner, my father will read it too. My grandma is the most educated person in the house, although as far as I know she owns only two books—a Victorian paperback about a young woman who drowned herself after losing her boyfriend, and a Victorian digest of the geography and economies of the English counties—the book she had to study in England when training around 1898 to become a telegrapher. She is teaching me the Morse code.

July 1943 . . .

My dad is growing potatoes on the road allowance between our lawn and the gravel road we live on. "Netted Gems" he calls them. It took him a whole day back in the spring to dig and level the dirt. Now he has a rake and is "hilling" the potato plants. If there is no blight we will have enough potatoes for the winter, he says. Blight is when the leaves turn white and the potatoes are no good. He is also growing onions and carrots and beets in our back garden because they too will keep all winter. We need them because of the war, because food is scarce and some things like butter are rationed. The more things we grow the more food there will be for our soldiers and our friends in England, my grandma says. To the south the snow has melted and the tiger or lamb has disappeared.

October 1943 . . .

A big console radio stands in the living room just outside the doors to my bedroom and my parents' bedroom. In the evenings my father sometimes listens to "Gangbusters" or "The Whistler" and the sirens and gunshots keep me from sleeping. In the morning after my father leaves for work, my mother turns it on so she can lie in bed and listen to "Breakfast with Brown" on CJOR. I go and lie on the bed beside her and wait for her to get up and make a real breakfast. "Brown" is Billy Brown, who has an English accent and plays mostly English music, although I don't know for sure that there are other kinds of music. He begins and ends the show with a rooster crowing—"Reddy Rooster." He plays a lot of Harry Lauder and George Formby, and Gracie Fields and Vera Lynn. "Knees up Mother Brown," George Formby sings to his ukulele, but about a different Brown family I think. My mother's old name was Brown. There are a lot of Browns. Gracie Fields sings "The Lord's Prayer" a whole lot, and when she does, my grandma Brown comes down from upstairs to listen. My mother enrols me in the Billy Brown Birthday Club. I get a membership card with my name and a large red rooster on it.

In the evenings my grandma has been teaching me prayers. At bedtime she sits me on her knee on the sofa to recite them. The first one was easy: "God bless mommy and daddy, grandmas and grandpas, uncle and aunts, and all kind friends, and make me a good boy, amen." It seems like an okay thing that they be blessed. And if God wants to make me a good boy, maybe it'll be partly his fault when I'm not. The second was also pretty easy, because it rhymed— "Gentle Jesus meek and mild, look upon a little child, pity my simplicity, suffer me to come to thee, amen." I think I know what it means and I don't like it. But I want to please my grandma. Sometimes she says she wishes she'd been "taken" when my grandpa died. Now we are working on the one Gracie sings, the Lord's Prayer. Why isn't God's will already done on earth, I wonder. Maybe he can't make me good. But grandma doesn't know and just shakes her head.

August 1944 . . .

My mother and father are taking me for a week-long vacation by the seaside in White Rock. We take suitcases onto a bus that takes us to Langley where we transfer to a smaller bus that goes to White

Rock. It is crowded, and my dad has to sit beside the driver on the box that covers the engine. Mr. Marshall who owns the White Rock Hotel comes in his little Austin 7 to meet us. My mother hangs a grey flannel blanket on string across the hotel room between my bed and theirs. We play some slot machines that are in a pavilion at the end of the pier. They take nickels—then a little crane inside sometimes picks up prizes or coins and dumps them down a chute for us. There are a lot of navy sailors. I catch small

My father and I at White Rock, 1944.

fish—my dad calls them "shiners"—off the end of the pier. I ride floating logs in the water. There are a lot of cars in White Rock parked behind buildings with sacks wrapped around their tires. I don't understand why. The hotel dining room serves wonderful slices of deep raspberry pie. On some days we walk down the railway tracks through Peace Arch Park to Blaine in the U.S. We have to walk carefully across a long trestle that has wide gaps between its boards. My dad listens for approaching trains. There's no railing on the edges. In Blaine there are more sailors, ones who wear the same blue uniform except it has a star in both corners of the back collar. They put the stars there so people can know they aren't Canadians.

September 1944 . . .

I am lying on my back on the front lawn watching squadrons of Liberators practise flying in close formation at various altitudes overhead. They are from our new airport, and are practising for bombing runs, my father says over a place in Germany called the Ruhr. Or over Berlin or Leipzig or Dresden. I can tell them apart— the graceful Liberators, the hunched-together twin-tail Lancasters and the smaller two-engine Mitchells. I have a little grey model of a Lancaster and also one of a Wellington. One afternoon in the 1980s on my way to Grainau to give a paper about *Tish* and *SwiftCurrent*, I sat down in the sunlight for lunch in Augsburg and complimented the waiter on the handsome triangular "square" we were facing. "Yes," he said. "We call it RAF Square. But it's okay." He smiled. "There was a big Messerschmidt factory nearby." "In Haunstetten?" I said, "Six km?" "Close enough," he said. Oops, I don't know about this in 1944, do I. I'm supposed to hate Germans. I'm supposed to think like a little kid. Sorry.

December 1944 . . .

It's almost Christmas. The tiger shines brightly in the snow on the mountain. I'm going to Vancouver with my mother and grandma on the interurban tram to see Santa. The tram is like a wooden streetcar only bigger and heavier and made up of two or three cars. It has woven straw seats that are worn on the edges and scratch the backs of my knees. The tram cars are thirty years old my father tells me. He gets free tickets for us because he works for the BC Electric Company which operates them. The tram takes us through Matsqui Prairie and Langley Prairie and under the amazing arch of the Pattullo Bridge across the Fraser River to the Carrall Street station in Vancouver—a two-hour trip.

I was born here in Vancouver, even though I have always lived in Abbotsford. My father was born in Vancouver too, in 1910. My mother arrived in Vancouver in 1913 with her mother and father, after crossing the Atlantic on one of the last trips of the *Empress of Ireland*. She was four years old. They met in Vancouver in the early 1920s, and married there in 1938. They wanted to marry earlier but couldn't because of the Depression. In 1939 my father was transferred by the BC Electric to Abbotsford. My mother didn't want to come. She came, but then insisted on having me in Vancouver with her old family doctor, Dr. Gillespie. They had bought a house in Vancouver when they got married. They have kept it, and rented it, even though they have bought another one in Abbotsford, in case they can go back. Houses are still cheap for people with jobs, because of the Depression. They have a bank account in Abbotsford, but also ones in Vancouver, in case they go back. Every few months my mother and grandma take me on the tram to visit these banks—carved stone buildings on Hastings Street and Granville Street that are larger than churches, and have lots of orange and brass lamps—to have their bank books "made up," they say.

I like the tram because it runs through fields and woods but stops every few minutes at crossroads to pick up passengers and there are new things outside the window. In Vancouver there are a lot of streetcars, some made of wood and some of metal. Their trolleys make huge sparks as they rumble around corners. My mother and grandma shop for Christmas things at Woodward's, which is near the station, and then go farther along Hastings to Spencer's for dresses and gloves. My father won't let us shop at Army and Navy, which is beside Woodward's, because it's blacklisted by his union. Each time we pass it I worry because there are bad people inside.

At Christmas Spencer's has a big window with people-sized toys that move. We go inside to an elevator. The young woman who runs it calls out "Going up!" We join a long lineup to see Santa. We go for lunch in Spencer's fifth-floor restaurant. There is a purple rope across the entrance that makes us wait. We get a table where I can see the boats in the harbour. We stop at Woolworth's and buy two goldfish which my mother suggests we call Jack & Jill. In the tram back to Abbotsford they sit in a carton beside me on the wooden windowsill.

June 1945 . . .

My mother thinks that one of the Liberators has crashed. In the mountains. That's what people are saying, she says. Maybe ten or eleven men. I bet they'll never find them, she says. The bears or the mountain lions will get them. I look out the window and wonder whether it crashed on Tiger Mountain.

August 1945 . . .

The war has ended. Mr. Truman has dropped big bombs on Hiroshima and Nagasaki. "I was in Nagasaki," my father says, "in

My father sails for Nagasaki, 1924.

1924." It was his first job, after he left school—he was a messenger boy on Canadian Pacific's *Empress of Asia*. Abbotsford however looks unchanged. It is still about three blocks square. But my mother has started sending me downtown alone to get small things that she needs. Some of the sidewalks are made of wood, like the trams are. Most people walk to work or to shop. You buy your vegetables and canned goods from the grocers at Modern Market, who pass the things you ask for from behind long wooden counters. You buy your eggs at the egg candlery in the alley behind the Glacier Café, your meat at the "Cold Storage" building where farmers and hunters bring dead animals to be cut up, frozen and stored. Many of these arrive on horse-drawn wagons. I watch out for both cars and parked wagons, because often the unattended horses can lurch— onto the sidewalk.

Besides the farms, the main places where people work are the Clayburn brick plant, the Canadian customs offices at the U.S. border two miles south, and the BC Electric Co., which runs both the electricity supply and the electric tram line from Vancouver through Abbotsford to Chilliwack, twenty miles east. Children close to my age often walk along the side streets leading single cows to nearby farms to be bred. I have to watch out for cows. There are farms on three sides of the block our house is in—Tuck's farm behind us, Aish's to the east and Conway's to the west. Our next-door neighbour is Reverend Tench, of the United Church—he has two lots and keeps twenty or thirty chickens under the fruit trees on the one beside us. A small pickup truck from Conway's farm delivers bottled milk, unpasteurized, every morning. My father is a "ground man" on the BC Electric's local line maintenance crew. That is better than being a "digger" but not as good as being a driver or lineman or a farmer.

Now the war is over, my mother says, we don't need to close your blackout curtain. It's a black flannel drape that my mother has sewed so that it runs on a drawstring across my window close to the glass. But at night the setting sun shines through the curtains, and car lights flash briefly from the alley. I want the blackout curtain closed. The next week she takes down the other blackout curtains from all around the house but leaves mine.

September 1945 . . .

My mother has decided that I should have piano lessons—maybe because when I am bored I sometimes play with the keys on our piano and already know middle C. Grandma doesn't play but my mother can play hymns like "Jesus Bids Us Shine" and "Work for the Night Is Coming," which Grandma has wanted me to learn to sing. And sometimes a song called "Down the River of Golden Dreams," which my mother sings to herself. I can tell however that the playing for her is hard. My teacher will be Frieda Nelson, from the Nelson family our road is named after. She and her sister have the original Nelson farm and still tend a dairy herd. My mother and I walk down the trail through the woods from our road to the highway, then up McCallum Road to the farm. My mother is carrying her childhood music case—a black leatherette one that rolls up and buckles. We open and close the farm gate because there are cows in the field, and walk up the long curving lane to the farmhouse.

November 1945 . . .

My father's mother, Minnie, and her husband, Uncle Charlie, arrive on the morning tram from Vancouver with my father's older brother, Uncle Orrie, for Sunday dinner. This seems like the first time I have seen them. My mother and grandmother have been saying bad things about them for the past week, including that they don't think Minnie and Charlie are really married. Minnie wants me to call her "Nana." She's tall and wears a large showy hat. She's brought Christmas presents and also brought my father a .303 Lee-Enfield rifle that belonged to her father, who has recently died. It was made for the Boer War, my father says. It has Queen Victoria's crest on it. He lies down on the living room rug like a soldier and aims it into the legs of our dining-room table. She says she's given Orrie her father's double-barrelled shotgun. I play "Dolly Dear" for them on the piano—the first piece I have learned. At dinner Uncle Charlie knocks over his teacup and makes a large stain on the white damask table cloth, and on the "silence cloth" underneath. My mother and grandmother nod to each other as if they knew this would happen. Then we all walk down the hill with them through the darkness to the evening tram. My father carries a metal flashlight. To get to the tram station we have to walk between some trees and some parked rail cars and a caboose. A stream of liquid spurts from the caboose as we pass, nearly hitting Nana. She's so startled that she stumbles. "That's a rude caboose," says Orrie.

December 1945 . . .

My mother and grandma and I take the tram to Vancouver once again to see Santa and do Christmas shopping. At Spencer's Santa gives me a toy gun, a black .45 automatic. My mother is unhappy and says I can't keep it. We go to the store's fifth-floor restaurant, where again I get to look at the CPR and Union Steamship boats in the harbour. I have my favourite restaurant meal, poached salmon.

At home that night I don't feel well and pick at my supper. Then in bed I throw up all the poached salmon. I've never thrown up before and so don't have words for it. I call out, "Grandma, I've spilled on the bed." I probably call my grandma because I think she knows more. "You've vomited, dear," she tells me. After that night I don't like eating salmon, but I have a new word.

March 1946 . . .

A quiet struggle among things American, British and Canadian simmers within our house. My grandma has grown up in a small vil-

lage in County Durham while my father says his family in Canada goes back to 1798 on his father's side and to a Métis "De Bois" in Thunder Bay in 1802 on his mother's. My grandma—who recounts growing up the youngest child of a village innkeeper— views herself as better than anyone not born in Britain.

My dad's mother Minnie (second from left), her brother Lester (far left), mother Betsy de Bois and father Robert Parkin on their farm outside of Lindsay, Ontario, around 1898.

Her brother Sim was chief engineer on a steamship that sailed to Rangoon and Vladivostok. Her brother Jack managed a tea plantation in Darjeeling. She likes to tell people she has always voted Conservative. My father, who completed only Grade 8, campaigned for the CCF before the war, and is sometimes shop steward for his union. On election day they unhappily joke about going out to cancel each other's vote. None of us knows how my mother votes. In 2003 I drop into my great-grandfather's inn, the Cross Keys, in Hamsterley, for lunch, and there on the walls are nineteenth-century photos of my grandmother and her family, all of them looking very solemn and conservative. She had lived here as a child, in the second-floor rooms. I find a photo on the wall of the inn from the time her father had retired and she was working as a telegrapher—around 1900. Her sister Alice, five years older, and her husband Tom Stephenson were running it. I photograph the photo.

Damn—I've done it again, pretended to know the future. Put that photo back on the wall!

I like my grandma. She is full of amusing stories about "the old country" and about her and her brother Jack climbing down an apple tree to sneak from their rooms above the inn, about riding

My greatgrandfather Kirkup's inn, the Cross Keys, in Hamsterley, County Durham, around 1899–1900. That's my great-aunt Alice, her husband and two of my cousins in the doorway.

a bicycle to her job at the telegraph office in Newcastle. As well as the Morse code she is now teaching me rhymes such as "tuppence and twopence, a groat and three 'appence, a penny and a penny and an odd boar bee." You say "twopence" as if the first part were "twop," and "'appence" as if it were "'oppence." But when I begin school she expects me to wear short pants in good weather, and riding breeches in bad. I have to wheedle her into visiting the school grounds before she can be convinced that in Abbotsford real boys wear jeans. In just a few years Daphne Buckle will have a similar problem with her mother in North Vancouver. Oh shoot!—my editor will hate me.

June 1946 . . .

Even before I begin school, Frieda Nelson sends me to perform at the Fraser Valley Music Festival. I play "The Blue Bells of Scotland" and forget that I am on stage and "count out loud" to the music like she has told me to do when practising. The adjudicator tells the audience how valuable counting out loud can be and ranks me second in a "novice" class of seven. His name is Burton Kurth and my mother says he is famous. She says this as if his name could help make me famous.

The festival is held over several days in the Legion Hall in Mission City, seven miles north of Abbotsford across the Fraser River, and draws its competitors from places like New Westminster, Langley, Mission, Abbotsford and Chilliwack. The hall seems to hold several hundred people, and is usually full. It has a wide deep stage with a dramatic mural of the Vimy monument on its back wall. My grandpa Brown was at Vimy—large pictures of him in his uniform hang in my room. That's Vimy, my mother whispers.

The adjudicators sit at a table near the front centre, wait for you to make your way onto the stage toward the monument, and ring a bell when they want you to begin. There is a very long silence as I sit at the grand piano waiting for the bell.

October 1946 . . .

I am in Grade 1 in a one-classroom school just south of the big elementary school. It's really the ground floor of a small wooden Masonic Hall but has a cloakroom and desks on runners and an oiled board floor just like the big school. And a pot-belly stove at the back. All of us children are strangers to each other. Our teacher, Miss Chappell, is very old and has silvery grey hair. She uses flash cards. I am the only one who can read "morning." If one of us is bad, Miss Chappell goes across the field at lunchtime to the big school to get the strap. She straps Rennie Harm forever because he refuses to cry. We are all watching—fearing her, admiring him. One recess I get really mad at Perry Long for pushing me off the stump that we pretend is a truck, and throw a piece of broken china at him and cut him over the eye. I will probably get the strap. I race inside and tell Miss Chappell, "I hit Perry and he's bleeding" and she rushes off to help him. Later nothing happens to me.

June 1947 . . .

I compete at the music festival in Mission again, playing "English Country Garden," and again in 1948, playing the march "In Rank and File." I win the class both times. The music is set for the classes by the festival board so that each of us plays the same piece, including Bill Walker who is also taking lessons from Frieda Nelson and will later major in music at UBC and be the official tape recorder of *Tish* poetry readings. But Bill goes to a school on Sumas Prairie and so I don't know him—except through my mother who wants me to dislike him.

On some festival days my schoolroom class competes as a choir, and often wins too. I have a boy-soprano voice and sing descant. There are individual singing competitions at the festival, and so one day I ask my mother if I can take singing lessons too, and she sends me to my godmother, Marie Lobban, who teaches singing. I compete at the festival, singing Shakespeare's "Hark, Hark the Lark," and place second—behind Bill Walker. It is very different to perform facing the audience than to sit at a piano unable to see whether people are sleeping or giggling. It is my first poetry reading. The next year I sing a Cavalier song "Boot, Saddle, to Horse and Away" and again place second behind Bill Walker. It's another poem. Maybe I am going to be a lyric poet.

September 1947 . . .

I am puzzled about Frieda Nelson—wondering why she wants to live in Abbotsford. She seems tall, dramatic, confident, even glamourous, and a lot younger than my mother. Occasionally she will play for me, something complicated by Bach or Chopin or Rachmaninoff, or other composers from big far-away cities. She makes the music seem rich—and very playable. Her farmhouse seems also from faraway. It was once lighted by gas—you can see the stubs of old tubing poking from the walls. From the high ceilings hang two tarnished brass chandeliers, now electrified, with one or two of the little white glass shades missing. There's vertical tongue-and-groove panelling partway up the walls. Just outside close to the house is a tennis court that is now overgrown with small trees. In the south window close to the piano is an old mahogany table with only two things on it, a crocheted cloth and a framed photo of a young Canadian sailor. Who is it, I ask my mother one day. Her boyfriend, my mother says, a Conway I think, they never married. What happened, I ask. The war, says my mother.

October 1947 . . .

Snow has started to fall in the surrounding mountains. The dim outline of the tiger on the mountain to the south of us has reappeared. My mother is listening on the radio to some American hearings about traitors who make movies. There is a lot of talk about something called a "Fifth Amendment." If someone at the hearings uses this Fifth Amendment, this proves they are communists or traitors. My mother says to my grandma that she doesn't know what to think. My grandma says what can you expect from Americans.

Old King Cole Junior.

November 1947 . . .

Sometime in the fall of Grade 2 I am called out by the principal, Miss Stenerssen. There are people from the village theatre club with her. They want a small boy to play "Old King Cole Junior" in their Christmas pageant. They give me a large ditto-printed script. On my way home I meet two high school boys, Kenny Turnbull and Ron Arnold, who notice the unusual piece of paper and grab it, rip it up and toss the pieces into the creek that runs beside Hazel Street. I go home and tell my mother, and she comes with me to the creek and helps me retrieve the pieces. She lets them dry and then tapes them back together. She was forelady of the Keystone Press bookbindery in Vancouver before she married my dad. She has a box of stuff for making books. I like this box. Ron and Kenny are usually okay, but are known to be uneasy about pages with writing on them. After the play is staged I pose for a photo, calling for my fiddlers three.

Why have I been asked to be in the play? Maybe because my teachers know I am used to being on stage? Or used to memorizing music and songs? I just think it's because I'm good—talented—and

Me as young Johann Sebastian Bach.

as far as I can tell the rehearsals and performance are fine. The next year the high school puts on a play supposedly based on the childhood of Johann Sebastian Bach—some painful orphan years he spends with a mean uncle and a kindly Tante Anna. Miss Stenerssen and my teachers again volunteer me for the role. Again all seems to go very well. And the following year the theatre group asks me to play Santa Claus Junior in another Christmas pageant. A year or two later there is a second high school play that needs a boy—and I expect to be asked. But instead my school sends the son of someone who has a senior position in the district school administration. I decide I must be no good at acting, and I never take part in a play again.

There is of course a class structure in Abbotsford, one more real than the one that my grandma imagines separates herself and my father. I don't have words for the concept but I know the concept. The doctors, the bank manager, the BC Electric manager, the teachers, business owners don't much socialize with people like my mother and father except on very special occasions when it would be rude to stay away. Maybe I've been lucky that none of them have had children in my classes. My father however would like to move up. He was "Chancellor Commander" my mother says, of a Knights of Pythias lodge in Vancouver and still owns the tux he had to wear there. It's the one in his wedding picture. He would like to join the Masons, but is starting by joining a newly founded "aerie" of the Fraternal Order of Eagles. His line-gang foreman, Lyle Lobban, is the founder and first president. My father is vice-president.

He has also become storekeeper for the line gang, keeping track of its cross arms, wire and insulators, and ordering what is needed. He now goes to work half an hour early to "do the stores" before working his regular hours as a ground man.

The line gang's 1947 Christmas Eve party, my godfather Lyle Lobban under the '24,' my father seated fifth from the right, and visitors from the business office standing.

December 1947 . . .

Whatever thoughts I have about words and books and reading have come mostly from my parents, my grandma, my father's brother, Uncle Orrie, who has visited with Nana and Charlie at least twice more, and from Jimmy Webster who lives up the street. "Kindergarten" is a word that people know but have no need to use in Abbotsford. But my father in early 1945 did build me a small wooden table and chair, and framed and painted a sheet-metal blackboard so I could spend mornings with my grandma learning to print letters and numbers and short words. When the war ended, she got me a subscription to a British children's magazine, *Wee Wisdom*. Now she has replaced it with one called *Open Roads for Boys*. I haven't liked either of them—they seem written by adults who think children like me are lucky to have adults think about them. "Pity my simplicity." This week, however, badgered by my grandmother, from one of these magazines I memorize a Kiplingesque poem called "How to Succeed"—"Drive the nail aright, boys!" it begins—and recite it at the annual elementary school talent contest, a contest that I win by also playing on the piano "The Evening Star" from Wagner's opera *Tannhäuser*. On the day of the talent contest I am in Grade 2 in a school with grades from 1 to 8. I don't have any special aspirations. Memorizing poems and playing the piano from memory are now among various things I happen to be able to do like running or batting a ball while playing "scrub." My classmates think I am unusual but don't blame me for it. They think I can't help it. I encourage this. I work a lot at making myself up for them. Or changing how my parents are making me up.

I walk to school, and back and forth as well to home for lunch, using a wooded path across the three rail tracks that interrupt Hazel Street, the road that would otherwise run directly from my house to the school. Often I have to scramble between parked boxcars, climbing onto and down from the couplings. It is safest to climb up rather than crawl under—and to remember to listen for whether there's an engine attached. Jimmy Webster, the son of the owner of the village's new Ford dealership, lives about a half-mile past my house, and climbs the couplings with me. Most days his dad is waiting for him just past the tracks in a bulbous '48 Ford sedan, and gives me a ride up the hill. Jimmy is enviably precocious—full of exotic information that he regularly volunteers in class. From him I learn that there is a Roy Rogers and a Gene Autry and a horse named Trigger. He has been by car with his parents to Yellowstone and the Grand Canyon. Mine do not yet own a car. Worse, he owns a set of the *Book of Knowledge*, which he seems to pour through daily. That's just an American book, my grandma says when I finally complain, and shortly after I am bought a set of the *Britannica*.

The Ford dealership will catch fire and burn one morning just after the astoundingly sleek 1949 models are released. Okay okay, I know I'm not supposed to know this yet, but I'll forget if I don't tell you right now. The dealership will be rebuilt but Jimmy's dad will lose the business, he'll be rumoured to have a drug addiction, he and his wife, a nurse at the village hospital, will separate, and around 1951 she and Jimmy move away to Greenwood, in the western Kootenays. The next I'll hear of Greenwood is a decade later when George Bowering tells me he once lived there. I'll forget to ask him about Jimmy.

April 1948 . . .

The people in Abbotsford are quite a mixture, my mother says. There are Canadian-born ones who come from long-time-ago British settlers—like the Conways who deliver the milk, my piano teacher Frieda Nelson, my godfather Lyle Lobban the line-gang foreman and his pal Bat Nelson, both of whom often arrive on weekends in an old pickup truck to see my dad, so drunk there is froth around their mouths from the beer they have tried to swallow. There are Hungarians and Ukrainians who arrived in the 1930s, and a large community of Mennonites who attend various kinds of Mennonite churches or even the United Church. There is a Chinese restaurant but it is run by a white friend of my father's called Bart Warner. He calls it the "Java Lunch" and has painted palm trees on the walls. My father says there are Indians but I never see any, although I am beginning to suspect that "Sumas" and "Matsqui" and "Chilliwack" might be Indian words. The beautiful and vivacious Gross twins in my class, Gerry blonde and Jackie red-headed, are Hungarian, and I secretly love them both even though my grandma insists that anyone not British is low-born. My grandma is often surprisingly wrong. Their father is one of the village barbers, his name anglicized from something like Grossinger. The cheerful barber my mother takes me to is also Hungarian, named Pete Robson, anglicized from Rabinczy or Rozsavolgyi . . . I can never remember. The first barber she tried, my father's barber, Ed Hansen, is Swedish—he burned my left ear with his cigarette and so she hauled me across the street without paying and got Pete Robson to finish the haircut. The smartest girl in my class, my competition, is cheerful Tina Wiebe, from a Mennonite family. Most Mennonite kids go to Mennonite-run schools, but Tina and Caroline Enns and Rennie Harm and Ernie Schroeder come to the public school—perhaps because they can walk to it. Some speak Low German with their parents, but no one thinks of them as German despite their surnames. They are Mennonites, who have come here because of their religion. Or maybe they are good Germans. *"Wie gehts?" "Wie gehtes ihnen?"* I learn to

say. *"S'gut."* *"S'ist wahr."* All this German is going to help me get to
UBC and to my future *Tish* friends a year early—and maybe is going
to be crucial in my finding them at all. But yes, I don't know that yet.

By Grade 3 other kids begin arriving at the school direct from
Europe. The Gross girls are excited because their cousin June is
going to arrive soon, and sure enough the next month the quietly
attractive June Kleininger joins us. From Holland comes Tony
Alberts, his father a doctor. He too is obliged to wear short pants to
school for several months until his parents become aware of local
customs. From England comes the very petite Jean Rhoda. This is

We dance a polka at the Fraser Valley Festival.

really interesting and it is part
of a huge post-world-war re-
location that is also bringing
my future friends Aritha Van
Herk to Alberta, and Daphne
Buckle, who will become
Daphne Marlatt, to North
Vancouver and Tommy Ima-
mura and Stan Fukawa back
to nearby Bradner from some

place they don't talk about. There is always more going on than
what I can find out. "In the midst," Warren Tallman will write. Our
Grade 4 class successfully dances a polka at the Fraser Valley Festival. There's Jackie Gross second from left in the front row, and then
Jean Rhoda, Gerry Gross, June Kleininger and Caroline Enns. And
there's me, second from right in the back, beside tall and happy Kay
Heppner, the village jeweller's daughter. You can see the Vimy memorial behind my right shoulder. And there's Jimmy Webster, framed by
a pillar in the middle. The polka is not a British dance. Jimmy's not
there in the photo the next time we dance—a Swedish schottische.

June 1948 . . .

The Fraser River, five miles north of us, is rising because there was
a lot of snow in the mountains and now the unusually warm spring

weather has been melting it. The tiger has vanished. People think the river will break the dikes beside it and flood. It is already picking up logs and old stumps upstream and floating these downstream, threatening the poles that hold up the power lines that cross it. My dad's line gang is working in shifts on a boat on the river pushing logs away from the pilings that guard the poles. Then the dikes break. We are okay because our house is on high ground and the waters come only to within half a mile north of us. But the water has cut the highways to Mission and Chilliwack and cut all three railways. My dad's gang can't get to their boat except by driving to Langley, which is halfway to Vancouver. They sleep at a hotel in Langley between their shifts. My mother and I walk down the back of our hill to where the flood begins, and a photographer for the local newspaper takes a picture but doesn't talk to us. The picture appears in the paper—"Two evacuees look back toward their flooded home."

Soldiers from the army come with amphibious jeeps and trucks from the war to help rescue people and dogs and cows and chickens. People call these jeeps "army ducks." They take the people and animals to the old Commonwealth Training airport where the Liberators were and where people can stay. When the water goes back down there are a lot of dead fish, many of them young salmon that were trying to get down to the sea. In three years' time Daphne Buckle will arrive from Penang via England but may never hear about the flood or how it is damaging the boats and docks of the gillnet fishers upstream from Steveston. When the water goes down there also are dark horizontal lines six to ten feet up the sides of barns and houses where the water level was. In ten years' time I will drive hopeful young poet Bobby Hogg around the once flooded land and show him these lines. In thirty years' time I will speak in Burnaby at a conference that editor and bibliographer Roy Miki has organized called "The Coast is only a Line." But Roy is thinking of other lines. Come on, Frank, back to the present. Most Japanese-Canadians are missing the flood because they still aren't allowed to live near the coast of BC.

July 1948 . . .

The radio and the *Vancouver Sun* have news all the time about an airlift in Berlin. Some planes have crashed. People in Berlin may starve unless the British and Americans can get more food there. I'm worried that the war might start again. I check the paper each day to make sure.

But my dad has bought a car, with my grandma's help because she will enjoy going for "drives." It's a 1947 Chev torpedo-back coupe, maroon on its top half and beige—"Hollywood Beige" my mother points out—on the bottom. "Two-tone" paint on cars is a new thing. All the prewar cars seem to have been painted all one colour, usually black. New-style things are good things, and my father is proud. Most Saturdays he washes and polishes it. My mother however isn't entirely sure about the car. Several times she says that people stop her in the street and suggest that it is one of the cars they saw that was caught in the Fraser Valley flood.

Our 1947 Chev, me and my dad in his Sunday suspenders.

Each Sunday now we go for drives. My dad knows every road in the Fraser Valley from Chilliwack to Langley because his line gang has repaired the wires and transformers on each of them. For the first time I see Matsqui Village and the lines on the walls where the flood reached. I see Huntingdon a mile south of Abbotsford where you can cross into the town of Sumas in the U.S. Why do they have a Sumas too? A few miles farther south in Bellingham I see an amazingly Art Deco movie theatre, the Mount Baker.

My dad also drives us across the Fraser River on the old railway bridge to Mission City. One of the spans of this bridge fell down during the Fraser Valley flood but has been raised and repositioned. I see Hatzic Lake and Harrison Hot Springs. I see the power dams at Ruskin and Stave Falls where my father first worked for BC Electric in 1936. I see the little boat the *Ruskin* on which my father and his workmates protected the power lines during the Fraser Valley Flood. I take a picture of it with the new German folding camera that Nana in Vancouver has sent me. I also see for the first time Forest Lawn Cemetery in Burnaby where my grandpa Brown, who was at Vimy, is buried. And some Sundays we visit Nana and Charlie's little house and she serves baked cauliflower and baked macaroni which I've never had before, and I meet their dog, a dark grey Pekingese named Hannah. Dogs are dirty, my mother warns. I find out that Charlie is an orderly in a hospital, and a Cockney, and that Nana cleans a jeweller's offices on weekday evenings. That my grandma doesn't like Cockneys. On each drive I am unknowingly doing research on some of the poems I will write in *Bridge Force*, *War Poems* and *Back to the War*. On each drive I also teach myself the names of all the cars and trucks we pass. Model A. Model T. Reo. Tatra. Terraplane. Packard. Studebaker. Prefect. Kaiser. Hudson. Henry J. Crosby. I am becoming a car person.

Most of my *Tish* friends will also be car people because they are growing up in small towns like I am. Here I go wandering forward again. I will go with George Bowering in 1961 to buy his first car which he will later abandon on Twelfth Ave. in Vancouver beside the Goodwill building. It will be a bargain at $125. But the friends who will grow up in cities, like David Dawson or Jamie Reid, I will never associate with cars. Do they even get drivers' licences?—I may never know.

August 1948 . . .

The airlift in Berlin is still scary. There are more planes, and some of the pilots are Canadians. Mr. Barrett the retired postmaster has bought the empty lot across the street from us and is building a strange new house—with two levels and a flat roof on each. Something new from Europe, my mother thinks. Mr. Barrett has travelled to Europe and to the Caribbean, and has relatives on St. Kitts and Nevis. He sometimes gives me the colourful stamps from their letters. The house catches fire when the roofers are putting on the

asphalt roof—I run to my mother and call out "All of Mr. Barrett's money is going up in smoke!" and make her laugh, because I don't know about insurance. The house is rebuilt and he and his wife move in as soon as it is mostly finished. I visit as much as I can. He never talks about how odd his house is. He talks to me like a grown-up and I wish I could talk that way back. I haven't heard about Bauhaus architecture but I really like Mr. Barrett for wanting a different house.

Me in 1967, my first wife Helen, one of my neat cars and Mr. Barrett's odd house.

September 1948 . . .

At the back of the Grade 3 classroom in Abbotsford is a shelf of extra books which you can read if you have finished everything the teacher wants you do with the textbook or purple-ink ditto worksheets. I have begun studying the literature of the Second World War—reading the several "Dave Dawson" books that can be found there. This is not the Dave Dawson I will meet in a few years' time in Vancouver and who will flirt with all the other *Tish* editors in a hopefully gay way. Oops. Dave Dawson is an eighteen-year-old American fighter pilot who shows no sign of understanding words like "flirt" or "gay." Which is fine, because neither do I.

Dave has gone to Britain in 1939 to fly with the RAF because his own country is stupid and doesn't understand the need to fight Germany. His best friend is the equally young and skillful British fighter pilot Freddy Farmer. They are best friends the same way that Britain and America should be best friends—the way they will be once the Japanese have attacked Pearl Harbor. I feel mostly British when I read these books, and enjoy the rare moments when

Freddy has to rescue Dave, but I also figure out that the author, Mr. Bowen, is an American and will usually give Dave the best assignments, despite being one of the good Americans who wants Britain and the U.S. to be best friends. And there are no Canadians in Mr. Bowen's books although I know that my cousin Bill Yates, from my grandma's sister's family in Calgary, died four years ago when his Lancaster was shot down by Germans over the Black Forest. He was twenty-three. And I can remember touching another Canadian Lancaster, and looking into its long metal belly, during the victory show at Abbotsford's Commonwealth Air Training base. If my cousin had flown with Dave Dawson or Freddy Farmer he would still be living.

Dave and Freddy fly Hurricanes and Spitfires and occasionally a Vultee or a Lockheed Lightning, and in one book steal a German Me 110 from the Brussels aerodrome and in another a Mitsubishi Betty from a Jap carrier. As long as I can remember I have had small plastic models of a Hurricane and a Spitfire, and also a P-40 and a P-51 Mustang.

And so I search for additional titles at the village public library and read *Dave Dawson in the RAF*, *Dave Dawson at Dunkirk*, *Dave Dawson at Singapore*, *Dave Dawson at Truk*, *Dave Dawson on Guadalcanal*, *Dave Dawson with the Flying Tigers*, *Dave Dawson on the Russian Front*. . . . As well as helping me understand what it is to be British or American, these books help me begin filling gaps in my understandings of recent history. I had seen my father's surprise when he read in the *Vancouver Sun* that the *Prince of Wales* and *Repulse* had been sunk; had listened to my grandma read a letter aloud in which her sister-in-law Minnie wrote from Southampton that she and Sim had survived an air raid by crouching under a staircase as their house fell around it; had panicked in August 1945 when the Abbotsford air-raid siren rang to celebrate the Jap surrender. I had pieced together information from comic strips in the *Sun* such as *Steve Canyon*, *Terry and the Pirates* and *Johnny Hazard*. But Dave and Freddy have zoomed over the battles everywhere.

October 1948 . . .

We are driving to my granddad Davey's house in Vancouver. He is sick and will probably die. In Vancouver my father takes Twelfth Ave. to Clark Drive, which becomes Knight Road, and then turns toward the cramped little cottage my granddad had bought for his family in 1912 on East Twenty-ninth Ave. The houses around are very poor. The Reid house next door has no glass on some windows—just tattered canvas. Orrie, who still lives here, meets us at the door. This is either the first or second time I have met granddad, although I have the silverplate baby spoon he sent when I was born, engraved "Granddad to Frank." He is lying in a single bed. He looks really grey. He had angrily disowned my father when he had left home in 1938 to marry my mother—throwing his blue Big Ben alarm clock across the lawn after him. The dented clock still stands on my father's dresser. As my mother caustically predicts, we will find out next week that he has mentioned only Orrie in his will.

December 1948 . . .

My father drives us a few miles out of town to Kilgard, to go past the Clayburn brick plant. There's a village here too, all the little houses made of red brick. They're the first brick houses I've seen—except years ago in my little pig book. "Company houses," says my mother, "for the miners." "Is there a mine?" I ask. Now I'm thinking of the seven dwarves. Kilgard is pretty amazing. And so close. "That's why there's a brick plant," says my dad. "Sumas Mountain has a bunch of clay mines, the best in BC for firebricks." We drive past a wide creek and a church camp and up a mountain road. "There's a mine," says my dad. "I thought Sumas Mountain was beside Sumas, across the line," I say, "the one with the tiger made of snow." "That's the American Sumas Mountain." He laughs. "No tigers here."

March 1949 . . .

Now that they have a car and can drive to the river, my mother and father have decided to take up fishing. They buy two telescopic rods and two large Penn reels equipped with forty-pound test lines, and go with me to the Ridgedale "bar" of the Fraser, just east of the Mission bridge at the northwest side of "our" Sumas Mountain. They want to catch trout, but my dad is also worried about catching sturgeon, which also live in the river and can be six feet long and weigh hundreds of pounds. My mother cannot figure out how to cast the line; my dad is not good at it either. His reel gets plugged with knots and snarls—a "backlash" he says. Sometimes they unwind much of the line from the reel and lay it on the river bank, and then my father whirls the sinker end round and round over his head before hurling it out over the water.

Sometimes the hooks catch on things that are stuck under the water. "Snags" my mother calls them. The line is too strong to break so my dad has to cut it, and we lose the beautiful sinker. My dad makes the sinkers himself. He brings home a blowtorch and old insulators from work, drills holes in old blocks of wood and melts the lead from the insulators. He puts loops of copper wire into the holes and pours the lead around them. "All your work is gone," I say, when he cuts the line. "All my work is here," he grins—and squats to rebuild the end of the line with swivels and hooks and another sinker.

They decide to switch to the newly invented spinning reels, which work only with lighter line. My dad is still worried about a sturgeon carrying off his line and rod, but less so because while they have caught a few catfish and several trout, they have not yet seen a sturgeon. My dad cuts the lower line guides from the rods and solders graduated ones suitable for spinning reels into their place. He buys my mother a $45 Airex reel that is known for accurate short casting, for himself a $40 Mitchell, known for its distance casting, and another rod equipped with a CAP reel for me, mainly because a CAP is relatively inexpensive—$12.

We bait two hooks with worms, attach an eight-ounce lead sinker, cast our lines out into the water, lean the rods on a forked stick and wait for a jerking of the rod tip to indicate that we have a fish trying to eat the bait. My dad calls this kind of fishing "nigger fishing." I ask what this means. He says it means you don't have to do anything, just sit back on the bank and wait. The only other time I have heard the word "nigger" spoken is when the men on the line gang use the small crane that is mounted on their truck—they all call it the "niggerhead." My dad also uses the phrase "let's call a spade a spade," and I assume that he is talking about shovels but I have also heard things that make me think he maybe isn't. I never do ask.

We all three quickly become accurate at casting—very important when there are often people fishing about fifteen feet apart all along a quarter-mile of riverbank, and it is impolite or worse to cast one's line across someone else's. Making a good cast is as good as catching a fish, my father says. He can cast about sixty or seventy feet from shore, my mother about forty feet, and I figure out technical ways to equal or surpass her. I find myself in a kind of sibling rivalry with her, something I've already experienced fairly often because of her mother living in our house and because of my father's favourite words for her are "my little girl."

I also notice that my mother uses a lot of fishing expressions. "That's real fishy," she'll say when she doesn't trust an explanation she has been given. "She fell for him hook line and sinker," she'll say about a woman she knows who has made a poor choice of a boyfriend. "She was quite a catch," she will say. "He fed her quite a line," she'll say. "She hooked him real good," she'll say. "She hooked him, and then just reeled him in." Sometimes we do catch a hungry carp that has swallowed both hook and sinker, and the line between. Once I catch a sturgeon, but it is only thirty-five inches long, and my dad says we have to throw it back because they have to be at least thirty-six inches long to be legal. "Keeping it would be dynamite," he says, using the expression he uses whenever he considers breaking a law.

June 1949 . . .

After school I wait for the thump—usually around four o'clock—of the *Sun* paper on our back porch. Here the clear black-and-white conflicts of comic strips such as *Steve Canyon* and *Terry and the Pirates*, both of whom fly somewhere near China, are dissolving. The war is over, and the strips' heroes have been getting involved in hard-to-follow transactions among warlords, probable criminals, glamourous bar girls and the duelling armies of Chiang Kai-Shek and Mao Tse-Tung. I keep reading mostly because I like the exposed thighs of the bar girls and the drawings of rivets on the aluminum airplanes. And so when in 1949 I read in the *Vancouver Sun* of North Korean tank shells "rolling down the highway toward Taejon," I am not surprised. That fall or maybe the next spring several boy students and I are papering the back wall of our classroom with dramatic coloured sketches of intricately riveted MiG-15s and Canadian Sabre jets exchanging bursts of gunfire over MiG Alley. Years later I will think of these sketches whenever I come across Greg Curnoe's cover for Bowering's *At War With the U.S.*—a Canadian-marked jet fighter shooting up a U.S.-marked Corsair. I'm sure I will.

AT WAR WITH THE U.S.

George Bowering

I have also begun reading Winston Churchill's history of the last war. I have got my mother to buy *The Gathering Storm* and *Their Finest Hour* from the Book-of-the-Month Club. They have indexes and maps and I can read them back and forth, and use the index to look up things I have already read and partly forgotten but now need to know. I will read these through 1952, having to wait impatiently for *The Closing of the Ring* and *Triumph and Tragedy* to be published. I am doing another part of my research for those books I will write, *War Poems* and *Back to the War*. I am probably trying to understand my past. Maybe I am trying to understand the childhoods of some of my new friends and some of my future friends.

July 1949 . . .

Friday is the first of July and so we have a long weekend. My dad decides to decorate our car with small Red Ensign flags—one at each front corner of the roof and one on the radio antenna. My mother wants us to drive to Bellingham and have a picnic in Cornwall Park, a big wooded park in the north end of the city with damp interesting trails. So my father replaces one of the Red Ensigns with a Stars and Stripes, to be polite, he says. But at the border in Sumas, where you cannot see Tiger Mountain, the U.S. customs agent is angry. The American flag has to be highest, he tells us. He makes my dad get out and tape the U.S. flag to the top of the antenna, and move a Red Ensign down to where the U.S. flag had been. A mile or so down the road, my dad pulls over and lowers the antenna, which is telescopic, to its lowest position.

It is this year that I begin thinking that all American men must be soldiers. The gas station attendants are wearing military-style shirts and jackets. The work clothes for sale in Sears and Montgomery Ward, and worn by most workmen, look like army uniforms. The bus drivers and waiters in restaurants and gardeners in the park all look like they are ready for war.

November 1949 . . .

I'm walking with my mother downtown and we stop to talk with Miss Chevalley, who was my Grade 2 teacher. They talk about school and what I'm doing in Grade 4. He doesn't like "Practical Art," says my mother. I start to create a poem. "Practical art, it's all a big farce," I plan to say. But I get the last word wrong. They both smile nervously. Language and poetry can take you where you didn't plan to be.

March 1950 . . .

I really like Uncle Orrie, although I saw him only once or twice before my father could afford a car. The more my mother and grandma have talked about what a "ne'er-do-well" he is, the more I have liked him. My father's parents were one of very few who divorced in 1914—not because my grandfather beat my grandmother, which I think he did, but because she had to pretend "adultery"—I'm not sure what this is—in order to shame him into divorcing her. She also had to give up her two boys. "Your mother fucks other men," is what Orrie will tell me, much much later, that his schoolmates yelled at him and my dad that year.

At home my mother often scoffs at his never having been able to keep a steady job. She tells us he's shiftless because he earns an unpredictable income by playing Hawaiian guitar and banjo in one of Barney Potts's dance bands, or playing the ukulele on local radio. She scoffs at him for taking creative writing courses at night school and aspiring to write short stories—"What money is there in that?" she asks. She rants about his having had a brief affair with his father's housekeeper, Mrs. Braiden, and then on his father's death having begun living common-law with a young Chinese woman, Eileen Wong. This is just after my father gets our car, and we begin visiting Nana and Charlie every few months for Sunday dinner. Soon Orrie and Eileen are usually there. In my young eyes Eileen is gracious and attractive. Orrie has a sardonic wit, which I will later recognize—as my poor father probably already does—as somewhat limited and immature, and enjoys teasing my father. He cannot resist awkward puns. One time I have a new cap, with a fold-down extension for the ears. "It comes down over his ears," my father says. "It comes down over his rears?" Orrie exclaims. "Surely not that far!" and laughs loudly at his own jest. Orrie seems basically good-natured, but I am the only one of us who thinks so. I would like to be like Orrie. I would like to have an intriguing name like "Orrie." I would like to play in a dance band and take creative writing courses and write stories. I would love to live with a young woman like Eileen.

May 1951 . . .

They've put up a tent in the main window of Mc&Mc's, our dry-goods store. A big tent for four people, with camp chairs and a camp stove and sleeping bags arrayed around it. It's the first window scene I've ever noticed in an Abbotsford store. Windows have been just to look in or out of, and tents I've seen only in books. I don't know any families that go "camping." I point the tent out to my mom and dad, who last fall replaced our car with a brand-new black 1951 four-door torpedo-back Chev, with a "Powerglide" automatic transmission. The next weekend they drive down and shock me by buying the tent. Mc&Mc's has to take down the window display—it's the only tent they have. Everyone in town will know who bought it.

We are going camping at Larabee State Park near Bellingham for the twenty-fourth of May holiday weekend. All we have is the tent, and some sleeping bags and air mattresses my mother has bought from the Eaton's catalogue. But on the way to the park on Friday night my dad stops at the Bellingham war surplus store and buys a Coleman stove and lantern, a tarp to use as a ground sheet and a bright aluminum icebox. We can bring them back duty free because we will be away more than forty-eight hours. It's my first night sleeping outside of Canada. The park supervisors and workers all wear military-style uniforms. On the way into Bellingham we pass a field in which there is a thirty-foot-high pile of World War II steel helmets. On Saturday we drive back into Bellingham so my mother and grandma can shop at Sears and Kress and Montgomery Ward. My dad buys a big bag of roasted cashews and takes me down to the second-hand shops near the harbour, where the gasworks smell really strong. He wants to buy some paperback westerns. There are a lot of old Victorian hardbacks here for twenty-five or thirty cents. I buy a *Moby-Dick* and a *Golden Treasury*.

July 1951 . . .

My mother and grandma are making their usual trip to Vancouver
to shop and have their bank books made up. But now they can't take
the tram—it stopped running last September. It was old my father
says. The cars were all built between 1900 and 1911. They couldn't
replace them because of the Depression and then the war. The BC
Electric has begun running a bus line from Vancouver to Chilliwack
called Pacific Stages. The buses are green and white. My father gets
free tickets for them too. My mother and grandma have to take the
bus to go to the banks because they don't know how to drive and
the banks aren't open on weekends when my father isn't working. In
Vancouver, the bus has a different terminal than the trams had, one
almost as close to Granville Street as to Hastings. Sometimes we
walk from the terminal to the Bay on Granville, and sometimes
down to Woodward's on Hastings. This time we go to Woodward's
and it is having a sale of boxed leatherbound Nelson and Collins
"classic" books from England for 99 cents. The Nelson books are
blue and the Collins ones maroon. I buy Stevenson's *Treasure Island*
and Dumas's *Three Musketeers*. I read these and on the next trip buy
Dumas's *Louise de la Vallières*, Wilkie Collins's *The Woman in White*,
Stevenson's *Kidnapped* and *Catriona*, Dickens's *Barnaby Rudge* and
The Meditations of Marcus Aurelius. Maybe I like the leather and the
gold stamping. When I meet Daphne Buckle in 1960 I confuse her,
I suspect, with Catriona Drummond. If the series had offered Darwin's *Origin of Species* or Marx's *Capital* or Freud's collected works I
would probably have bought and read them too. Then I might have
realized that I have been confusing Catriona with my grandma. But
I'm still a kid and don't realize much. And while the books are ones
of adventure they are not part of an adventurous series.

September 1951 . . .

Daphne Buckle has recently arrived in North Vancouver. George
Bowering has completed his first summer of picking fruit near

Naramata and is nursing a sore back from having stepped too quickly from a ladder. Gladys Hindmarch is delivering newspapers, the *Vancouver Sun*, along a muddy half-completed stretch of the Trans-Canada Highway north of Ladysmith. Of course I don't know any of this because I am still in Abbotsford, entering Grade 6. With the Grade 7 and 8 classes having been sent to a different building, my class is now the senior one in the school. I have a new fountain pen, a Parker 51. Our teacher, Miss Leask, is soon replaced by the much younger and quite attractive Miss Gourlay, who often looks inexplicably tired in the morning, sometimes slumped at her desk with her head on her arms when we come in. But she smiles and jokes about it. This is the first year that my classmates and I talk about what our teacher might be doing at night. In arithmetic Miss Gourlay lets us work through the textbook at our own paces—I will manage to finish by early March. My mother and dad have sent off for a sex education book—for me—but when it comes they read it and are shocked and hide it in their closet. I have found quite a bit to read in the *Britannica*, in the volume I call SARS to SORC. I have also found the hiding place in the closet.

March 1952 . . .

I have another cousin who fights in wars, from the same Regina family as Bill who died. He is a captain in the PPCLI in Korea—that's the Princess Patricia's Canadian Light Infantry I tell people, the Princess Pats. His name is Ted. He has survived his unit's service, and has got married, and is going to be briefly in Vancouver. His family is ashamed, my mother says. But we go down to Vancouver anyway to meet him and his Japanese bride. I am astonished. She is more beautiful than I could ever have imagined a woman could be, even from reading *Terry and the Pirates*.

My grandmother still has me sit on her knee each night and recite my three prayers. I am increasingly resentful about this and rattle the prayers through as rapidly and as meaninglessly as I can. No one has reproved me and so the ritual has continued. Several recent nights I have been impatient or exuberant about getting away and have pushed myself off after the final "amen." Today her doctor has told her she has two cracked ribs. She will be seventy at the end of this month.

May 1952 . . .

Something big is happening at Peace Arch Park. A Negro singer is there that the U.S. government doesn't like and won't let come to Canada. His name is Paul Robeson. My mother says he is one of the greatest singers ever and listens to his concert on the radio. She doesn't like Frank Sinatra and has always turned the radio off whenever he sings. Paul Robeson sings from the back of a truck parked just inside the U.S., while thousands listen on the Canadian side. A union just like my dad's has arranged things. He sings "Ole Man River" and my mother gets teary. The concert has something to do with the last war or maybe the war in Korea but it is all very complicated. War is easiest to understand when there are soldiers shooting each other.

June 1952 . . .

My mom and dad are listening to the radio results for the BC election. My dad thinks the CCF could win—its leader, Harold Winch, is one of the politicians he once handed out leaflets for in the thirties. But he and my mom are both dismayed. The three parties with educated members have all lost. A new party called "Social Credit" has won. Our riding has been won by an auto mechanic who works for a garage on Sumas prairie. Two school dropouts are the party leaders. The next week one of them is premier and the other, Phil Gaglardi, is minister of highways. I could have been premier, says my father, or at least a minister. The garage mechanic has become minister of agriculture. In North Vancouver, Arthur Buckle is most likely wondering what sort of country he has come to. In Oliver, George Bowering is listening to jests

he will include in his "swashbuckling" history of British Columbia. I am hearing the name "W.A.C. Bennett," which will be that
of the library in which my letters from George and other papers
will some day be stored. You will get to the library by driving up

Kelowna in 1908.

Gaglardi Way. You're get-
ting ahead of yourself again,
Frank. What I'm actually
thinking in June 1952 is
that this election is all part
of the end of the war. The
defeated coalition government of Mr. Boss Johnson
was in power since 1941.
Now there will be a new
BC, full of highways and cars and discarded trams. Mr. Bennett,
who has owned a hardware store in Kelowna, is setting out to run
the province like a hardware store my mother says. Two hundred
miles away, my future friend George is starting to write, "Then
an eastern businessman named Bennett came to town, and then
Bennett's party got a superhighway built between Kelowna and
the Coast. Now Kelowna is a shopping mall with parking lots full
of sports utility vehicles." Not all the less educated people are the
same, I am thinking, nor all the educated. Mr. Bennett is not a fan
of Paul Robeson.

July 1952 . . .

My mother has the kitchen radio tuned to the Democrat convention in the U.S. She had listened to the Republican convention a
week or so ago but it wasn't very exciting, she said. Everyone
knew that General Eisenhower would be chosen. There are a lot
of speeches but they all sound much the same and use the same
words—"from the great state of," they shout. When one of the
speakers nominates Adlai Stevenson, who was not expected to be
nominated, he stresses his honesty, calling him "Mr. Integrity." Does

this mean that the other candidates are dishonest I wonder. Aren't politicians expected to be honest? I don't like Senator Kefauver— I have heard that he is a bad man. The convention chooses Mr. Stevenson to run for president. I don't think he will win. General Eisenhower has a much simpler platform—it's called "I like Ike." I also think he will win because all this seems to be another part of the end of the war. He is being demobilized. People will stop calling him General Eisenhower.

September 1952 . . .

Daphne Buckle has learned to say "sweater" in place of "jumper." In Nelson, a town I have not yet heard of, Lionel Kearns is beginning his first year of high school; he has joined the school's dance band, the Kampus Kings. Fred Wah is nearby, walking through a Kootenay forest, doing research for a book he will call *Tree*. The land is not flat like it was in Swift Current. He is also wondering when people will stop thinking of him as Chinese. I am getting on a school bus, #7, to go to junior high school. It has a young woman driver. I don't think I've seen a woman drive even a car before. Some of the kids think she must have learned when she was a teenager in the army during the war.

I should be going to the new junior high school that is being built on land that the village has bought from Frieda Nelson, part of the old Nelson farm, but it won't be ready until January. The bus is taking me to a temporary high school in the barracks at the old Commonwealth Air Training base on Mount Lehman Road—I wonder where the Liberator bombers have gone. The school gathers students from all the district elementary schools, and so I am meeting for the first time kids who have lived all my life only one or two miles away. Instead of only one room for each grade, there are six or more Grade 7 rooms, seemingly selected by ability. Many of those I went to the elementary school with are in other rooms. I have another new fountain pen—a Schaefer "Snorkel." My best friend this year is Melvin Szigety. I visit his farm on weekends and sleep over. He teaches me to handle his .22 rifle. We shoot at a target set up against a stump. He shows me a place in the nearby woods where some boys our age have put some old sofa cushions so they can take turns having sex with their twelve-year-old sister. I have been daydreaming about sex, usually with some exotic partner like Princess Margaret Rose or Dorothy of Oz. A Brit and an American. He trades me a paperback novel called *Kitty* that has lots of descriptions of sex for a Porky Pig comic book. At home I no longer have to say my prayers for my grandmother. She thinks her ribs have healed.

I have also been playing badminton for the past two years, mostly on Saturday mornings in the gym at the old Philip Sheffield High School—the school that the new junior high is going to partly replace. I am only moderately athletic, and so I have been studying the game as if it were a sonnet or a math problem—how to turn my body fully sideways to make backhand or forehand retrievals. How to aim overhead drives at an imaginary point high above the back line so that the shuttle drops straight down barely within the court. Another way that I can make myself up. I join the junior high badminton club which has numerous girl members who look almost like Princess Margaret Rose in shorts and sweaty T-shirts.

November 1952 . . .

As usual, the tiger has started to reappear on the mountain. But I am used to it. I have used my father's new 8 x 30 binoculars to look at the rocks and trees that help shape it.

April 1953 . . .

Up in the Kootenays Lionel is wishing he could be a pro hockey player. He is playing tenor sax for the Kampus Kings. The girl who was my partner in the Swedish schottiche is pregnant. The father isn't Lionel—although later I'll be sure that he wouldn't have minded—it's a boy I played badminton with last year when we were all in Grade 6. They are both a year older than me because they had both once failed a grade. Their parents are arranging for them to get married. I look back at the schottische photo. She and

I are in the second row, far left. The father-to-be is in the back row immediately behind her. They are the two saddest-looking ones in the photo, although on this day they have not yet found each other. "May 30, 1952" I have written on the back with my

We dance a schottische.

fountain pen. I have unwittingly started research on my study of family relations, *Edward and Patricia*.

August 1953 . . .

We are going on a two-week camping trip here in BC. We are going to places where my father and a partner mined on their own for gold in 1934 and 1935, building sluice boxes on the Similkameen and Tulameen rivers. "We didn't make much—maybe $1,200 a year—but it was good to be working," my father recalls. When you say "Similkameen" you accent the "milk." I didn't know there were any government campgrounds in BC, but there are—very small with only nine or ten campsites at each, and pit toilets. But only three or four sites are ever occupied, and the picnic tables are made of shining slabs of varnished natural wood. Eight years from now I will sit at an identical table near Oliver and type the stencils of the first issue of *Tish*. I will sleep that night in the same tent. Hmmm.

We camp at Stemwinder campground on the Similkameen near Hedley where I have my first close look at sagebrush and Jack pines. There are big black and white birds in the pine trees that my father calls "Whisky Jacks." He says that Roosevelt raised the price of gold in 1934 from $20 to $35 an ounce. But it's hard to find. We camp at Antler Beach near Peachland on Lake Okanagan. We ride the ferry from Peachland to Kelowna, where Mr. Bennett is plan-

THE TIGER ON THE MOUNTAIN 39

ning to build a bridge. We drive through Enderby where this summer's polio epidemic is most intense. My mother won't let me drink the water here, or talk to people, or let my father stop to camp. No one knows how you get polio. But if you get it you are crippled for life, or trapped in an "iron lung," or you die. In each town I buy a felt pennant with the town's name on it. My father buys a souvenir decal in each and glues it to a rear window of our Chev. We camp in Mount Revelstoke Provincial Park which also has pit toilets—we are almost in another part of Canada—the part my grandmother calls "Back East" where her eldest sister Kate's family lives in Calgary and Regina, but there are five hundred miles of bad gravel road to drive to get there. My grandmother has still not seen Kate since they both left County Durham in 1913.

September 1953 . . .

I begin Grade 8 and fall secretly in love and begin unwittingly gathering the material for a poem I will someday write called "In Love with Cindy Jones." It will be the best thing I was ever able to do for a certain girl, or write for any girl or woman, and I will hope she knows. In English we study Scott's *The Lady of the Lake* and John Drinkwater's *Abraham Lincoln*. My father says that he studied *The Lady of the Lake* in Grade 8 too, the last year he was in school, along with "The Wreck of the Hesperus." "The boy stood on the burning deck / Eating peanuts by the peck," he recites. Maybe this is why he left school. My mother is listening to radio broadcasts of Joseph McCarthy's hearings on communists in the U.S. Army. She has decided that Senator McCarthy and someone called C. David Schine are bullies. They are some of the ones who have kept Paul Robeson from singing in Canada. I have decided that I am still pretty good at writing and so enter the provincial BC Pulp and Paper Association essay contest, and win second prize. The prize is $50, with which I buy a "7 drawer kneehole desk" that I have coveted in Eaton's catalogue. My father says the top is fragile and gets a sheet of plate glass cut to fit it. My grandma buys me a desk blotter. For Xmas I get an

"Arrow" stapler, which I will someday use to staple copies of *Tish* and grant applications for *Open Letter.* And maybe to staple parts of this manuscript.

In the spring of 1954 I would like to earn some money berry picking or bean picking like many of the other kids. George Bowering is bored by his year at Vic College in Victoria and is thinking of going back to fruit picking or maybe enlisting in the U.S. Marines or maybe the RCAF. And back in Oliver his girlfriend Wendy doesn't want to see him. Gladys is playing saxophone in Carter's Teenage Orchestra, at dances in Crofton and Chemainus and Parksville and getting $10 each time. It would be useful to have known some of this. My dad is saying I'd enjoy doing something. But my mother and grandma say berry picking is menial work, grubby work, and forbid it. I make a little money putting leaflets under the wipers of parked cars.

July 1954 . . .

I go with my mother and grandmother once again on the bus to Vancouver—another trip to shop and make up their bank books. We walk along Pender Street from the bus station toward Granville and look in the windows of second-hand bookstores. This time I pause also at the Peoples Cooperative Bookstore which has numerous new books that are low-priced because they are printed in Russia. For sixty to seventy-five cents each I buy hardback translations of Chekov's short stories, Turgenev's *On the Eve* and Pushkin's *The Captain's Daughter.* The books are generous in size and the typography clear and spacious. "Mockba 1954" the Pushkin title page says. The Peoples Cooperative Bookstore is supposed to be run by Communists but you can't find books like these in other stores.

September 1954 . . .

It's Grade 9, and if you want to stay in the "top" class you have to study French. I still think I'm pretty good at writing and so I apply to also take typing—instead of music. I've also completed the Theory, Harmony and History exams from the University of Toronto music conservatory, and the Grade VII piano examinations—all more advanced than the music course. But typing is a "commercial" subject, the counsellor tells me. If they let me take it I'll be depriving a young woman of the typing skills she'll need to get a job. He doesn't mention that there's never been a boy in the typing class. But he does let me skip most of the music classes and still get the credit.

My English teacher, Mrs. Paul, lets me write on different topics than the other students write on, and reads some of the short stories I am trying to write. After school one day I ask her very seriously whether it is better to use an adjective or a phrase to modify a noun—"a leather coat" or "a coat of leather"? I feel I need a black-and-white answer. She tells me "it depends" but isn't very clear about what it could depend on. She is of course correct but I am impatient. We study *Romeo and Juliet*. She gives me Willa Cather's "Paul's Case" to read, probably because of my saccharine short stories in which young and misunderstood boys and girls always find true love. She also gives me Maugham's *The Moon and Sixpence*. On a trip to Bellingham I buy second-hand copies of Abrams portfolio books of Van Gogh, Utrillo, Rembrandt and Cezanne.

I enter the school public speaking contest, which requires the writing of a script. I write a stirringly clear right-wing speech praising the heroic resistance of the Nationalist Chinese on Formosa, and win the contest. The winners compete in Chilliwack against similar winners from the other major Fraser Valley high schools. I place second, although the official photograph makes it look as if I won. The attractively self-assured young woman on my left—your right—is the winner. I'd like to get to know her, even though I'm

Why I took up public speaking.

Lionel Kearns (centre) playing with the Kampus Kings. 1954–55.

still secretly in love. Lionel Kearns is hoping to play hockey in Mexico. My father has a position in the provincial "wing" of the Eagles lodge and often has to drive to Vancouver. George Bowering has joined the air force. Fred Wah is still in Nelson and is now playing a trumpet as a junior member of the Kampus Kings, while Lionel plays a lead sax. Fred is also unwittingly gathering material for *Diamond Grill*. This is menial work but no one tells him that.

April 1955 . . .

They are tearing up the streetcar tracks in Vancouver—replacing the red streetcars with beige trolley buses and diesel buses. The buses are noisy and smelly. This seems like another end-of-the-war event, another long-delayed modernization, but I'm not sure I like it. The streetcars with their straw seats and clanging bells and one open-top observation car were for me part of exotic Vancouver. There were square wooden streetcars, and square metal streetcars, and a few sleek "President's Cars" that had been new when I first remember seeing them in 1943. By the time I get to UBC they will all be gone.

My godmother Marie Lobban gives me a copy of Earle Birney's *Down the Long Table* for my fifteenth birthday, signed by Mr. Birney and signed again by her. Earle Birney is BC's most famous writer. My godmother has never before given me a present—why has she given me this one? The book seems to be about the McCarthy investigations and about Mr. Birney and workers like my dad and godfather Lyle during the Depression.

In the summer we go camping in Banff and then down in Yellowstone. On the way we pass through Virginia City, Montana, a silver-mining ghost town where Mark Twain once interviewed an outlaw, Bad Jack Slade. There's an old Wells Fargo stage coach on

the street, and some carts that carried silver ore. Writers can have interesting lives, I think. My mother buys me a Kik Cola at the Bucket of Blood Saloon. My own interesting bad habit is getting too close to bears with my German camera. Sometimes my dad pulls me back by my collar.

September 1955 . . .

It's Grade 10 at the brand-new senior high school, a school that also offers "senior matric"—a very compact version of first-year university. I again apply to take typing and, when again refused, decide to take German instead of music, despite being warned by the teacher that all of the other students will be from Mennonite families that speak Plattdeutsch at home. We complete a full-year course by Xmas, and then a second full-year course, in which we read most of Baron Munchausen's *Wunderbaren Reisen*, by June. I get an "A" in both. My English teacher thinks I am bored, and suggests to the principal that I move up to Grade 11 English. He agrees, but then discovers that this is against provincial regulations. He offers a plan. I will remain enrolled in Grade 10 English but do no work—instead I will spend the time working in the school library on a provincial Grade 11 English correspondence course. I decide to stop taking piano lessons—even though I am close to completing an ARCT and qualifying as a private music teacher. I have vague ideas that it might be interesting to work for External Affairs and write some things on the side. The high school organizes a dance band and I am asked to play piano. We have a sax player, Buck McConnell, a violinist/drummer,

Mike Siska and an accordion player Donna Nissen. When Buck plays, we play rock 'n' roll versions of "Shortnin' Bread" or "In the Mood," or dreamy waltzes like "Allegheny Moon" or "I Walk Alone"; when Mike plays violin we offer square dances—and I struggle with the drums; when Donna solos we do Swedish waltzes and schottisches. Far beyond hearing, Gladys Hindmarch goes on playing sax in little towns on Vancouver Island—the group is now called Wally Carter and his Western Canadian Dance Band; Fred Wah in Nelson plays the trumpet and marimba, with a sigh; Daphne unwittingly collects material for *Ana Historic* and *The Given*; George makes jokes as he looks down at the world through a camera. Here in Abbotsford, my mother is worried that I may be socializing with girls at the school dances and warns me that Catholic girls are instructed by their priests to lure Protestant boys like me to get them pregnant—so the boy can be converted and the church get another member. At the year's end none of the beautiful Catholic girls are pregnant. I win the silver cup for top male scholar in the grade.

July 1956 . . .

I get a summer job in a store owned by two of my father's lodge friends—it's a Woolworth's knock-off that they call the "5 Cents to 1 Dollar Store"—on a red-and-gold-lettered sign that looks just like a Woolworth's one. It's one of the most prosperous stores in town, employing six or seven young women in candy, clothing, housewares, notions, fabric and other departments. Each young woman has her own cash register. They hire me to help with the annual inventory, and then keep me on to work in the basement receiving and pricing large shipments of toys that are arriving from Japan for Christmas—more complicated work, they hint, than many of the "girls" can do. They pay me $25 a week. Most of the young women get between $27 and $35 a week. On my breaks I go out to the alley and talk to the real girl I am still secretly in love with—she is working at her father's store just up the street. Meanwhile my father has been teaching me to drive—first on his brand-new Plymouth Belvedere four-door hardtop, with a push button automatic transmission, then on various standard-shift cars he borrows from friends. I pass my test driving Bart Warner's 1955 Studebaker Commander. My mother is still caught up in our sibling rivalry, and decides she wants to learn to drive too, but he is sending her to driving school. She hints strongly that she has mixed feelings about this. In Nelson Fred has bought himself a 1930 Model A coupe. I know I don't yet know things like this but I also do.

A lot of the older boys are heading north to work on the new TransCanada Pipeline near Dawson Creek. All spring there was a fierce debate in Ottawa about how to build this pipeline and whether it will be all-Canadian. My mother thinks the Liberal minister in charge of it, Trade Minister C.D. Howe, is a bully. I kind of think so too.

September 1956 . . .

I have completed the correspondence course, and am now in the top Grade 12 home room, although I won't complete Grade 12 until the next year—along with some senior matric credits. I am enrolled in two Grade 12 English courses—the general one and the major, in the French major course, the required Grade 11 science, math and PE. There are great kids in my home room, although the fact that they are a year older makes all the attractive girls seem as much maternal as sexy. Or maybe like big sisters. That is sad—and is probably due to my perception of things rather than theirs. The English teacher is Alan Dawe, who was a student of Earle Birney's in the 1940s, and published poems back then in *Raven*, the UBC student literary magazine. He has a guitar and sometimes plays Weavers songs—Pete Seeger songs—to his classes. He will later become head of English at Langara College in Vancouver, and include one or two of my poems in a college anthology that he edits. I imagine myself in a writing class taught by Birney. Dawe also has subscribed to the newly launched *Tamarack Review*, and brings me the early issues to look over. There are poems there by people called Jay Macpherson, Eli Mandel and James Reaney but they seem old-fashioned to me, like word exercises, and not very interesting. Alan Dawe shrugs when I say this. But I do order a subscription.

October 1956 . . .

My father has been elected president of the Eagles for all British Columbia. He and my mother are leaving to make a driving tour of the province's Eagle lodges in a car that the local Hudson dealer has provided for the occasion—a blue 1956 Hudson Jet. In the spring my father will have to fly to New York City to represent the province at the North American convention. Although he has also joined the Masons, and for a couple of years been president of the Abbotsford Association for Handicapped Children, this is likely to be his biggest achievement. The positions however don't seem to be opportunities to *do* anything important. The handicapped children's association raises money to buy wheelchairs and things but doesn't lobby the government to change laws or even to redesign the sidewalks. An Eagles president doesn't change the direction of the Eagles. My father has told me that he doesn't like the rule that an Eagle applicant can be only a "white Caucasian" but he knows enough to keep quiet. I would want to change things. I reflect on how my father uses racist slang—he calls the list of alcoholics who are barred from drinking in local bars "the Indian list," he still talks about "nigger fishing" and "calling a spade a spade"—but nevertheless believes in the legal equality of all races. Language can be insidious, I think. You can consciously want to be a good person and yet have language lead you to speak meanly.

November 1956 . . .

On a trip to Bellingham I buy a black leather motorcycle jacket for $10 at a liquidation store. But later I don't wear it much. It doesn't feel like me, or like how I want to be me. In the Wahl's stationery store in Bellingham I buy one of the new "ball-point" pens—a "Wahl ball." I also buy Everyman editions of Turgenev's *Fathers and Sons* and a Modern Library one of Tolstoy's *War and Peace*. Our band (I play piano and sometimes drums) is occasionally playing at weddings—we get $10 or $20 each for the evening. The weddings are mostly in country halls, and the guests get very drunk, some get hurt in the fights that break out.

January 1957 . . .

My best friend for the past two years has been Benny Jacob who competes provincially at table tennis. He taught me how to play, and in return I taught him how to play badminton, and now he plays better than me. His mother and uncles and cousins speak Hungarian and attend the Catholic church, although I wonder, without asking, whether he may be ethnically Jewish. He has an older cousin, Benny Papp, who wears strides and has been working on pipeline construction, and who warns me about which wedding halls have the worst reputations and advises me on how to avoid fights. Our high schools have a long-standing ban on wearing strides—the baggy gabardine dress pants with narrow cuffs that tough guys like to wear to show they can fight and might have a switchblade. "Zoot-suiters." The two Bennys are also curious about people who may be about to arrive at the Abbotsford airport—three thousand refugees from a failed revolution last month in Hungary. I had followed the news reports hoping the revolution would succeed but Benny had been pessimistic—or admiringly cynical—from the start.

My father and mother are getting ready for their trip to New York. They will fly in a Lockheed Super Constellation, a "Super-Connie"; it will be their first flight. "This is for all the work your father's done," says my mother. "I enjoyed doing it, kewpie doll," says my dad. They are almost as excited as kids get at dances.

At school some of the Grade 12 boys and I begin lobbying for a boys' cooking class. I am not the only one disappointed by having been excluded from classes the school assumes should be only for girls. A number of us who plan eventually to go to university wish we had been able to take both typing classes and cooking classes— these are things we will have to do for ourselves, we complain. Some of the other boys who expect to have construction jobs up north join in—they will be "batching" too they say. In February one of the home ec teachers—Miss Cyr?—tells us she has volunteered to teach a seven-week noon-hour cooking class for boys. She seems to regard it as a possible adventure—which in some ways it becomes. The class fills almost instantly. She begins by teaching us to bake muffins from scratch, and concludes by having us cook a full-course meal for the teachers. For high school it is an unusually serious and self-regulating class—something I won't see again until I am in third year at UBC and in the English department's honours seminar. We boys are briefly school celebrities.

May 1957 . . .

The Hungarian refugees are now living at the airport where I once went to school, but we don't see them much. I have been counting the high school credits I will have at the end of the year—because of having taken the extra German course and English correspondence course, I will have 115 credits and 2 majors, just one major course short of the required minimum of 120 credits and 3 majors. I have sort of known this for a while, but been resigned to spending another year both finishing the requirements and getting some advance credits for university. I am restless, however, and begin reading and rereading the provincial graduation rules. Most students accept a pass in their enrolled courses on the basis of their year's work. This is called being "recommended" by one's teacher. There are provincial examinations in the Grade 12 courses but the only ones who write them are those who would otherwise be failed by their teachers or who wish to win university scholarships. As I reread the description of this process, I notice that there is nowhere a requirement that a student have been enrolled in a Grade 12 course before writing its provincial examination. It seems I could merely write an exam and earn the missing credit. I take my discovery to the principal, Colin Mackenzie. He warily agrees. He doesn't think the question has come up before—because few would want to take an exam they hadn't received preparation for. I tell him I would, and he suggests that in order to retain my eligibility for the scholarship that the BC Electric offers to children of employees I should write the exams as well in the courses I *have* taken—a somewhat larger task than I'd considered.

So that's what I decide to do, write four exams including one in a major history course that I haven't taken. I read the history textbooks and borrow and copy by hand the class notes of the young woman, Sonia Thomas, who has been forever the outstanding female student of her grade. The average I obtain is not outstanding—eighty-five percent—but pretty good for one based entirely on arts courses—two English, a French and a history. I have received eighty-three percent for the history. The average earns me both a small UBC entrance scholarship and the BC Electric one. The teacher of the history course jokes that I have proven him unnecessary. Colin Mackenzie seems surprised. The four beautiful young women—Sonia Thomas among them—who edit the school yearbook are not surprised—they have already included me among the graduates, writing "Talented, straight-A student Frank Davey need not worry about his future. He plans to take an English major and write short stories. . . ." I am slightly worried, but I am on my way.

George Bowering is also on his way, having finished his three-year hitch in the RCAF. Gladys Hindmarch is planning to come from Ladysmith on Vancouver Island. She thinks Victoria will be too British. Lionel Kearns is already on campus. Betty Lambert, who in 1976 will write the notable comedy *Sqrieux-de-Dieu*, has just graduated but will stay another year to qualify for graduate study. Another future dramatist, Carol Johnson, who will write and publish as Carol Bolt, is only fifteen years old but has just been accepted. She has zoomed through school because her mother is the teacher of a one-room twelve-grade school near Fort St. John. Fred Wah and Pauline Butling are also on their way. And the whole Sopron University faculty of forestry will be there, from Hungary, and speaking Hungarian. And I'll discover most of all this very soon. I just can't wait.

POSTSCRIPT

*

These things happened. But how did I happen? I made myself up as these months went by from the available possibilities. Made myself differently to my mother, father, grandma, teachers, friends, employers. Made myself positions on the international news. Convinced the girls of my graduating class that I had not to worry about my future.

I recall reading a *Star Weekly* novella around 1950 about a boy named Rab who excitedly joined the American rebels in 1776 only to be mortally wounded at Bunker Hill and spend the last pages protractedly and bravely dying. I was glad an American was dying and sad that a young man like me was dying. For several weeks, I fantasized a different ending—one in which he was rescued by a young British woman and survived. I was fantasizing myself.

One of the sad aspects of my Abbotsford years was that although I knew some of my own inner life I knew little of that of my classmates. I sometimes knew when they were upset or fearful, as when Patsy came to me early spring of 1952 to ask me to be her schottische partner—usually we accepted teacher-assigned pairings. But for the most part we all pretended happiness, or stoicism. We kept our fantasies to ourselves.

*

Did my dimly knowledgeable teenage self unfairly generalize Abbotsford onto the rest of the world? Maybe not. What I hoped I was leaving that summer of 1957 was not just a small town but also an air of cultural stagnation that seemed everywhere around it.

Nothing seemed to me to have been created in BC or Washington State by my parents' generation—that is, nothing much seemed to have been created since the 1920s, a period which both my parents recalled with some nostalgia. My father especially recalled that era's extraordinary automobiles—the Moons, Pierce-Arrows, Duesenbergs—that could be bought for twenty or thirty dollars in 1930 because no one now could afford to operate them. My grandma recalled losing thousands of dollars that year on once profitable second mortgages she had invested in and which had been defaulted. The Star automobile that she and her husband had bought in the twenties had had to be their last car purchase. My mother joked about how my father—unable to afford streetcar fare—would walk thirty blocks across town to see her and then offer to take her for a walk. All the interesting electric lights on our Christmas tree—the glass Santas, the clusters of fruit, the imitation roses—were from the 1920s. The new ones were just plain coloured glass.

Most of the "new" structures I had encountered were of 1920s modernist design—the Art Deco Marine Building and City Hall in Vancouver, the Burrard Street and Lions Gate bridges, the numerous Arts and Crafts houses of West Point Grey and Kerrisdale—or else they were, like Abbotsford's new high schools, functional but pedestrian boxes. The only recent architectural gem in Vancouver was the BC Electric Building on Burrard Street, completed in 1955, only six years before *Tish*—which later became the first postwar building in Vancouver to receive heritage designation. In the U.S. the only new structures seemed to be from Roosevelt's "New Deal"—the Grand Coulee Dam and numerous small concrete bridges with 1930s dates embossed on their abutments. The tallest and most famous building in the world was the Empire State Building—completed in 1931. The most famous new poem Eliot's *Waste Land* of 1923, the

Abbotsford's new senior high school, 1955.

most famous new painter Picasso. The Reaney, Macpherson and Mandel poems I had read in the *Tamarack Review* seemed to be still working out of Eliot's poetics. It was as if, because of the Depression and world war, the world had stood still—for more than thirty years. There had been creativity, but in things such as the MiGs and Sabres I had drawn for my Grade 5 and 6 classrooms, the monstrous six-engine B-36 bombers that overflew Abbotsford on their way to McChord Field, the Avro Arrow that was being developed in Toronto, in pop-up toasters and cameras and plastic fabrics and push-button transmissions, and the atom bomb. "I have seen the best minds of my generation . . ." someone had written just last year.

It wasn't so much the old monuments themselves, like the Marine Building, that both impressed and troubled me, it was the way those buildings testified to hopeful lives, engagement in

ongoing process, implications of what could have come after. They were testimonies more than they were monuments. They were much like the gold my father had accumulated with his sluice boxes on the Similkameen—it was the pleasure and hope of doing fruitful labour that my father recalled, and not the product which that labour had created.

My father (left) beside the Similkameen in 1932-33.

The war of course hadn't simply ended with Nagasaki in 1945, or in 1947 with the introduction of brightly coloured cars, or in 1957 with seamless nylons. Its spasms had continued with the Nuremberg trials, the Berlin airlift, the murder of Jan Masaryk, the Chinese civil war, the founding of Israel, the Korean War, the blacklisting of artists such as Hellman, Robeson and Pete Seeger, the Mau Mau terrorists in Kenya, the execution of the Rosenbergs. In 1958 I would be able to attend a marvellous Seeger concert in UBC's Physics 100 amphitheatre—the blacklist was still limiting Seeger's performing career to left-sympathizing campuses and small coffee houses.

Not allowing him all the possible pleasures of his work, but bringing that work to us. "Put a bobbin in my hand, so I can keep on a-workin' in the Promised Land," he would sing. Fred Wah remembers being turned toward music and the arts during the early 1950s by "a music teacher who was one of these American music people from Hollywood who was rushed out of the country during the McCarthy era and ended up in Nelson and had written for movies for years and was a good musician" (Fee interview). The war and postwar decolonization of the British Empire had profoundly unsettled Daphne Buckle's life—causing her to be born in Australia during her family's displacement there from Penang, and to endure a lengthy journey later from Penang via England to North Vancouver.

I don't believe one can overstate the impact of that war, and its Cold War aftermath, on the writers who would become the *Tish* group. One consequence was for us to be simultaneously attracted and repulsed by both British and American nationalisms, whether literary or military. Much like the West was attracted by anti-Soviet writers such as Solzhenitsyn, Yevtushenko and Pasternak, we tended to be attracted to anti-nationalist Americans such as Olson and Ginsberg and to cosmopolitans such as Stein and Duncan, and to the least British (and the least celebrated within Britain) of the British— David Jones, Samuel Beckett, Harold Pinter. We were suspicious of nationalisms, including Canadian ones. Most of us had Japanese-Canadian schoolmates who had been interned. A very attractive young woman I met at UBC—a housemate of future dramatist Carol Bolt—had spent four of her first five years imprisoned in a Japanese camp at Hong Kong and was at the very least physically marked by those years. Daphne Buckle's family had barely avoided similar imprisonment. She would later write explicitly about these connections, and their repercussions within her family, in her poetry tripycht *Ghost Works* and novel *Taken*. Bowering's attraction to the left-wing editors of *El Corno Emplumado* and to the Cold War materials of his novel *Harry's Fragments*, Jamie Reid's decades of commitment to the Communist Party of Canada (Marxist-Leninist), Lionel Kearns's hockey-playing years in Mexico and his support of the Cuban Revolution all had their roots in World War Two's upheavals. We were suspicious also of consumerism—of a culture that produced toasters, cars, clothes, films and poems as if they were widgets to be displayed on countertops, in driveways and in museums. We had seen the well-wrought steam iron. "How about a little capitalistic affection," one of my Korean War comic book heroes had asked, not entirely ironically.

*

None of those airplane-flying comic book heroes had been women. In Abbotsford men's jobs had been for life and women's jobs were to tide them over between high school and marriage, or to supple-

ment the family income in hard times. Men had to work, women could avoid it; housework was a sort of natural hobby that they had been genetically programmed to enjoy. Such sexism of course was normal—it was both systemic and structural. My father's Eagles lodge had a "Ladies Auxiliary" which the men had organized and of which my mother eventually became a president. The Masons had organized a similar "Eastern Star" lodge for its women, and a man desig-

My mother, Worthy Matron.

nated as its "Worthy Patron" had to be there to advise its putatively presiding "Worthy Matron" at each meeting. My mother became a "Worthy Matron" too. The discomfort of women with this system was reflected mostly in the routine sarcasm they directed at their male partners, and in the fairly steady stream of materially comfortable housewives who were sent to Crease Clinic in nearby New Westminster for four-week visits occasioned by "breakdowns." In Abbotsford "breakdowns" could be only a female ailment. That such rigid roles could adversely affect both men and women struck me only when I realized that I needed to learn to type, or when the boys of my graduating class realized that cooking was going to be for them a more useful skill than wood-work or metalwork. Only among my teachers did I meet a signifi-cant population of ostensibly happily working women.

But at UBC the faculty members would be overwhelming male, and the secretaries entirely female. Young men were seeking degrees; young women were popularly perceived to be pursuing their MRS's. Many seemed to believe, along with Hardy, his "maid and her wight," that "all this will go onward the same though dynasties pass." Male dynasties, that is. Could one have a female companion whose capabilities and achievements one admired? What kind of life would the 1955 winner of the Fraser Valley Public Speaking Con-test have? Would I want to have accompanied her? Wouldn't one be better off with a happily achieving woman than an unhappy and impeded one? That was a puzzle that I would later find out I was not alone in pondering. Pauline Butling had already unconsciously begun research on her essay "Hall of Fame Blocks Women"—an essay I could have no idea I would eventually publish. I was inch-ing my way toward writing a longish poem on Abelard's Héloise, bpNichol and Camille Claudel. I would one day have a fantasy infat-uation with Isabelle Adjani.

*

Except for remembering the Vimy monument, I have written almost nothing here about my maternal grandfather, Pte. Albert Frank-land Brown, and his serving in the Canadian First Division in 1917–1919 at Vimy, Ypres, Passchendaele and Mons, and after the Armistice at Godesberg, near Bonn, on the Rhine. About how parts of our house, including my bedroom, were a shrine to his memory. In an ornate brass frame, a tinted 19-by-13-inch photograph of him in his uniform gazed benignly from the wall that faced the foot of my bed. His just-in-case "hero" portrait. An even larger frame hung over my bed enclosing his battalion colours and a small sepia photo of him in the middle. A third photo of him in uniform stood on my dresser enclosed in another brass frame engraved in colour with cannons and the flags of Britain and France. There were various family stories about him—that he had been an army cook, that he had been a machine gunner, that he had been such a good machine-gunner that the air corps had asked him to move up to a biplane's rear cockpit. He had declined. Two canvas and brass belts from a .303-calibre water-cooled machine gun, probably a Vickers, hung in my closet. That he had helped a French-speaking Belgian family recover their silver heirlooms from where they had buried them during the 1914 invasion. In 1993 I discovered a long letter of gratitude to him from that family; he must have given them his Vancouver address. At various places in the house there were also a tall brass pitcher made out of a 9 mm shell and an ashtray made from the base of a Belgian shell stamped "FN Nov 1917," both of them decorated with the brass badges of Canadian soldiers who had apparently no longer needed them. A crucifix made from four 7.92 mm cartridges. Art. Folk art. There was the story that in 1939 when war had broken out again he had volunteered for further service. There was also the story that his death a few months after my birth had been due to the effects of wartime injuries. My father said to me several times—and not always in front of my mother and grandmother—that he was the finest man he had known.

There must have been at least some family plan in all this—perhaps an undiscussed one. My name "Frankland" had already been engraved in 1917 among his battalion colours. The seven wooden packing cases that my grandfather had made in 1913 for immigration to Canada were preserved as our jam cupboards, with his hand-painting of his name "A.F. Brown" still visible on their doors. In my early years I had difficulty not conflating the two world wars. My grandfather's woodworking and garden tools were the best and most carefully stored of my father's tools. I think my father had internalized him as a role model, even—especially?—when calling my mother "his little girl."

Perhaps the most important relic of my late grandfather was my grandma herself—the "most educated" one. In late 1940 after his death she had become dangerously depressed. Had lost weight, stopped caring for herself. Her doctor, the one who had delivered me, gave her about a year to live. My parents had invited her to live with them, helped her sell her large Kitsilano house and move most of her furniture—including her Mason & Risch piano, those jam cupboards, her military photos of my grandfather, two large landscape paintings that had once hung in the Cross Keys, that letter from Belgium—to Abbotsford. Almost at once she took over the family laundry and cooking, began teaching me to read and to "remember" my grandfather, and lived another twenty-three years. This was probably one of *Tish*'s founding moments, and I almost forgot it.

*

Is there a contemporary literary culture? Is there a contemporary culture of design? The year is 1953, and I'm thirteen years old, and

In my Art Deco shirt, 1953.

I am wondering this, but I have no idea. The answer of course was yes—wherever there is humanity there is culture—although this particular culture's materials seem pretty ordinary, as if sourced from W.A.C. Bennett's hardware store. There is considerable pop culture—the dazzling Art Deco–derived nylon shirts that boys have to wear this year—Clarice Cliff on steroids—the white poplin jackets that will be equally necessary in 1954, the pink shirts and pink suede shoes of 1955. There is Eddie Fisher's radio show, "Coke Time" and on the new CBC-TV "Our Pet, Juliette." But has any resonant literature been written since Frost or Eliot or Hemingway or Faulkner? My mother subscribes to the Book-of-the-Month Club and Reader's Digest Condensed Books and so I read *The Caine Mutiny* and *Marjorie Morningstar*, *The Razor's Edge*, *The Old Man and the Sea*, *The Stillness at Appomattox*, *Seize the Day* and—more valuably—a book written by a woman, *The Sea Around Us*. Canadian literature is barely noticeable—I have read some William Henry

Drummond, Bliss Carman and Charles G.D. Roberts in my grade school readers, and somewhere Pratt's "Dunkirk." And then *Down the Long Table* and the first issues of *Tamarack*. On my parents' forty-eight-hour camping trips to Bellingham to buy inexpensive clothes and appliances, my father and I drift repeatedly down to the second-hand stores near the harbour where for less than a dollar each I buy old leather-bound editions of Byron, Hemans, Burns, Coleridge, Wordsworth, Irving, Arnold, Newman, Tennyson, George Eliot, Melville and Thackeray. "The tea rose, tea-gown, etc. / Supplants the mousseline of Cos, / The pianola 'replaces' / Sappho's *barbitos*"—when I read Pound's lines at UBC in the spring of 1958 that is what I will think of—the "orlon" dresses my mother had been buying in uptown Bellingham while I was finding discarded gold-stamped editions of Christina Rossetti and John Henry Newman down by the harbour mission.

*

Where are the admirable models?—who might one learn from? It was a question my father must have had in his struggles just to earn some income, but which had become enormously larger for me as my life began moving away from his, encountering the luxury of larger aspirations. Pound was a Fascist, and Eliot "the most bank-clerkly of Englishmen." Yeats was a Victorian misogynist, and Thomas a bellows full of musical wind. "Beans, beans," Robert Kroetsch would write a few decades later. Conflicted views of Britain and the U.S. run through *Tish* much as they ran through my childhood and adolescence. Most of us had emigration from Britain somewhere within family memory—Daphne Marlatt has written about her tradition-bound uncles and aunts in England, George Bowering about his grandfather from southern England and his mother's "Okie" American family, Lionel Kearns has spent much of the last decade researching his father's service in the RAF in the First World War and the Kearns family's history in Ireland and the U.S. Baseball-loving George, who has lamented the influence of "all the stiff-necked Brits and their toadies" in his hometown of Oliver

(*Magpie* 132), would have begun doctoral work in 1966 at the University of Sussex rather than Western Ontario except for a secretarial foul-up at the British university.

Disgust at "official" United States would permeate *Tish* much as it permeated my childhood. The U.S. that had executed the Rosenbergs and persecuted Paul Robeson would be in the *Tish* years the U.S. of the Bay of Pigs invasion, the Cuban missile "crisis," and of increasing intervention in Vietnam. George Bowering became increasingly incensed by U.S. culture's attempts to monopolize the word "America" for itself—and began insisting on calling it "USAmerica" rather than "America." Yet the U.S. dissident cultures would attract us, much as the Rosenbergs and Robeson and Seeger had intrigued me.

For me during my childhood the only "hero" of the Second World War had been Churchill; afterward I continued to admire a Britain that had fought against Germany for a year and a half before the U.S. entered the war—to admire it over a U.S. that had entered the war only because it had been attacked at Pearl Harbor. Those Dave Dawson books had done their job. I grudgingly admired Britain also for its opposition to the founding of Israel. At first I had been overwhelmed by the romantic propaganda that the U.S. media circulated about Israel's "heroic" founding, but I also became increasingly troubled by what I was discovering about the vicious bombing of the King David Hotel. The creation of a new and often ruthless ethnic/religious nationalism immediately after a disastrous clash of other nationalisms began to seem astonishingly stupid. My grandma treasured her much-worn Victorian sheet music for "Rule Britannia" but Britannia wasn't going to rule, nor Germany or Japan. Israel could survive only with a militarized populace and right-wing policies—some of which we would now call ethnic cleansing. I had much greater admiration for Jews who had attempted to continue to live as members of a non-national or transnational culture.

My father had a belated admiration of Britain for its election of a Labour government in 1948. But my intuitive sense that those children's magazines, *Wee Wisdom* and *Open Roads for Boys*, talked down to me—that British children were infantilized in ways offensive to a young Canadian—remained with me. The "Angry Young Man" hooded coats that I would see students wear on campus in 1957–1958 would seem to me offensively colonial. The "Angry Young Man" novels I would read would seem narrowly specific to Britain—i.e. parochial. George Bowering signals a similar view when he recalls welcoming that year "the end to the illusion cherished by some elders that our proper influences were Auden and Spender and other Brits who were tilting at windmills we had never seen" (*Magpie* 200). One couldn't in good conscience identify with Britain any more than with the U.S.

Daphne Buckle's extensive experience of this conflict between North American BC and Britain—despite their common misogyny—was to a large extent encoded in her own family dramas, and has been worked extensively into both her novels (*Ana Historic* in particular) and poetry *(How Hug a Stone)*. As for other writers associated with *Tish*, this conflict showed itself mostly in their attraction to continental European writers, philosophers or painters. Jamie Reid's favourite painter, for example, was Chagall. In any discussion he would inevitably invoke Nietzsche, Kierkegaard, Rimbaud or Artaud. And it wasn't only *Tish* writers who had these interests. Throughout the UBC campus one could hear references to philosophers such as Sartre, Jaspers, Heidegger and Unamuno, painters such as Chagall, Modigliani, Klee and Kandinsky, dramatists such as Brecht, Beckett and Ionesco and political theorists such as Adorno, Arendt and Marcuse. Plays by Chekov, Brecht, Beckett, Sartre, Betti, Ibsen and Ionesco were all produced by UBC's Freddy Wood student theatre group during my years on campus. These were loose, seemingly prosaic, enigmatic texts, with ambiguities that invited not so much admiration as imaginative work by those watching.

*

And then the invisible and seldom mentioned First Nations—the Sumas and Matsqui Sto:lo. Where had they been? One of the

labourers on my father's line gang was a son of the early BC anthro-
pologist Charles Hill-Tout but I didn't know anything about Charles
Hill-Tout and neither did my father. In 1957 I also hadn't yet fig-
ured out that my father's Metis grandmother might have also been
called "Indian." I don't think my father had. I was only beginning
to realize that "Mission" and "Mission City" had once been words
that indicated a Catholic "mission" to Christianize "Indians."
There was still a residential school there—I had occasionally seen
uniformed young girls scurrying down side streets beside it. But
had I ever *met* an "Indian"? I still don't know. There were apparently at least three hundred in the general Abbotsford area in 1991
(Riggins 6). My father had occasionally mentioned one who tried to
join the Eagles. Maybe they looked a lot like the rest of us. I had
been right about a few words—"Sumas," "Matsqui," "Chilliwack,"
"Similkameen," "Tulameen," and a few words approximately like
them—that they really once had been Indian names. People were
mysteriously somehow "proud" of them, like they were of souvenir
totem poles, or like my mother was of the intricately woven Capi-
lano Indian baskets she had bought in the 1920s and now used to
contain her needlework. Long-ago Indians were apparently more
interesting than on-the-street Indians. It is long-ago Indians that
some of my *Tish* friends will become interested in writing about in
poems with titles like "tentative coastlines." Me too.

*

Were there vast empty cultural spaces in Canada for one to fill?
That was my impression, and probably that of my future *Tish* com-
rades too—although not a huge amount of big-time cultural information could reach one in Oliver or Nelson or Abbotsford or even
Vancouver in 1956. We of course were surrounded by local cultural
information but we weren't sure that this counted anywhere else.
CBC Television had barely begun broadcasting in Vancouver. *Tropic
of Cancer*, *Sanctuary* and *Lady Chatterley's Lover* were still banned
books—banned since before the war. Earle Birney, Eric Nicol and
Roderick Haig-Brown were the only BC writers I had heard of. If

this was naiveté, it was at least extremely useful naiveté—useful in building hubris if not confidence. And was it naiveté? Had much happened in BC writing since Floris McLaren, Doris Ferne and Allan Crawley's founding of the magazine *Contemporary Verse* in 1941? Writers such as Earle Birney, Dorothy Livesay, Ethel Wilson, Jane Rule and Phyllis Webb had had individual careers that they carried on mostly elsewhere—in Ontario, with publishers whose books rarely appeared in BC bookstores and were rarely celebrated in the *Vancouver Sun*. As far as I could tell they had done little work to build literate networks, or literary descendants, in their own province.

Were there any young BC poets or novelists in the generation immediately ahead of us? None that I knew of. One oddity of Birney's presence that we had not yet had the opportunity to notice was that his writing students—while sometimes becoming "big" on campus—had tended so far not to develop significant post-graduation careers. That generation would eventually take shape mainly through the arrival of late developers such as Pat Lowther and Roy Kiyooka, and immigrants such as Robin Blaser, Robin Skelton, J. Michael Yates, Stan Persky and Stan Cooperman.

The empty cultural space I was sensing in 1957 in BC points once again "back to the war," and to the Depression years that led up to it. F.R. Scott, Dorothy Livesay and A.J.M. Smith had had their poetry careers violently interrupted by these years. Smith and Scott would first publish in magazines in the late 1920s but not be able to publish their first books until the 1940s. Livesay would publish her first book, *Green Pitcher*, in 1929, her second in 1932 and her third not until 1944. BC was not alone in its gaps, delays and silences. Some of these reflected the difficult economics encountered in the 1930s and '40s by publishers. But they also reflected the difficult financial and ethical choices would-be writers had to make in a time of high unemployment, growing global conflict and rudimentary social services. In 1937 Birney had advised his fellow leftist writers not to allow even their reading of literature "to interfere with the much bigger job of helping to organize . . . fellow workers toward the establishment of a society where writers will be free to express themselves without starving or turning intellectual traitors" (Birney np). The delayed emergence of the Scott, Smith, Livesay and Birney generation in the 1940s and '50s in turn delayed the emergence of the Page, Layton, Dudek and Mandel generation until the late '50s and early '60s. Our generation of poets—elsewhere in Canada as well as in BC—was the first since the 1920s to have the possibility of emerging in its own time. When we did abruptly go public, it was, interestingly, older non-BC writers such as Robin Mathews, Al Purdy and Milton Acorn, ones still seeking audiences, who would be the most troubled.

And that empty cultural space points back even more tellingly to the mostly silent and still ongoing wars of sexism and of colonization. Millennia of gender warfare had left almost only male authors on the universities' bookshelves and reading lists. Three centuries of colonization had created a culture in which the colonizers could see First Nations culture only as museum-eligible— the museums of white people's poems and place names and basket-selling tourist shops—and their own strange communities as shabby reflections of wealthier or finer lands elsewhere. Some of us will someday write novels that make these wars more visible. In 1957 it was becoming desirable to own an Emily Carr painting, but would one really want to have lived a life like hers?

PART 2 LISTEN TO THE SOUND OF IT

Studying Poetry, First Meetings, First Commitments (1957–1961)

July 1957 . . .

I work again at the "5 Cents to 1 Dollar Store," although the owners are preoccupied with building a small shopping centre by filling
in ravine land two blocks west. It's the wooded ravine with a small
creek that my mother and I had crossed in 1945 to get to Frieda
Nelson's, and that I had crossed every day to get to high school.
The village water had come from that creek during the 1940s. The
project is an early sign that Abbotsford is to be no longer a village.

I drive my mother and myself to Vancouver, to the UBC housing
office to look for a place to stay. On the main boulevard to the campus, workmen are starting to erect the remains of early-nineteenth-
century totem poles to help celebrate an 1858–1958 centennial.
Most of the poles have been removed from Queen Charlotte Island
villages abandoned after the smallpox epidemics of the 1830s. Some
celebration. I don't want to stay on campus in one of the dormitories—they are expensive. They also seem annoyingly parental. I'm
tired of the small panopticon that surrounds one in a small town—
the sense that the town is an audience that watches you whether or

not you want to "play" to it. Every child famous among children. We look at a number of rooms for rent just outside the university gates. There's a bus that runs the two miles from the gates to the campus. We settle on a basement room in a house in the 4400 block on West Sixth. It is owned by an elderly woman, Mrs. Akrigg, the widow of an RCMP officer. There's a police-issue bed in my room. She is very frail, hunched over from osteoporosis, and depends on a middle-aged housekeeper, also a widow, Mrs. Dale. Mrs. Akrigg's son is a professor in the English department at the university—the Shakespeare professor, "G. Philip Akrigg" and sometimes "G.P.V. Akrigg." The rent is $25 a month. I can cook my meals in the kitchen once Mrs. Akrigg and Mrs. Dale have eaten, and have half a shelf in the fridge. This seems to be a standard arrangement for student rooms. Mrs. Akrigg is pleased that I am a "normal" student. The student she rented to last year, she says, was an Arab, and cooked strange-smelling foods. The smells made her ill. Mrs. Dale says it was especially bad when he cooked at night when they were trying to sleep. He claimed he had to cook "after dark" because of his religion.

From there we drive to East Hastings Street and the famous pawnshop, BC Collateral Loan. I've been thinking of teaching myself the guitar and looking for one with a good sound. I find a Gibson LG-1, with a case, and buy it for $85.

August 1957 . . .

I decide to accompany my mom and dad on their "camping" trip to Oregon and the Olympic Peninsula. The previous year they bought a sixteen-foot travel trailer and are planning to take it through Walla Walla in Washington State and Bend, Oregon, to the California border and then come back up the Oregon coast to Washington and do a circle tour of the Olympic Peninsula coast. My dad likes to stop for two or three days in each place so he can sample the local wines without having to drive. He lets me sample them too. This is edu-cational because U.S. wines are mainly varietals—so I learn to distinguish Zinfindel, Cabernet, Pinot Noir, Grenache, Merlot. He doesn't care for whites. It's the last trip I will take with them. Everything goes well until we are camped near Port Angeles, and I meet and spend most of the evening in the dark woods with a tall seventeen-year-old young woman from Coos Bay. Jeannie. My dad had been planning to spend the usual three days. But when I get back to the trailer around 2:00 a.m., it is already off its jacks and hooked to his car. We pull out of the campsite at once, leaving Jeannie with only tire marks to contemplate in the morning. My mother is certain that her son was about to be "trapped." I write to Jeannie after I get home—to my mother's horror we had exchanged addresses.

September 1957 . . .

The UBC campus has only a few recently built modern buildings—the War Memorial Gymnasium, completed three years ago for the British Empire Games, the University Hospital, the engineering building, the education building and a number of dormitories—but none that will regularly concern me. The core of the campus was built in the 1920s and early '30s—the library and the chemistry and physics buildings of stone, and the large but "temporary" arts building, agriculture building, registrar's office, auditorium/cafeteria and armouries of wood frame and grey stucco. The sudden enrolment of thousands of veterans after the war had been dealt with by the importing of a hundred or more large military huts from various then unnecessary army and air force bases. Thus much of the campus looks like the streets of airport barracks in which I had begun junior high. The vets must have felt right at home. Some huts have been turned into classrooms, some into student laboratories, others into faculty offices. The war still resonates. My Philosophy 100 class will be three-hour-long lectures in an army hut filled with around a hundred students.

Before classes begin, however, is an orientation or "frosh" week with events organized mainly from the dorms and including some hazing. Frosh are required, according to leaflets distributed by the student organizers, to wear identifying beanies. This seems excessively like the panopticon of the small town I have just left. Although younger than almost all of the first-year students, I decide to look older. I buy myself a tweed overcoat. I smear dirt on my new brown-leather briefcase—male university students in 1957 carry cowhide briefcases much the way 1990s students will carry backpacks—so that it will look at least a year old. I keep my newly bought first-year textbooks out of sight. I find that anonymity is surprisingly easy—my first university success.

As well as English and French, and biology to fulfill a compulsory science requirement, I have enrolled in Latin, thinking it will expand my vocabulary, psychology thinking that it will help me create fictional characters, and philosophy hoping that it will make all this thinking incisive. There is an introductory creative writing course, but entry is restricted to second-year students who have submitted a qualifying portfolio of writing. A counsellor tells me that a hundred or more usually apply for the course's twenty places. I will need to do a ton of writing this year to create that portfolio. I also have enrolled in golf—the university requires first-year students to do two units of athletic activity. Most students try for bowling or archery—but these fill up early.

My parents have little idea of what I am doing. They imagine that any university degree is a ticket to lucrative employment. My father suggests that I take practical courses, but doesn't know what these might be. Neither of them have attempted to read the university calendar. My father is only now realizing that I have graduated from high school without any of the math and science credits necessary for the sciences or engineering.

Overall, UBC is as crowded as it was back in 1946 when swamped with veterans. The English department is especially stressed. The university requires completion of its first-year course by every one of the approximately two thousand incoming students regardless of degree program, and completion of its second-year historical survey by every arts student regardless of major. The approximately thirty-five-member department—which at this point has virtually no graduate program—must staff many of the around fifty sections of English 100 by part-time hiring. Almost every faculty spouse with an English literature background has been drafted to teach. The department also cuts corners by hiring British university graduates with dubious Masters degrees—both those granted automatically two years after completion of a baccalaureate and those given as compensation for a failed doctoral thesis. Many Canadian universities are doing this. A Canadian annual salary of $4,000 seems enormous by comparison to 1950s academic salaries in Britain. I figure all this out very quickly—I am curious about my professors' backgrounds. I am curious about how UBC compares to other universities. There are shelves of university calendars in the library. I figure out also that most students don't care about such things.

However, I have improbably good fortune with my courses. My Latin course is taught by Malcolm McGregor, chair of the classics department and a theatrically dynamic campus figure. My biology course, one designed for non-majors, is taught by someone involved in the new field of DNA research and who brings to many of the lectures excited news about the latest discoveries. My French literature course is taught by a Parisian poet, my philosophy course by the future department chair Barnett Savery and my English course by Ruth Humphrey who—despite having what appears to be one of those honorary Oxford M.A.s, earned in 1926, is passionate about the modernist literature on which English 100 focuses. She is also a close friend of Emily Carr and Sheila Watson.

Near the end of the month is Club Day—the day that campus clubs mount displays in the armouries building to attract new members. Among the clubs is the Writers Workshop, which meets monthly in the basement recreation room of an English department faculty adviser. An interesting word, "workshop," I think. It suggests tools and sawdust and metal filings. Santa's workshop. That we make things. There is a locked wooden Writers Workshop drop box in the lobby of one of the army huts on West Mall that has been converted to offices. Workshop members leave their manuscripts anonymously in the box. The adviser clears the box the week before a meeting and creates enough copies for everyone. I join. The club may help me create my portfolio.

October 1957 . . .

I seem to be the only one who has come from Abbotsford to UBC. Others in my graduating class have stayed at the high school to do senior matric. Most of the other students here are Vancouver residents, for whom moving from high school to UBC is as unremarkable as moving from junior to senior high. That galls me— that what is logistically so difficult for some can be so routinely, even banally, easy for them. I have a hard time liking any of them. They gather together in the same chattering clusters that they did in high school. They hang out at the student union building, Brock Hall. They "rush" fraternities and sororities. They run for student council. The older males go to law school. I know I'm exaggerating but these are unfortunately the most visible local students.

My mom and dad have been coming down every Saturday morning to take me home for the weekend, do my laundry and then bringing me back Sunday night. Most Saturday nights I get together with Bud Blinch who graduated with me and is now working for a septic tank cleaning company. He has a car and we go down to Sumas, Washington, beside the mountain with the tiger, and enjoy a pitcher of beer. His dad is a customs officer. I persuade my parents to come to Vancouver only every other week—sometimes I need the weekend for reading or writing.

What I miss most is having a piano to play. I am realizing that at home I had played not just to practise but also to create a space within which I could make the demands of the day disappear. There are a lot of demands here. My room is large, so I browse the used piano stores and for $400 buy an old Gerhard Heintzman upright from Eaton's. The delivery men create deep gouges in the back lawn in dragging it to the ground-level basement entry and my room.

My landlady, however, does not enjoy music—not even the half-hour or so I limit myself to playing. She doesn't tell me this herself.

She may not have told Mrs. Dale—who does, however, hint that I should play more softly. Instead she complains to her son, the Shakespeare professor G. Philip Akrigg. Whatever she says enrages him. One afternoon I hear him storm into the house and stomp across the floor. Near the top of the basement stairs he trips, and tumbles down the narrow wooden steps to the concrete outside my door. I look out, then down and there is his round bald head and beside it a pair of wire-framed glasses. I ask if he is okay. He is both furious and incoherent. A minute passes before he can stutter that either I go or the piano. I don't help him up. The next day I persuade a reluctant Eaton's to retrieve the piano and give me a full refund. It seems I will never want to take a UBC Shakespeare course. There are soon even more ominous gouges in the back lawn. I become resigned to quietly teaching myself to play my new guitar.

But I am curious about Akrigg. The older students tell me he runs a joyless classroom. Mrs. Dale tells me that he refuses to let his teenage children dine with him and his wife, Helen, because he believes them still "incapable of adult conversation." How does he expect them to learn, I wonder.

I write and submit a story anonymously to the Writers Workshop drop box. I should probably write about Professor Philip tumbling down the stairs, but I don't think of that. Instead I write about a fight at one of the wedding dances our band played at last summer. The narrator has sentimental longings for one of the young women at the wedding. At the Workshop meeting most of the members are in third or fourth year or a graduate-qualifying year. The young men are affecting British accents and wearing Angry Young Man coats. Many of them say this story is one of the worst things they have ever had to read. To keep myself covered, I add my own condemnations to theirs.

November 1957 . . .

I am rushing to the physics building to get to the big lecture theatre before classes change. Pete Seeger is giving a concert at noon—

12:30 to 1:30. Admission is twenty-five cents. The foyer is already unusually crowded. Seeger and his group The Weavers used to play at Carnegie Hall. Now for a few dollars he plays in a 1920s classroom in Vancouver. I push into the room and get a seat—soon people are sitting on the steps of both aisles. But we have to wait—apparently he has been held up at the border. Perhaps predictably. Seeger finally comes through the lower doors and begins tuning his five-string banjo. He sings the "Winsboro Cottonmill Blues"—a bitterly amusing labour song. He sings "The Ballad of Sherman Wu"— about the Taiwan-Chinese student at Northwestern University who only a year ago was denied entry to a fraternity—to the tune of "The Streets of Laredo." At the end he has us join in a repetition of the opening verse—"As I was out strolling the streets of Northwestern / I spied a young freshman dejected and blue / And when I asked him why was he dejected / He said I'm Chinese and I can't join Psi U."— in effect having us all sing from the perspective of the abject Sherman Hsiu-huang Wu. He sings of mass-produced architecture—of houses that are mere "little boxes on the hillside . . . all made out of ticky-tacky" and all looking "just the same." For psychology students he sings a rousing version of "The Ballad of Sigmund Freud"—"Oh Dr. Freud, Dr. Freud, how I wish you had been differently employed!" He leads us in choruses of "Wimoweh." And as probably an allusion to his political difficulties—and his being delayed at the border?—he sings the 1930s German leftist song *"Die Gedanken sind frei"*—"thoughts are free," he translates, "you can't put them in jail." We are all on our feet cheering—probably in equal measure for his amazing facility with the banjo, his passionate voice and his committed humanity. It is the most extraordinary hour I have yet lived. I'm sure that for years after I will sing these songs to myself as I walk or drive or shower. *"Die Gedanken sind frei."*

Mid-November 1957 . . .

I have to read Conrad's *Heart of Darkness* for my English course. I am finding most of it dull and repetitive. I get through it by playing a forty-five of one of José Iturbi's recordings of *Au Clair de la lune* equally repetitively. In French we are reading more interesting things—Voltaire's *Candide*, Gide's *La Symphonie pastorale*, various poems by Paul Verlaine. The professor is François Fleury, who has just had a book of poetry, *Jours d'Arès*, published by the prestigious French publisher Gallimard. He is young. Such things are possible. In my philosophy course Barnett Savery has given me one hundred percent on my mid-term. He is having an argument with the administration about grades. He says that if the top grade in math or physics can be one hundred percent then the top grade in arts courses can be also.

The literary hero on campus is a fourth-year student named Desmond Fitzgerald. He writes cleverly Yeatsian poems that are published in *Raven* and is one of the most influential of the Angry Young Man crowd who attend the Workshop. He has an aggressively polite English accent despite his Irish name. He is rumoured to be from a noble family. He says he is planning to do graduate work at Harvard. I am curious and seek out more info. I discover his full name: Desmond John Villiers Fitzgerald, twentieth Knight of Glin.

Another senior student, however, Betty Lambert, who has just graduated and enrolled in a qualifying year toward graduate study, is generous and helpful in the Workshop discussions. She won UBC's Brissenden writing award in 1956 and its Macmillan Award this past spring for a short story but doesn't even hint at pulling rank on the other members. She and I become friends, at least in the context of the Workshop, and after the meetings sometimes have our own brief meta-discussions of the responses various texts have received. She often drives me back to West Sixth. Sometimes I think that it's only the possibility of talking to her that keeps me coming to the meetings.

I don't encounter George Bowering at the workshop this year. I just sometimes hear the name. There are usually twenty-five or thirty students—he could be here but I don't think he is. Besides, all the young men pretending to be Brits would likely put him off.

A young woman from my first-year Latin class is sometimes here. But most seem to be upper-year. Sometimes I see myself as a small military beachhead from the future. Salerno, Anzio.

January 1958 . . .

In English we have been studying mostly fiction and drama. As well as *Heart of Darkness* we've read Lawrence's "The Rocking Horse Winner," Faulkner's "The Bear," Mann's "Mario and the Magician," Joyce's "The Dead." They all seem troublingly old—the literature part of English 100 is supposed to be twentieth-century, and it is, but it is all pre-war, much like most of the buildings on campus. Ruth Humphrey knows these stories really well—it is the writing she grew up with at Oxford in the early twenties. But the readings in my French course have been entirely different—now Camus's *L'Etranger,* and Marcel Aymé's *"La Carte."* Are there such works in English? Would they be as formally different as these are from Lawrence and Joyce, or as Lawrence and Joyce are from the writing of my leather-bound Nelson and Collins classics?

One late afternoon after my biology lab I am riding the old diesel bus from UBC's Main Mall to the gates. Darkness had fallen before the lab ended. The bus is crowded with tired-looking students. I begin a poem about the bus "growling from the darkened campus" and finish it in my room. I take it to the drop box for the next Writers Workshop meeting where the Angry Young Man coats call it a "mood piece" and criticize it for its pessimism and for using the pathetic fallacy. But Betty Lambert likes its sound. It's the first poem I've written at UBC.

February 1958 . . .

In English we've begun looking at poetry. Hardy, Housman, Eliot's *The Waste Land,* Pound's "Mauberley." Auden's "September 1 1939" is the most recent poem. Ruth Humphrey knows these poems like a jeweller knows the intricate structure of watches. I've discovered a journal called the *Explicator*, the journal that most English 100 students rely on. Its short articles disassemble poems like these—ones likely to be taught in university courses—and reproduce them as prose summaries. It's useful in identifying allusions and translating the bits of Latin, Greek, Old French, German—languages that the poets all seem to know but few of us do. But it's also somehow offensive—"a prose kinema" Pound would call it, one that lets you read "with no loss of time." Of course if Ruth Humphrey hadn't explained "kinema," I would have had to look for it in a dictionary or the *Explicator*. It also seems to assume that poems should be obscure—ciphers to be decrypted—and that poets should write in code, like those seem to do that I read in *Tamarack*. I don't believe this. I feel as if I am somehow betraying poetry each time I use it.

In my Latin class, where it's normal for texts to be old and inscrutable, I have become friends with two students—Ann Campbell, the young woman who also goes to the Writers Workshop, and Paul Tennant, who shares my preference for a back-row seat. Paul has joined the campus Conservative club and is urging me to join. The new Liberal leader Lester Pearson has rashly demanded that the Diefenbaker government resign, and "Dief the Chief" has responded by calling a snap election for March 31. Paul thinks that the seat of the first Chinese-Canadian ever elected to Parliament, Douglas Jung, could be in danger. Jung was elected only nine months ago, in the Conservatives' surprise victory.

Douglas Jung in 1957.

Paul is the first Canadian nationalist I have met. He will go on to get a Ph.D. from Chicago and to write books on Quebec politicians and BC Aboriginal land claims—and to become chair of political science at UBC. There I go again. The Conservatives, under leader John Diefenbaker, won their minority victory in last June's election by promising Canadian ownership of the oil pipeline projects, a new "northern vision" that stressed the development of the north and the Arctic, and their inclusion socially and politically. Rarely in Canadian history had the Conservatives proposed progressive social policy. But they had at times been nationalistic—defeating Laurier's Liberals in 1911 under the viscerally satisfying slogan "no truck or trade with the Yankees." I have trouble with the idea of helping the Conservatives—they have always seemed a stuffy British party to me, probably because my grandmother had automatically supported them. But Doug Jung's election last spring was electrifying. It had happened only ten years after Canada's Chinese Exclusion Act—a 1920s act that barred further immigration and denied voting rights to Chinese-Canadians—had been repealed. When Jung had come back in 1945 from serving in the Canadian army in Burma, he had had to wait until that repealing to receive the grants that other veterans had already received to attend university. Not till 1953 did he receive his law degree. Jung himself seems young, personable, courageous and progressive, part of a future I want—not at all "conservative." He has been working to expand Chinese immigration, and to give citizenship to the up to twelve thousand Chinese who somehow managed to enter Canada during the Exclusion Act period. Paul's invitation is tempting.

Meanwhile I have still been going back to Abbotsford almost every other weekend, and joining Bud Blinch for a night across the border in the taverns of Sumas. You can buy a pitcher of beer for ninety cents, and pee in a porcelain bowl over which someone has written, with Cold War humour, "In case of A-bomb attack hide in urinal—no one has hit it yet." Also no one has checked anyone's ID. On one of these visits, I meet an Abbotsford kid, Dan Code, who has a Norton motorcycle. We go back and I trade my chrome-laden motorcycle jacket for his .22 rifle, a Cooey. Another evening I'm in the Legion café in Abbotsford when an older guy we know, a guy with a drinking problem, wants to know if anyone will buy his gun. He has a Winchester Model 94 .32 Special—a nineteenth-century lever-action rifle with a saddle ring. I go out to the parking lot and buy it for fifteen dollars. The gun club has a shooting range out near the garbage dump, a range that is unfenced and unmonitored. Bud Blinch and I go there the next Sunday morning and shoot fifty or sixty rounds at targets. We adjust the sites on the Winchester. There are no laws against carrying long guns in cars or trucks as long as they are unloaded, or against carrying them discreetly on the street from house to vehicle.

March 1958 . . .

I have joined the campus Conservatives. I have signed up to campaign for Doug Jung in Vancouver Centre. The party thinks that the sight of white kids coming to the door to urge support for a Chinese candidate will win support from all varieties of voter—especially the Chinese. I am eager to begin. Vancouver Centre extends from Stanley Park to Main Street, from the harbour south to Broadway. It includes the wealthy West End, the downtown business area, the lands around False Creek, and Chinatown. For two or three nights a week I distribute Jung's campaign leaflets door-to-door in apartment buildings in both the West End and Chinatown. It is easy work—almost everyone seems glad to see me. Many curious food smells in the narrow apartment building corridors. Outside other campaign workers are using stencils to spray-paint trails of footprints on the sidewalks, and the slogan "Follow John." Reporters are following the painters with cameras. And Canada does follow John—Jung retains his seat by an increased margin and the Conservatives win the election with the largest number of seats so far in Canadian history. But I miss the victory party—I have to study for final exams.

June 1958 . . .

I read in the *Sun* that in Hungary several of the leaders of the 1956 revolt have been executed, including Premier Imre Nagy. "Nawj" his name is pronounced. There is an elderly man with this name in Abbotsford, a notary, and we have always called him "Mr.

Naggy"—even my Hungarian friends Benny and Melvin. I wonder whether the premier was a relative. I read also that the U.S. Supreme Court has supported the State Department's withholding of passports from Communists and others of "doubtful loyalty." I guess that includes Paul Robeson.

July 1958 . . .

I've decided to stay on in Vancouver and take second-year French literature at summer school. I haven't been able to find any summer employment, except outside of Vancouver where I would need a car to get to the worksite. French had been a world-opening course for me last year. I have my marks now. I've managed A's in all six subjects, with an A+ in philosophy my highest grade—and English the lowest. French was my second highest.

There's a Jean-Paul Lemieux exhibition in the UBC Art Gallery in the basement of the library. Last term I saw a small Jack Shadbolt exhibition there and was amazed that such formalist colour-dominated work had been done in BC—or in Canada. I coveted every painting. The Lemieux here is equally startling but so austere, even penitential. I wish I could create such things. I wish Miss Blatchford, my high school art teacher, had told us about Jack Shadbolt, here in Vancouver, only forty miles away.

August 1958 . . .

My portfolio application to the creative writing class, English 202, has been accepted—probably by the instructor, Jake Zilber. I'd been worried. Except for the bus poem, it was almost entirely narrative prose similar to my story that had been savaged by the Angry Young Man boys at the Workshop. I have also enrolled in the required English lit survey, a philosophy department course in symbolic logic, a social psychology course, another Latin course and a religious studies one on the Old Testament. I don't need another six-course load, but there so many fascinating things to study. I imagine myself as a Hungarian refugee turned loose in one of the new Vancouver supermarkets. I would like to take courses in Russian literature, art history, the history of architecture, the theatre of the absurd, political science, Renaissance history, logical positivism, existentialism, phenomenology. Some students at the Workshop last year talked about wanting to study just writing— about how they wished there were a creative writing degree. I could see them becoming clever writers who were ignorant of almost everything.

Students choose their majors between second and third year, and I am not yet sure of my choice. So I am taking the prerequisites for a major in any of four departments. For much of last year I leaned toward philosophy and French. Perhaps I still do. At least in a few years' time I may be the only UBC writer to have taken a course in religious studies.

September 1958 . . .

The new Buchanan Building has been completed—it will house arts faculty offices that used to be in the army huts, and classes that were in the old arts building. But the old buildings will still be needed. Most of my courses, however, will be in Buchanan—which on the outside looks long and boxy like my senior high school. But it has large lecture theatres on the bottom level.

A number of Abbotsford students have arrived—mostly from the 1958 class that I would normally have graduated with. My friends Benny Jacob and Charley Piddocke are among them.

The creative writing class is surprisingly big—twenty-five or thirty rather than the twenty I'd expected. For some reason Gladys Hindmarch and I notice each other and sit together. The course is going to have a series of required assignments—a biographical essay, a first-person narrative, a novel chapter, a one-act play, a haiku and a lyric poem—plus a number of "open" assignments. She tells me about an English professor, Warren Tallman, and his wife, Ellen—Gladys had happened to get assigned to his first-year class last year. She sometimes baby-sits for them. It was Warren who persuaded her to take this writing class. She has also met George Bowering and another writer, Barry Hale, and some of the crowd that hang around the *Ubyssey* and *Raven*. She says she's thinking of taking Tallman's 400-level poetry course next year. She suggests that I should too.

The Writers Workshop holds its first meeting and all the senior students from last year are gone. Only Ann Campbell and myself are back. Instead of a membership in the twenties there are fewer than ten. The new members include Judy Copithorne, Mike Sin-

The first Writers Workshop meeting of 1958-59: Ann Campbell, Caroline Friedson (with ball), Mike Sinclair, Ann Long and Judy Copithorne.

clair, Ann Long, my friend Charley Piddocke, and Mary Miller and Janna Hill from off-campus. Mary and Janna are fashion models who also want to write. Janna is on the cover of the current BC Tel phone book. I am elected president—by acclamation. The Workshop also has a new adviser—Tony Friedson, a U.S.-trained Brit newly hired to teach the playwriting course and modern drama. Tony's wife, Caroline, a lively, lithe retired dancer, will be teaching a section of first-year English. Ann Long, at whose house the first meeting is held, will be much better known a decade later as the conceptual artist Anna Banana. Just couldn't hold that bit of the future back either. The Workshop meetings are relaxed and cheerful. We no longer use the drop box. People put their names on the work they submit, just like writing students do in classes.

October 1958 . . .

My course on the Old Testament has been the only compelling one so far. My section of English 200 is three dull lectures a week to a class of some seventy students. Symbolic logic is interesting but

hardly inspiring. Social psychology has little concern with the individual—groups of people are presumed to be predictable and mea-
surable, as long as one can find the right grounds on which to
predict and measure. Latin is just Latin, despite the continued good
humour of Malcolm McGregor, whose class I am in once again.
Creative writing is stressful—there are several would-be prima
donnas in the class who imagine themselves already worthy of
fame, and writing a means of displaying one's worthiness.

UBC has three small affiliated theological colleges. My Old
Testament professor comes from the United Church one, and is
an ordained minister. I had seen the course merely as a chance to
familiarize myself systematically with most of the Bible and thus
the Biblical references in English literature. Here, to my great surprise, I am taught to read the Old Testament anthropologically and
textually—to read it as a work constructed by the social practices of
nomadic agricultural bronze-age peoples. We have already exam-
ined the Ten Commandments and identified some of their class
and gender biases—how the writers were older property-owning
males—men who had houses, wives, cattle and servants that they
feared less fortunate men would "covet," and children whose
rebelliousness they also feared. The writers were not the young
or the poor. We have learned that the verb translated in the sixth
commandment as "kill" was in Hebrew more narrowly "murder."
We have learned about the health dangers of the time that made
useful and reasonable the prohibition of "traife," the mixing of
milk and meat, and the consuming of blood.

January 1959 . . .

In Cuba Fidel Castro's rebels took over the government on New
Year's Day. It's the end of a nasty dictatorship and probably the
end of a lot of corrupt American-owned casinos I think. However
the only Cuban I know is Desi Arnaz on the *I Love Lucy* show—and
the bandleader Xavier Cugat. I think he's a Cuban. Some of the students in my religious studies class believe the new government is

a good thing—that it may at least end prostitution at the casino hotels. I realize that I don't know much about prostitution, or prostitutes, although back in Abbotsford one of the girls in my Grade 6 class is now rumoured to be one.

The big news at the creative writing class is that Gladys Hindmarch has won second prize in a continent-wide *Mademoiselle* writing contest—for a prose piece she wrote for our course. We are all extremely impressed, but Gladys modestly shrugs it off as a fluke. I think Jake had given it only seventy-five percent, but she tells me now that he's raised that. I tell her that she should start coming to Writers Workshop meetings, and she says she will.

February 1959 . . .

With my friend Charlie, I go shopping for a car. We find a 1947 Ford coupe with a broken transmission. I buy it, and during the spring break we pull the rear end, pull and dismantle the transmission and reassemble it with higher ratio Lincoln-Zephyr gears inside a pickup-truck gearbox. A floor shift. Charlie does most of the reassembly—he has helped repair transmissions before. He says he enjoys doing the work.

The creative writing course has been getting more interesting. For the one-act play assignment I have adapted a short story by Kildare Dobbs that was published in one of the early issues of *Tamarack*. Jake Zilber thinks that it is produceable, and recommends that I send it to the CBC. I have recently bought copies of Allen Ginsberg's *Howl* and Lawrence Ferlinghetti's *Pictures of the Gone World*. Ferlinghetti's sardonic voice seems close to my own sense of things, and I write a cynical poem about the recent disarmament conference in Poland. It begins "Oh they're having a ball in Warsaw / talking about disarmament and all that jazz . . ." It is the first poem I feel somewhat pleased with. I like the pun on ball, the "ball in Warsaw" allusion to George Viereck's novel, the contrast between the formal music of aristocratic balls such as those in *War and Peace* and contemporary jazz. I like its engagement with current politics. It's fun to read aloud. Jake Zilber likes it too. Gladys is less happy this term, having now to write poems. For my additional

assignments I write parodies of some of the poems other students have submitted—including some by Gladys. Jake likes these as well. She is offended that I get higher grades for them than she does for the originals. She thinks I have exploited her. She tells Jake

Gladys Hindmarch (bottom). Alec Annan (far right) at Jake Zilber's end-of-term party.

she should get a bonus for having inspired my parodies. Indeed these will probably clinch my getting an "A" for the course.

The biggest event of the course, however, belongs to Alec Annan, an older student who Gladys and I have tended to perceive as vain and patronizing. He has written a three-or-four-page poem in which every line is packed with internal rhymes and half-rhymes and insistent rhythms—a kind of syllabic fugue that extends the musical effects of Poe's "The Bells" almost—in my opinion—to absurdity. Calling it a "tour de force"—which indeed it is—Jake has given it a grade of one hundred and offered to publish it in a new magazine which he and department members Jan de Bruyn, Elliott Gose and Heather Spears are planning to launch on campus next fall, to be called *Prism*. Gladys and I both feel very uneasy about this poem and its intricate verbal pyrotechnics. To us it seems to have been written not out of belief or insight, or to make the world more understandable, but for personal aggrandisement. A show-off text. We will both have similar reservations, along with Fred Wah and Jamie Reid, about George Bowering's "Meatgrinder" poems in the fall of 1961. Nope, delete that—got to save something for later. Annan's poem appears the next spring under the title "Faux Pas de Deux" as the lead offering of *Prism* 1:3. It may be the only text that Annan will publish.

March 1959 . . .

I meet Bobby Hogg in Abbotsford. Charlie and I are looking for Ford parts, and have heard that he has a non-running 1948 Ford. It's a coupe, sitting in his parents' driveway with the flat heads removed so he can install new head gaskets. He is waiting to borrow a torque wrench. He has a maroon 1947 Ford four-door sedan as well that he is driving while he works on the coupe. Bob refers us to someone else who has a two-carb intake manifold for sale. But he mainly wants to talk about creative writing at UBC. I offer to bring him some course descriptions and also to loan him some books.

Carol Johnson (Carol Bolt), George Bowering and Gladys Hindmarch at the Writers Workshop, spring 1959.

Carol Johnson, who is also in Jake Zilber's writing class, and George Bowering have started coming to some of the Writers Workshop meetings. It's the first time that I'm sure I've met George.

May 1959 . . .

I have reserved Mrs. Akrigg's room for next year and returned to Abbotsford for the summer. Bud and I go out almost every night in one of our cars and meet up with guys I used to go to school with. Sometimes we hang out at the Watson farm, half way down the highway to Sumas. Or we meet up with Bill Walker's jolly cousin, Johnny Walker, who is rumoured to have once lifted a V-8 engine from his Ford and carried it to a workbench, at the Wee Drop tavern. From some of the guys I learn that the hop farms on Sumas prairie are hiring. I drive out there and get hired. The work pays $1.25 an hour—slightly better than the "5 Cents to 1 Dollar Store." Many of the other workers are refugees from the Hungarian revolution—including architects and doctors. They have taken the work to help pass the time until they have learned enough English to resume their careers. Working to be able to enjoy time—I have to think about that. It's part of what I do when I write. I learn a few words of Hungarian, none of them polite. I also learn to fit the speed of my labour with the general rhythm of the other workers. The Mennonite foreman wants us, of course, to work quickly. Each of us has a row of hop plants to trim and train to grow up toward the overhead wires. He will fire anyone who lags behind the group's average progress. So we never let anyone lag behind. None us gets significantly out in front; all of us temper our speed so as to stay close to the slowest. We do this without words—with nods, and pointed looks. It's a lot like playing music together.

I've loaned Bob Hogg some of my Ferlinghetti, Corso and Ginsberg books, and had a look at the health-food store his mother runs from a corner of their living room—the business seems to offer mainly cereal grains with strange names, grains that look a lot like bird food. It's the only health-food store in BC outside of Vancouver. Bob is pretty skeptical about his mother's health-food beliefs—as is his father. Both see the stuff as prissy and unmanly. One Sunday his parents invite me to dinner. His mother has cooked a beef pot roast for Bob and his dad—a roast which she and Bob's older brother George do not touch. I'm with Bob.

June 1959 . . .

We are partway through another tour of the hop fields. Once we finished trimming and training, we were sent back to where we started, and asked to "tie in" the two vine-entwined cords that run from the roots to the wires above. When we complete this we will be sent back to the beginning again for yet another procedure. My dad, however, has been trying to get me a different job. Three men read all the BC Electric Company's meters in the Fraser Valley, from the Vedder Canal to the Langley–Surrey border, and from the Fraser River to the U.S. border. Each of these men receives two or three weeks of summer holiday. The company has decided to hire someone to replace them during their holidays. Oddly this is a job that my grandfather Davey did when he first came to Vancouver in 1902, and which my uncle Orrie did for a while in the late 1920s

before drifting back into music. I don't need to apply for the job—my dad one day tells me that it's been arranged, and that I will have to go to the new BC Electric Building in Vancouver at the end of the month to do the paperwork. The pay is around $375 a month—a union rate. I start work at the beginning of July. It's good that I have a driver's licence—most of the meter reading is done from a car window.

My Uncle Orrie setting out to read meters in Vancouver in the late 1920s.

Bud Blinch's dad, Wilf, invites me to go golfing with him next Sunday, in the U.S. near Lynden, south of Sumas. He has difficulty finding people to golf with, and has heard I have taken "golf" at UBC. Abbotsford is still primarily a working-class village that sees recreation as fishing, hunting, bowling, dancing and drinking, though there is some talk of building a curling rink. Here Wilf, who has served in the Canadian army and seen something of the world, is ahead of his time.

July 1959 . . .

The meter readers have three cars—two 1956 Chevs painted in company colours and one 1957 Chev that is plain green. The full-time readers have uniforms, which I don't. But for some reason I usually get the plain car. Only the meter-reading book identifies me. I am a student. I am a writer. I am a marksman at the shooting range. I am a musical worker. I am a golfer. I am a meter reader.

We go out in our separate cars in the morning and read meters as fast as we can. We find a vacant farm or quiet lane in which to park and eat our lunches. Then we read the rest of the meters as fast as we can. By 2:30 we are usually finished and drive to our homes for a quiet hour. At 4:00 we meet at the office and do the paper-work—reporting houses that are newly vacated, meters that have begun registering dramatic increases or decreases, houses that appear newly occupied, angry dogs that have kept us from a meter. The company probably wouldn't care for this work pattern, but the regular readers insist that I follow it, and for the first week or so take part of my route until I am able to match their speed. Monty, the oldest of them, is notorious for cutting through fields or backing his Chev at high speed into invisible fence posts. Near the end of the month I have my own legendary mishap. I drive into a pasture to read the meter on a pole beside a pump. I drive slowly between the Holsteins so as not to upset them. But as I stop, one turns abruptly to look and bangs her hip bone into my rear fender. Everyone in the office pretends not to believe my accident report.

When we have town meters to read in Abbotsford and Langley, we read mostly on foot, and take two cars. I usually ride with Monty, who fought with the First Division in Italy and then in Holland. He is one veteran who likes to talk about the war. But all his stories are comedies. He and his buddies are fighting room to room in a house in an Italian village, and suddenly German soldiers fill each doorway of the room and shout *"Raus!"* Monty and his buddies are captured. Then just as abruptly Canadian soldiers appear in the same doorways and loudly shout *"Raus!"* and all the Germans are captured. In another story Monty's platoon is scouting in advance of the front line and encounters a group of Germans—sunbathing in the nude. The Germans jump up and run and Monty's platoon starts firing their Sten guns but are laughing so hard they can't manage to hit any of them. Monty's is a Goon Show war. He's a Catholic and has seven or eight children. He says he reads the meters fast in the mornings so he can go back to his wife at twelve and have a "nooner." Everyone laughs, including Monty, and pre-tends to believe him.

August 1959 . . .

Now that I can walk to work, I take my Ford to a body shop that removes all its chrome and paints it "refrigerator white." Bob Hogg has a summer job working for the village's shoe repair shop. He

My 1947 Ford chick magnet.

has worked there part-time for the past year. Bill Walker is working for the summer at the village's radio and TV repair shop—doing many of the repairs. I occasionally drop by both their workplaces. Bob tells me that his family has decided to move to a farm out-

side of Langley, where his father has worked for the past few years as an accountant for a car dealership. Bob has his coupe running, and has sold the sedan, but meanwhile has bought a 1941 Ford coupe for a few dollars for parts. He has to figure out how to tow it from Abbotsford to the farm.

I am trying to work out what courses I want to take the coming year. My highest mark, a high A, was surprisingly in English, and my lowest, a B+, in philosophy. The rest were low A's. I've applied and been accepted to honours English. I'm going to enrol in Warren Tallman's poetry course, as Gladys had suggested, and in Tony Friedson's playwriting course. Birney is not offering his poetry-writing course this year. So I will enrol in his Chaucer course, and in a Restoration drama course—a lightweight substitute for the Shakespeare that Philip Akrigg, unfortunately, still teaches. In addition I'll take a course in Russian literature (in translation), a survey of the history of western art—and the bibliography and critical methods course that is compulsory for English honours—approximately six and a half in all.

One evening Bud and I are out in my car and pick up two very attractive teenage girls we know who have suspect reputations—they were probably hoping some guys would drive by. The one I know the best had climbed out her bedroom window to join her friend. They would like us to find something to drink—a request which will later have literary ramifications. We drive up an obscure road on the south side of the Canadian Sumas Mountain to a small farm where a reclusive young German man that we know often makes sake, and purchase a bottle for six dollars.

Over the next few weeks we buy some more, and our new friend offers to give us his recipe. He creates his sake in part by keeping his fermentation barrel warm inside a large pile of fir sawdust. I create my first batch in a used twenty-gallon olive barrel kept warm behind my parents' furnace. My dad buys me pressure-releasing caps for the gallon jugs in which I bottle it. I will take these jugs to Writers Workshop meetings and later to gatherings at the Tallmans' house. No, I'm not being clairvoyant about this—I'm just being logical. Moreover, bless Gail for climbing out her window.

September 1959 . . .

Back in Vancouver there have been big changes at the elderly Mrs. Akrigg's house. Mrs. Akrigg has been taken to a nursing home. Professor G. Philip has decided to keep her house operating with Mrs. Dale as its housekeeper, me in the basement and his mother's old room rented to a second student. The student is Dick Allison, a freshman from Waterton Park townsite, near Pincher Creek, Alberta. His father owns the Shell station in the townsite, and his mother's father is an Anglican archbishop. Dick introduces himself as "Dick the prick from Pincher Crick." Meanwhile Gladys has begun living at the Tallmans' house—she'd lived in one of the dorms for the past two years, but had been at the Tallmans' house several times a week for much of last year. She tells me that Professor G. Philip's eldest daughter, Daphne, has enrolled at UBC but has moved out of her parents' house because of some dispute. The story has been making its way through the English department faculty, but not all the details. We're now both in Tallman's fourth-year poetry class and whisper these things in the back row. She's also worked

Gladys Hindmarch and Rosemary Kent-Barber at the Writers Workshop booth on Club's Day, fall 1959 – my briefcase on the right.

with me to build a garish Clubs Day booth at the armouries for the Writers Workshop.

Akrigg is controversial within the department—which is not at all democratically run, and is bitterly split among its younger members who are mainly from U.S. universities, its older members who are largely British trained, and a handful from Canadian institutions. Students have to be careful what combination of professors they become affiliated with. Akrigg sits on the executive or "senior" committee, which officially advises on virtually all administrative and curriculum decisions—advice that Roy Daniells, the long-time head, often tries to ignore. Many of the ex-Americans try to avoid both Akrigg and the committee, and to deal directly with Daniells. The living situations that Gladys and I find ourselves in rather amusingly parallel the main fissure in the department—she now living with the Tallmans and I still rooming in Akrigg's mother's home.

I am finding that Birney's Chaucer course is going to be a big challenge. He himself is a delight—a performer as much a teacher. He prowls the front of the room as he speaks, and moves effortlessly from broad humour to extreme seriousness. He obviously enjoys Chaucer's sly sexual humour, and seems to identify with the characters' frequent moments of lechery. But UBC English has recently launched an expanded M.A. program, and to minimize the demands on its faculty has designated all of its 400-level courses as both honours and graduate credits. The students in the course range from third-year ones like me to second-year graduate students. Most of the latter sit in the front row and constitute themselves as a little club with Birney as their leader. Sometimes they manage to cause Birney to forget that there are other students in the room. I sit in the back row and observe. After class I go to the library and research some of the mysteriously coded questions Birney and the front-row club have discussed.

October 1959 . . .

The first issue of *Prism* has appeared. The lead editorial announces that it will publish only imaginative writing—no critical articles or reviews—and that its selections will be "prismatic," including "all possible ranges" of "the literary spectrum." It welcomes "good writing . . . wherever it comes from" and points out that this first issue has "writing from across Canada, and from parts of the United States." Among the contributors are Henry Kreisel, Raymond Souster, Wilfred Watson, Dorothy Livesay, Earle Birney and Margaret Laurence. Gladys complains to me that what Vancouver really needed was a local magazine—one that had beliefs about writing, a program. She says that Warren Tallman thinks the whole direction of the magazine is wrong. I gather that it's not so much the contents that offend Warren as the editorial and its liberal-humanist eclecticism.

Meanwhile I have been elected to the Letters Club. It is a solemn and hallowed club several decades old that the English department has sponsored. Promising English honours students apply for membership in their third year and in their fourth year must present a scholarly paper to a club meeting. At the end of the year the papers are collected into a leather-bound volume and shelved in the departmental library.

November 1959 . . .

Warren Tallman's course is quite eccentric. We have spent the first two months on Marvell's "To His Coy Mistress." It's possible, Gladys tells me, that we will read only six or seven poems all year—but read them very closely. Tallman is much more interested in the poems, and in having them read and reread than he is in any English department understanding of coverage or curriculum. He's also more focused on the process of reading poetry than on having the students accumulate a list of poems "read." For most of the class he sits at his desk, twisting his thin body into anxious shapes that parallel the awkward questions that he finds the lines of the poem raising. Some days we look at only three or four lines. I have met Lionel Kearns here—he and Gladys and I invariably sit together. Sam Perry is also in the class, and sits nearby. Lionel and I compete at offering off-the-wall interpretations, mischievously trying to add to Tallman's declared perplexities. In turn Tallman always considers our remarks very seriously, while Gladys shakes her head at the two of us in exasperation.

Earle Birney is hosting a visit to the campus by George Barker and has invited some students that he knows to a reception at his

George Barker at Earle Birney's home, November 23, 1959, with George Bowering and Betty Lambert.

house. I'm invited because he knows me from his Chaucer class. I have not been impressed with Barker—a pre-war New Apocalypse poet whom Birney probably knew when he was in England with the Canadian army. He seems like a relic from more understandably colonial times. Most of our curiosity is about seeing the inside of Earle Birney's house. My old friend Betty Lambert is here. She and Birney seem close. George Bowering is here too. He took Birney's poetry writing course this past year.

The car I bought is making my life much more interesting. When I go home to Abbotsford on a weekend, I will often drop in to visit Bobby Hogg in Langley who wants to know what is happening at the university. He wishes he were already there. Often I will give rides to other students from Abbotsford, particularly to my old piano and singing rival Bill Walker, who is now a third-year music major and rooms just outside the university gates too. But the RCMP in New Westminster, which I have to drive through after crossing the Pattullo Bridge, don't appreciate its loud mufflers. I satisfy one ticket by showing my receipt for having replaced them—with even louder ones. At least they haven't searched the trunk for sake.

December 1959 . . .

Lionel comes to Warren's class with copies of the second issue of *Prism*. It has five poems by him and one by George Bowering. There is no editorial but there are four pages of congratulatory letters—including ones by Kenneth McRobbie, Ethel Wilson, Henry Kreisel and Roderick Haig-Brown. McRobbie suggests that the first issue demonstrated the increasing superiority of eastern Canada's poetry over that of the west and characterizes Watson's and Birney's work as "very poor," "unexciting." All the letters, perhaps not surprisingly, praise the editors for their eclectic stance. Gladys and I, however, are delighted to see the poems by Lionel and George, and hope that this indicates that *Prism* will at least have a local emphasis—and not simply be a magazine from nowhere.

But upstaging all this is a visit by San Francisco poet Robert Duncan—not an "official" visit and "official" reading at the university, but a visit to the Tallmans and a truly underground reading in a hastily tidied section of the Tallmans' unfinished basement. Duncan is a friend of Ellen's from the 1940s when she was a grad student at Berkeley. He's published more than seven books and is about to be included in a major anthology as the leading theorist in San Francisco poetry. He talks about the serial poem and reads from his books *Medieval Scenes* and *Letters* and his more recent "Poem Beginning with a Line by Pindar"—a stunning text which he says he began by listening to, and following, the rhythmic and tonal implications of the Pindar line—"The light foot hears you and the brightness begins." The "brightness" that I sense is the opening of new possibilities of poetic form and ways of writing.

January 1960 . . .

Gladys has learned through Warren that Prof. G. Philip has again distinguished himself with some of his colleagues. His daughter Daphne has been having difficulties in first-year English and has gone to him asking for help. He has refused.

February 1960 . . .

They have started to build the Highway 1 Vancouver-to-Hope freeway about a half-mile to the south of Abbotsford, permanently cutting a deep trench across some of the roads on which I learned to drive. A former high-school classmate, Garney Borris, who lives two doors west on my parents' street, has a few drinks and gets into a drag race on one of these roads with an older man. Both vehicles crash through the barriers and into the freeway's newly cut trench. Garney is taken to hospital where he complains of pain but is told his injuries are superficial. He dies the next day of internal bleeding. His father is one of the workers at the brick plant. This accident could have happened to a lot of us.

My year at UBC has become increasingly split. The honours English seminar, overseen by Edmund Morrison, one of the senior profs, has been a professionalization year in which we memorize various bibliographic resources and standard journals, their coverage and acronyms—CBEL, MLS, JEGP, etc.—and commit ourselves to standard research methodologies. Birney's Chaucer course, despite his entertaining humour, has been an introduction to the scholarly world of graduate study. Tony Friedson's playwriting course has been entirely about contemporary models—Pinter, Beckett, Ionesco—and creativity. Warren Tallman's poetry course has been a year of questioning how literature is read, and has repeatedly valorized new readings over received ones. We are now reading Denise Levertov's "The Earthwoman and the Water Woman." Levertov is a younger English poet who has immigrated to the U.S. and become known there for innovative poems structured similarly to those of Duncan. Of my new writer friends—Gladys, Lionel, George, Sam Perry—I am the only one in English honours.

March 1960 . . .

For some reason automobile prices in Vancouver are oddly depressed. I buy a 1957 Ford coupe for $700 plus the trade-in of my older Ford. Soon, with the addition of Turnpike Cruiser fender skirts and spinner hubcaps in front, it is almost as attention-getting. Dick

My 1957 Ford, and the Abbotsford skyline.

Allison has been spending a lot of his time shooting eight ball in the student union building, Brock Hall. I have played with him, especially this term after his closest friend, a freshman from Whalley, dropped out in order to get married and work in his dad's landscaping business. Now that I have a more reliable car, Dick is suggesting that I go to Waterton with him and get work there for May and June—my meter-reading job is only for July and August. What he's probably angling for is a ride back home to Waterton.

May 1960 . . .

It's seven in the morning on May 2 and Dick and I have arrived in Waterton. We left Vancouver late in the afternoon after my last exam, driving to Seattle and over Stevens Pass to Wenatchee, before cutting up to Canada just south of Cranbrook. We had a desperate time finding gas stations—almost none were open overnight. We ran out of gas just inside the Waterton Park gates and had to call Dick's dad to come in his '48 Ford pickup truck to rescue us. Making things even more interesting is that Waterton received two feet of new snow the day before, and my Ford is sporting summer tires. Dick's mother, the archbishop's daughter, considers how long it took us on the road and predicts to Dick that I will not live to twenty-five. I stay with them for a few weeks while looking for work, but there isn't any. Dick, I think, was exaggerating. The main employer here is the Prince of Wales Hotel, but it won't open until late May and prefers that its young employees live in the hotel staff residence. It also doesn't let those in the residence own cars. Wary of overstaying my welcome at the Allisons, I pitch my tent in the campground once the snow has melted. A University of Alberta student named Barney, who also lives in the townsite, invites me to brew a batch of sake in his family's boathouse. So we drive to Lethbridge and "borrow" an aluminum beer barrel from behind a hotel pub. But the boathouse is cold, and the sake ferments very slowly. Toward the end of May I manage to get a job as a kitchen porter at the hotel, but continue to camp in my tent so I can keep my car. The rangers encourage me to change sites occasionally so I am not noticeably breaking their rules.

In the hotel kitchen one of the "salad girls" is a future wife of Winnipeg short fiction writer Dave Arnason—who will co-found a publishing house, Turnstone, which will publish three of my most influential books. But again I don't know about any of that yet, so I shouldn't be recalling it here, should I? Moreover, Dick's mother still thinks I'm very soon going to end this story and die. Maybe I am. The only things the salad girls and I ever have time to talk about are crates of lettuce and cucumbers.

What with my car and Barney's, we are able to have loud bush parties at remote campgrounds—something the hotel management probably doesn't like. I have brought an old banjo that I learned to play after my piano fiasco. Everyone wants to sing "Kumbaya," "We Shall Overcome," "Jamaica Farewell" and "Roll Me Over in the Clover." We do all these plus "The Ballad of Sigmund Freud." At the end of June, I set out for BC and my meter-reading job. Near Ellensburg, Washington, I have difficulty starting the Ford, and it backfires through the carburetor, setting itself on fire. I hurriedly open the hood and smother the fire with an old winter jacket I had reserved for camping. I try starting it again, and it starts and runs, but roughly. I drive on toward Abbotsford. There a mechanic—Dan Code's dad—discovers that a valve lifter has broken and nearly fallen into the engine.

July 1960 . . .

Bill Walker and I go to Vancouver to look for a big place that we could share. We find a large basement room with a private entrance, bathroom and rudimentary cooking facilities, and rent it for sixty dollars a month. The owners are a young family that live upstairs.

I discover that I have received A's in all my courses except Restoration drama.

I'm told by someone about a new poetry anthology that was published last month—Donald Allen's *The New American Poetry 1945–1960*. It has poetry by Ferlinghetti, Levertov and Ginsberg, by Duncan, Robert Creeley and Charles Olson, and essays on poetics. It's from Grove Press, the publishers of *Evergreen Review*. I started subscribing to *Evergreen* last summer. It's the anthology that Duncan had mentioned on his visit last December.

September 1960 . . .

This should be a good year. I have only four courses to complete, and the graduating essay. I am taking a seventeenth-century survey from Jan de Bruyn, an Anglo-Saxon and history of the language course from Meredith Thomson, a directed reading course from Tony Friedson and another mandatory honours seminar. I decide to have Jan de Bruyn supervise my honours thesis, which will be on Pope's "translations" of Donne's four satires.

I encounter Dick Allison. He tells me that a month after I left Waterton the weather warmed up and my sake matured. Barney threw a big party for all the young hotel workers and some of them got blasted and wandered loudly around the townsite. The police came and arrested Barney and some of the others, and seized what was left of the sake. They all blamed me. He thinks the police may now be looking for me.

October 1960 . . .

No sign yet of the police, but the Writers Workshop looks as if it will be lively. First-year students Jamie Reid, David Dawson and Bobby Hogg are here, and George Bowering and Carol Johnson are back, as well as myself and Judy Copithorne and Gladys. Tony Friedson tells us he has another first-year prospect—a young woman in his new first-year class who he says is an astonishing talent in both prose and poetry. She's articulate—and poised and beautiful too, he says with his usual impetuous grin. It's Daphne Buckle.

There's also a buzz at the first few meetings about Allen's *New American Poetry*. Many of the members, including me, have bought a copy—from the campus bookstore, which had ordered it for Warren's 400-level course. Arguments break out over the meaning of parts of Charles Olson's essay "Projective Verse." Jamie mischievously accuses our interpretations of "sprawling"—alluding to Olson's warning in the essay not to "sprawl," i.e. not to interpret the world narcissistically. I am especially struck by Olson's declaration that a poem can be viewed as an "action" that the poet does—"the act of the poem" he writes (Allen, 390–391)—rather than as a "closed" or "over-all form" (386–387), which the poet makes. Doing something has always felt more significant to me than the thing done.

Cathy Batten, Bonnie Erikson and Daphne Buckle at the "Projective Verse" party.

November 1960 . . .

Tony tells me that Daphne is coming to the next meeting and says more intriguing things about her. I feverishly begin writing a series of eight or ten poems to have ready to present. They are short, terse verses that ironically juxtapose classical philosophy and auto mechanics, ones I model after Ferlinghetti but that I will realize later more resemble Jack Spicer's work, which

I haven't yet read. Daphne does attend, and is very much as Tony described. I decide I must figure out a way to ask her out. Within a week I have a plan—Bill and I will hold a study party on Olson's "Projective Verse." We'll invite all the student writers we know, as well as some curious academic students. We'll invite Daphne.

January 1961 . . .

Our "Projective Verse" party—Gladys, Lionel, George, the fun-loving Carol de Angelis, Sam Perry, Bob Hogg, David Dawson, Jamie Reid and Daphne all turn up—Daphne driving her father's blue 1956 Pontiac. Some people bring beer. I have several gallons of recently finished sake—but which I have unfortunately not had the time to siphon from the sediment that settles on the bottom. I warn people not to disturb it. We have a useful discussion of the essay that at the very least identifies its problematical passages— the "private soul at the public wall," the arrogant "sprawl" that lyric poetry invites, the advice that one perception should lead immediately to further perception, the emphasis on the syllable— where it "all begins," the breath as the basis of line structure.

But as at Barney's party in Waterton, some people drink a fair amount. By 11:00 p.m. Jamie can no longer find a bottle opener for his beer and staggers out to the street and opens a long-neck bottle by smashing the top of its neck off against an edge of the sidewalk. Lionel forgets my warning about sediment and, using a nearly empty gallon that has more sediment than sake, demonstrates how to drink directly from a jug. Later that hour he becomes disoriented and leaves by climbing through our bathroom window. However I do manage to talk to Daphne as she is leaving and arrange that we will go to a play together.

Sam Perry, Carol de Angelis, George Bowering and Bob Davis at the 'Projective Verse' party.

The next day someone calls to tell me that Lionel had to be taken to the emergency ward and have his stomach pumped. People are teasing Jamie about having "sprawled" beside that sidewalk.

Late January 1961 . . .

I have been seeing Daphne as often as I can, taking her to a play, a movie, for coffee at the Black Spot—a dark candlelit beatnik-style coffee house on Dunbar. I am wanting one perception to lead immediately to a further perception. I have been writing more poems, most of them addressed to her. Some I give her, some I mail to her. When I am not with her I am thinking only of how I will next be with her. My version of one perception leading immediately to another is a headlong rush of associated images and exclamations. One of the poems is called "Love Among Flying Roses" and is inspired by Chagall but also rewrites the Jesse James legend—like a *really* early bpNichol Billy the Kid poem. We go to see *The Good Woman of Setzuan* at the Freddy Wood.

February 1961 . . .

Daphne and I both go to Robert Duncan's poetry reading and public lecture at the new UBC Festival of the Contemporary Arts, at which a more conventional American poet, Dewitt Snodgrass, is also reading and paintings by the modernist Vancouver artist B.C. Binning are being exhibited. At his lecture Duncan stresses a distinction between a "path poem," such as by John Donne, in which the intellect leads other faculties through the field of possibilities, and a "field poem," in which the intellect coordinates the other faculties—hearing, sight, speech, motion—which themselves control equally where the poet goes in the field of possibilities. I am taking careful notes. Later there is a party at the Tallman house for Duncan and Snodgrass. We watch in amazed amusement as midway through the evening Duncan begins making extemporaneous parodies of Snodgrass's poems and manages to attract ninety percent of those at the party to the Tallmans' front room—leaving Snodgrass with the companionship of only two or three. I am writing poem after poem this month, and listen especially attentively to Duncan when he fields questions about the Allen anthology and about the Olson and Creeley essays there on poetics. But Daphne has remained skeptical about this new "open field" poetics. She wonders whether I could write a sonnet. I write more than seven, including this one, which I give her on Valentine's Day.

Part of my notes at Duncan's February 8, 1961, lecture.

What's that? Write sonnets? Would you have me read
By candle? Heat my rooms with coal? My verse
Must be projective, follow Olson's lead,
Must race and roar; not ride a horse-drawn hearse.
Just fools ignore the oscillator's wail
And waste their talents on a harpsichord.
Though Dogpatch uses mules to carry mail,
A wise man keeps all funds and faith in Ford.
The sonnet's pretty rooms were meant for love,
Now who believes in that? Rave on, John Donne,
It's sex, not love! Give love back to the dove!
But wait. The form's not dead—its lines still run,
I yet may make the end: and if I do,
Love still will live, and owe its life to you.

March 1961 . . .

Nana is in hospital and not expected to live. I dropped by her house, as I often do, last Sunday night on my way back from Abbotsford. She knew I might be coming. But I was late, it was after dark, the only light in the house was in the upstairs bedroom, no one answered my knock. I didn't know that she was alone—that Charlie had got blood poisoning in a cut on his right hand and was in hospital. She had visited him Friday night but not since. Orrie found her Monday, unconscious in the upstairs bathroom, after Charlie had phoned to ask him to check. It may have been only a dizzy spell, Orrie says— at the beginning. I feel guilty and useless. Charlie comes to the funeral, a bandage on his right hand and arm.

I am still spending more time writing poems for Daphne than I am working on my courses and graduating essay. We go to hear Louis Armstrong at the Queen Elizabeth Theatre. We see *La Dolce Vita* at the Varsity Theatre. But while she enjoys our discussions and the large overlapping of our interests, she does not care for the intensity with which I appreciate her. Her high-school boyfriend Alan is coming back soon from a year in Spain. She says she promised to marry him back in high school. In my imagination he is Maud Gonne's Major McBride. I continue to write poems and send them to her by mail. I am evidently doing research for my books *D-Day and After* and *Bridge Force* but it feels much more wonderful and much more awful than research. As I read Olson, research is the field of events you are stumbling through and to which you must attend.

Bill asks if I want to go with him to Carol Johnson's apartment a few blocks away to play Monopoly with her and her roommate, Maureen Wallace. Carol has had him over to repair their fridge, I think. He occasionally does odd fridge and radio repair jobs— including at our favourite Chinese restaurant, the Varsity Grill. Maureen—"Mo"—has a curious background. She was born in Hong Kong just months before the Japanese invasion, and spent her infancy and early childhood with her mother in a prison camp. She still suffers from the after-effects of malnutrition.

April 1961 . . .

This is the first time, the very first time I have failed to achieve any-thing I have keenly wanted. I have never met a young woman like

Daphne—so intensely communicative, so passionate about creativity and with such quick intelligence. I try to force myself not to think such things. Fortunately I have not also utterly failed my academic year, although now that I am half-heartedly returning my attention to it, many parts of it seem unrecoverable. I can see that I will pass everything, but with mostly B+ grades. I've also indirectly contributed to a mess at the Letters Club—it looks as if the papers won't be collected and bound this year, for the first time in forty-odd years. I'm not even sure the club will continue. But I do have a growing folder of poetry, almost a hundred new poems in the past three months—and a discovery that writing such texts has given me more pleasure and satisfaction than anything else I've done. I doubt that I'll be able to stop. I try hard to persuade myself that this discovery is greater than anything else that might have been.

And the poetry scene has been heating up. The disagreements about Olson's essay "Projective Verse" have become particularly intense. Now that classes are over, Warren Tallman has offered to host open meetings at his house every Sunday afternoon until "we"—meaning mostly himself and the young writers who have come to make his house a meeting place—have come to an understanding of it and the other essays on poetics in the Allen anthology.

However, when CUSO—Canadian University Students Overseas—comes to campus to recruit students to teach in Sarawak, on the island of Borneo, I fill out an application and am offered an interview. It would be satisfyingly ironic to move beyond my disappointment by going partway around the world to work in a region that Daphne left eleven years ago. Despite the vicious and confused fighting in the Congo and Lumumba's murder, and the various duplicities involving the new President Kennedy and the Bay of Pigs invasion, I entertain images of Gaugin, Maugham, Durrell, Graham Greene. Meanwhile my roommate, Bill, is looking into doing independent research into Mexican folk songs, and wonders whether I would join him in a year-long song-collecting expedition. Nothing comes of either possibility.

May 1961 . . .

I decide to accept an offer of a place in the UBC English M.A. program. My mixed grades are acceptable—probably because the
department is even more in need of teachers for its first-year
composition and literature courses than it was when I arrived.
Possibly also because my pursuit of Daphne has been so public—as
Leonard Cohen is already thinking of writing, everybody knows.
I will be given a section of first-year English to teach, and be paid
an assistantship of two hundred dollars a month for eight months.
And now both Warren Tallman and Elliott Gose are playing at
match-making—trying to find another literary-minded young
woman who might attract me. Bill and I have spent a couple of Sunday afternoons playing Monopoly and consuming pizza and sake
with Carol and Maureen. Carol's irrepressible wit populates the
board with absentee landlords, railway wrecks and suicidal finan-
ciers. Mo is lively too but seems difficult to get close to. Bill and she
occasionally go to music concerts together.

We attend the first Sunday meeting at Warren's house. I bring
a gallon of sake—well siphoned and filtered. I had thought I knew
most of the people interested in the Allen anthology but there are
new people here, from the poetry class that Warren has recently
completed—among them Fred Wah and Pauline Butling. I wonder
whether they are serious people, or just hangers-on. Fred keeps
talking about starting a magazine, as if that would make something
happen. But he and Pauline seem hardly to know any of the more
productive of the poets here, such as George or Lionel. And only
Lionel seems interested in his magazine idea. At the meeting also
are David Cull, Peter Auxier, Sam Perry, Jamie, Gladys, Lionel,
George, Daphne, Judy Copithorne, David Dawson, Bobby Hogg,
my roommate Bill.

Bill and I drive to most of the meetings from Abbotsford, and
drive back after. He has his usual summer job at PM Radio in
Abbotsford and I am awaiting the start of my meter-reading job.
Sometimes Carol Johnson is there. Sometimes Bobby Hogg isn't.

Gladys sometimes misses meetings because she is working, as she has the past summers, on one of the freight steamships that sail the west coast of Vancouver Island. The meetings continue with Warren overseeing them in his usual non-directive way. Much as he can spend a full course discussing six or seven poems, he can spend numerous afternoons considering a variety of readings of Olson's essay. I find the discussions frustrating—although I enjoy the companionship. Some other people are frustrated too—Pauline thinks we are going around in circles. Myself, I think that I personally have a workable understanding of Olson's essay—workable at least in the sense that I can use it to enable my writing.

So Warren's pushing for a consensus doesn't interest me—and maybe doesn't work for him. Otherwise he wouldn't be making his suggestion that we offer Robert Duncan travel expenses to come— by bus—to give our group a series of lectures on the "new American poetry," its poetics and historical background. It's an off-the-wall suggestion—a bit like the ones Lionel and I used to make in his class.

July 23, 1961 . . .

". . . [I]f you're going to live as long as most of us live, you'd damn well better find a form of poetics that permits enough development that you're still doing something interesting to yourself when you're eighty-two." Duncan has agreed to come and is here in the Tallmans' living room. Bill has set up his Phillips reel-to-reel recorder. Duncan talks about how he met Olson at Berkeley in 1946 and that they had talked about ecology rather than specifically about poetry, and how in 1950 he had read "Projective Verse" and misunderstood it—he had thought its references to "field" had meant merely that a poet should read his poems aloud to an audience—a "field" of listeners.

He offers the usual summary of the imagist manifesto but expands it into a distinction between those imagists who saw the image as only sensory (Sandburg, Aldington, Flint, Amy Lowell) and those who saw it as potentially numinous (Pound, Lewis, Lawrence)—as a possible location of energy, as in the dynamics Olson seeks to show among "things in a field."

He digresses into discussions of Thomas Aquinas's attempts in the thirteenth century to assign the numinous image "to heathendom" in order to prevent people from thinking that "there were real trees and real angels," of Protestant iconoclasm ("their whole fight has been against the image"), and of the philosopher Alfred North Whitehead's goal of "establishing the maximum energetic relationship to the world" and thereby transforming conflicts into contrasts—to Whitehead, he suggests, "every conflict is a failure to see order." The Vorticism of Lewis and Pound tried to work from Whitehead—to achieve "a violent bringing together of things" by examining "how to get a force from two things that have not been together before."

What happened to this modernism? Duncan is blunt and often sardonic. He says that the failure of socialism in the U.S. in the 1930s sent most literary people fleeing to grad schools where "Jewish non-religious groups" founded the *Partisan Review* and "small-town Protestants" such as John Crowe Ransom and Allen Tate, who had an "absolute abhorrence of [the] numinous, of image and of image worship, founded the *Kenyon Review*." "Logic re-emerges." Any vital passionate thing is excluded—"because the Board of Regents [of their university] wouldn't like it." "What if you started to speak with voices in the middle of the classroom?—you start talking with voices and there is someone in your class who is going to run away to say there was a whole class which was not what we were supposed to be studying." We laugh, many of us thinking of Warren's classes.

He returns to Whitehead, paraphrasing from memory from his *Aims of Education* of 1929: "the congress of saints is a great and august body but it has only one place to meet and that is the present moment." Like Olson's poet open to his field, "you are a machine of things happening," he says—"otherwise Greece isn't there, . . . Greece is only there in the way it floods your life. But that doesn't mean you are the centre." He segues from this into a discussion of

Olson's "Projective Verse" essay as a text in which the "propositions are not even meant to hang together"—a remark that might have curtailed some of our arguments a few months earlier. Things hang together in a logical coherent way only in what Olson there scornfully calls "the universe of discourse." Here Carl Sauer, the ecologist, "is one of Olson's masters." An ecologist watches a plant in its field, but does not call it good or bad—something I will recall in 1969 when writing my serial poem *Weeds*. Similarly, Duncan says, one cannot call literature good or bad, or contrasting civilizations good or bad. As William James had believed, the world holds "a whole series, a plurality of realities." The world of Lear and that of *The Pickwick Papers*, he says, are one. "The experience of not liking a writer is that of not liking another man's religion."

"Magic's greatest enemy . . . is fantasy." Duncan is now explaining Olson's *The Maximus Poems* and how Olson has rigourously grounded them on actual events—"there must be an actual occurrence. . . . You've got to know what is there." The map on the book's cover, he says, shows the specificity that Olson insisted upon. In *Maximus*, Gloucester is a numinous place because its field of historical events reveals the meanings of humanity's relationship to a continent. Duncan stresses the non-national aspects of *Maximus*. "Gloucester is a place upon a continent, not in a country, not in America—it's on a continent. America's just one of those things in the universe of discourse, it could disappear and the continent would still be there. It's a locus—it was once a locus on a continent where there was no America, and it was a locus that had a continuity that he could trace all the way to Mexico."

Duncan's first talk is marked throughout by a puzzlingly semi-religious vocabulary. The numen "is the place or the thing where the god was," he tells us. "Gloucester was one of the holy places of the world," because its present and historical events echo and reveal patterns from ancient Greece to contemporary Mexico. Olson believed "that human history is right here, eternity, that's it," he says. When speaking about poets generally, Duncan tells us "The community of poetry is . . . a group of people who can even recognize each other as . . . living in eternity, or as living in this place as if it were one of the holy places." And later, when discussing creativity, he says, "Now this is the meaning of a creative act, that it is a spiritual event, it can't just take place, something has to be done, something has to be enacted. . . ." The puzzle, I realize, rests on Duncan's taking for granted that the eternal is not some distant realm, but is literally the here and now. For him the eternal and the material are the same. The word "cosmos"—which includes the planet Earth— is his equivalent of "heaven." When he uses the word "god," he is referring to the processes of the physical universe. Here he cites Whitehead once more:

[I]n Whitehead's universe god is a cosmic god, not a human god, and the human beings are cosmic beings, not human. So one of the funny effects in [Olson's essay] "Human Universe" is its anti-humanism; the "Human Universe" is really saying that the meaning of your humanity is to be found in the cosmos. The meaning of your humanity is in no way separated so that when you so much as change a phrase in a poem you are as much of a cosmic event as when the wind blows—that's an erosion process, something is happening there, and your poem has no place to be except in the cosmos.

Much of Duncan's language seems that of a physicist who has borrowed a theological vocabulary.

July 24, 1961 . . .

Tonight Duncan reviews his own writing, beginning with his serial poem *Medieval Scenes* and what he learned from it about revision. "It had a kind of necessity of its own and if you didn't get it right when you were working on it, there was no way to repair it any more than there's a way to repair a love affair or meeting somebody, or being very foolish at a party or any of the other things that happen to you in life." We press him on this question. "I tried to rewrite or correct . . . except what I had to do in that *Medieval Scenes* had only that time and that place to be done and ten years later you can't call upon the influences that were around that made the poem."

In recalling a section of that poem, "The Mirror," he talks about the need to go on writing even when the lines you are discovering disturb you. "I myself was terrified by what happened in the course of writing the poem. . . . Something in me in a sense did not want to be the poet of the poem." He is saying this in the context of his conviction that each poem has its own tonal and structural potential beyond the will of the person writing it. "When you start a sentence with the word 'the' or the word 'a' aren't you under a law for some time, because that word 'the' started something, and until it is ended, you are under a sentence. . . . And if you start a poem . . . you're under a law to keep those sounds, not to have them reoccur, but you've got to keep all of them so that when they recur they recur as part of the form." The sentence, he says, "is an inexorable law, one you can't escape at all. . . . When you are obeying the sentence, you are in the freedom of writing. Otherwise you have a writing block." Living and even writing creative texts within the demands of academic deadlines, most of those in the room listening to him are all too aware of so-called "writing blocks."

He then distinguishes his own writing practice from that of Olson, which he had so sympathetically outlined the previous evening, and indirectly makes Olson's practice even clearer. "The condition of *Maximus* was that there had to be no imagination in it. . . . Now what he meant by imagination was that he always had to have this objective correlative, and what I was doing in [his recent serial poem] 'The Structure of Rime' [a sequence based almost entirely on retaining and listening for the recurrence of sounds] was . . . trying to throw myself completely out where I would no longer check things in this way, and I would allow a certain area of my poetry to really do things that were forbidden by the immediate people that I was concerned with. Forbidden by Olson . . . That wasn't really allowed by Denise Levertov's insistence that you really register the life you're in in the immediate city."

Of particular interest to me, who had spent the spring writing poems that I hoped would both communicate my emotions and instrumentally influence my life's directions, were Duncan's concluding remarks on self-expression. "Of all the absurdities, to try to express something or want to express something when you're writing, when you only have to follow what you're saying when you write—because your writing is ultimately such a neutral document that you and anybody else, once it's there on that paper, are in the same relation to it to read," he exclaimed. I imagine Daphne "neutrally" reading many of my poems. "You don't really care after you have written it, and nobody else does," he continues, "if something of you gets expressed or not. What you read and what is fascinating is the world that emerges there." That worries me some. He also talks about the wish to create impressive poetry—the "feeling, oh, I ought to perform in here or something, and you don't go ahead with what it was you'd started to do, you keep thinking it ought to be better." I think of both some of my poems for Daphne and of Alec Annan's splashy "Faux Pas de Deux."

Bill and I are commuting each evening to these lectures from Abbotsford, leaving directly after work, a one-and-a-half-hour drive each way. The narrow highway between Cloverdale and Langley is crossed diagonally by railway tracks that almost run parallel to it. The crossing is unlit and without signals. As we are driving back that night, Bill abruptly cries out, "There's a train!" and I slam on my brakes and come skidding to a stop on the right shoulder just inches from the ghostly, slowly moving boxcars. The train was heading east, as we were, and was invisible except for our headlights. It had been a Duncan moment that there would have been no opportunity to repair.

July 25, 1961 . . .

Many of us have questions for Duncan that have arisen for us from his last two nights of talks, but he has prepared to talk about composition—about how to write. He recounts having visited with a middle-aged and diligent poet who has never had much success. The poet's little daughter is playing with a doll, and Duncan asks her a question that implies the dolly might be alive. Her father says, "She's past that kind of silliness." Duncan tells us that he knew immediately why this poet had never written well.

"One of the earmarks for me . . . of the school that has dominated in teaching in schools about poetry," he says, "and has dominated, for instance, in the school of masters who write poetry, is the idea that the poet's own powers and the poet's own choice, and the poet's own cleverness . . . is what happens; but it is a matter of cooperating with the thing and in a way you come into tune." I assume that he is talking about poets such as X.J. Kennedy, James Wilbur, Dewitt Snodgrass, James Dickey, the various poets of the Yale Younger Poets anthologies whose work fills establishment journals such as *Poetry* (Chicago). Duncan can see meanwhile that some of us have troubling questions about how this works in practice. "There is a difference between *trying* a word and seeing what happens with its use, and *choosing* a word," he explains and, a few sentences later elaborates: "You do not do things with words. [. . .] Words are real things and when they are in a place where you can see what it is they're doing and you cooperate with them, then something unfolds. And you can feel it's in you but it's really unfolding in the language. And you have suddenly entered a realm so much larger than your own mind because language is all of human experience."

Someone asks him about Olson's recommendations about making the line a "breath unit," and why the line structures of Olson, Creeley and Duncan poems are so different. We have known at least since the Allen anthology that the three have been publicly grouped together as part of a single "Black Mountain" school. Are their poems so different only because their writers breathe differently? Duncan replies that while Olson's lines do reflect his own short breath, he himself structures his lines purely for linguistic reasons—his long lines enable him to achieve what he considers an "exact notation." He says that each Creeley line is like a fragment of a verse in which the entire form of the verse is reflected. He jokes that Creeley has enough breath to be able to run around the block between lines, without altering the form of the poem.

What Creeley shares with him and Olson, he says, is that there is no conforming to a known pre-existent form. The comment reminds me of something Duncan said the first evening—that both Williams in *Paterson* and Joyce in *Ulysses* had borrowed a framework—had chosen a form before they began, but in Olson's *Maximus* there is no "over-structure"—"the form has to be in every single locus of the poem, and the reason it does this is because that form which Joyce borrowed from Vico, that form on one, two, three or one, two, three, four is a very definite idea about what the universe is like and a very definite idea about the meaning of human history. And for Charles, or Whitehead, he believed, no, that human history is right here, eternity, that's it." Duncan had gone on from there to talk about literary conventions—"there is no such thing as just a convention," he had said. "The figure I use for such a man is that he puts a fancy set of chains on himself and says, now this is just convention."

These three evenings have been provocative and even potentially liberating. I am already thinking of how I might "follow" my recent disappointment into a larger sense of my geographical and historical context, and have begun writing notes for some of the "bridge force" sequence I will write later in the year. Duncan's ideas have also made it clear to me how distant I have been from writing the kind of poetry he values. Fred, however, still wants to start a magazine. I'm not eager, but I also wouldn't want to leave myself out. Perhaps Fred has detected a potential energy flow in the local field.

July 30, 1961

Warren has arranged to conclude Duncan's visit with a reading by the young writers who attended his lectures—in the lofty space of the Buchanan Building penthouse, usually closed to students. Gladys is not there—she's back at her summer job on the boats. We have a party and an impromptu meeting after. Fred has persuaded Warren that starting a magazine is a good idea, and the discussion has moved from whether to how. What to call it?—a number of us have taken serious note of Duncan's remarks about Olson and Carl Sauer, and Sauer's landmark use of fossilized human excrement to determine the date of the domestication of grains in the Amazon basin, and so "shit" becomes one suggestion. Duncan, the poet who studies linguistics, has another idea—call it "tish" he says. Who will volunteer to be editors? Only Fred, George, Jamie, David and myself step forward. None of the young women. Of course almost all of the talk about starting a magazine has been between Warren and us guys. The apostrophe-s of Fred's "Let's start a magazine" hasn't been a shifter that necessarily addressed Pauline, Carol, Gladys, Judith or Daphne. Lionel, whom it did address, and who had been initially eager that a magazine be founded, declines. Who will lead the editorial team—everyone wants to defer, so we have a secret ballot. Embarrassingly for me, the vote is unanimous.

SECOND THOUGHT, JEST THOUGHT

*

Likely Stories, George Bowering and Linda Hutcheon would somewhat ironically title their anthology of postmodern fiction in 1992. I'm thinking that this is a bit of a "likely story" too. The seventeen-year-old who greeted Professor G. Philip in a heap on a cold basement floor did not expect that four years later he would be about to take charge of an independent literary magazine and a section of first-year English. I really should have written up that story about G. Philip.

The key event back in 1957, however, was not my witnessing Akrigg's less than happy fall. It was more likely my decision to persist in going to the Writers Workshop meetings and suffering Desmond Fitzgerald and his UBC version of the Celtic Twilight—a decision that eventually led to my classroom friendship with Gladys Hind-march and, through her, to Warren Tallman.

It is remarkable to me now how much my early years at UBC recapitulated my years in Abbotsford. The reverberations of war evident there, and the creative stagnation that seemed all around, were reflected by both the motley architecture of UBC's buildings and the general overcrowding of its programs. It was still in many senses dealing with the aftershocks of 1946's influx of returning veterans. Many of the faculty who had been recruited in Britain were refugees from that country's postwar years of austerity. Many of those recruited in the U.S. were happy to be north of the post-war McCarthy and House Un-American Activities investigations that had engaged the curiosity of my mother. Many students had, like Daphne, arrived at UBC because of the postwar upheavals that were wracking the colonies of Britain, France, Belgium and the Netherlands. The year Daphne enrolled, Fanon was about to pub-lish his *The Wretched of the Earth*, Belgian colonial intransigence was tearing apart the Belgian Congo, and Castro's guerrillas were implacably advancing toward Havana. The last and most tragic phase of the Indo-China colonial wars were about to begin. Amus-ingly, the main Canadian correlatives to this anti-colonial unrest were the 1956 pipeline debate and Diefenbaker's election wins of 1957 and '58.

In many ways, however, the "moment" of 1957–1961 at UBC was—perhaps accidentally—an extremely kind one for arts students. A pedestrian and pragmatic BC government was expanding a post-secondary education system that few of its members had experi-enced and fewer understood. While the general culture was focused on material enrichment, at the university the prestige of the arts—as a kind of finishing school for the upwardly mobile—continued, and with it the prestige of the English department as a purveyor of a necessary genteel literacy. This prestige assured the department tidal wave after tidal wave of enrolments in its first- and second-year general courses, and an unquestioned continuance of its role as the most influential of the university's departments. The size of

English's community of full- and part-time teachers and its student body determined what library resources were the most visible, what areas of the bookstore were the largest, what kinds of books the store stocked beyond required textbooks. What did they stock? The City Lights "Pocket Poet" series, the current lists of New Directions and Grove Press, vast arrays of Penguins and Pelicans, everything newly translated by existentialist philosophers, absurdist playwrights, or writers of the *nouveau roman*, Angry Young Man novels, Durrell's *Alexandria Quartet*. That swollen community around the English department in turn gave young writers not only a significant potential audience for readings but also a large and varied number of potential friends, advisers and sounding boards. For visiting poets, audiences of from three hundred to eight hundred were normal. So indeed something was moving beyond the war years.

*

The tension in UBC's English department between older faculty trained in England and younger ones trained in North America replicated in a more elaborate and verbally sophisticated way the arguments between my English-born maternal grandmother and my father whose Canadianness went back through uncountable generations into the Metis past. I often felt right at home. But that tension was never for me a simple dichotomy. I both enjoyed and mistrusted the overstuffed and over-furnished old West Point Grey house of William Robbins in which most of the Letters Club meetings were held—it was like meeting inside an English Christmas card. The lively Tony Friedson was amusingly British—Tony who indulged all of his writing students in wanting for them what they wanted for themselves. But there persisted in me a sense that British culture, no matter how rich, entertaining or quaint, was irrelevant to the place in which I lived. I still did not want to wear riding breeches.

The British literary presence that I encountered at the 1957–1958 Writers Workshop meetings did not instantly disappear with

Desmond Fitzgerald's departure for Harvard—despite the very different Writers Workshop that followed. There was still the occasional visit by an obscure British poet such as George Barker—who would be much better known in Canada in the 1980s not for his poems but for having, five decades earlier, made the impressionable and obsessive teenage Canadian writer Elizabeth Smart his long-term mistress, and begun siring her four children, while also continuing to live and have children with his English wife, Jessica. Imperialism in miniature. And there were still young poets on campus who preferred British forms and rhetoric—Michael Sinclair, Michael Matthews and David Bromige among them. Many of these affiliated themselves not with the Workshop but with the literary pages of the *Ubyssey* and the campus literary magazine *Raven*. Historians may someday note that of the original *Tish* editors only Bowering published in *Raven* or the *Ubyssey*. Both Fred Wah and I consciously mistrusted both publications. For us they were part of the Brock Hall establishment. Brock Hall for us was the privileged Vancouver students who moved easily from high school to university. It was the fraternity and sorority kids. It was the gathering place of people who ran for student council and had enough family money to paper the campus with campaign signs. I hoped Sherman Wu would someday be ashamed of having wanted to join Psi Upsilon.

Much of what we experienced as "British" was thus also a class phenomenon. Higher education in Britain had been until then largely restricted to the upper and upper-middle classes. The British literary culture that we encountered—both genuine and imitated—was an upper and upper-middle class one. In Britain to go against that culture was to create comedy—as in the 1950s novels of John Wain, John Braine and Kingsley Amis. Rebellion led to comedy because the genteel classes were still the norm—and were still these novelists' readers. The writers I was closest to wanted neither to create comedy nor pass as "gentlemen" or "ladies"—whether British or Brock-Hall Canadian. When I later began teaching at other institutions, I encountered a number of Canadian-born faculty—some not all that older than me—who had trained themselves to speak BBC English in order to pass as more-than-usually cultured. "This book is pre*fer*able," I reported at one department meeting. "I *raw*ther think it is pre*fr*able," a certain W. Barry Thorne, the acting chair, born like me in Vancouver, sweetly countered. I was reminded of a day in Abbotsford when I took my Grade IV pianoforte exams under a Royal Conservatory examiner. "Please play a D-major scale in *con*-try motion," he said. "Whaaat?" I replied.

Daphne was both colonial British and already determinedly North American. Given my Christmas card nostalgia for the England of my grandmother's village mixed with my determination not to wear riding breeches, it is perhaps not surprising how viscerally I became attracted to her.

When Daphne's wedding was about to happen in 1963, several writing students joked about the contrast between her usual costume of pedal pushers and canvas sneakers and the rather formal and traditional wedding preparations they had heard rumours about. Gladys quipped to me that she expected Daphne would wear sneakers to the ceremony—that is, that her preferences for lower-class clothing would appear incongruous in the life Glady believed she was about to enter.

Critics such as Pauline Butling and Lynette Hunter have identified the five first editors of *Tish* with working-class backgrounds. It's possibly a fair identification, despite George Bowering's father being a small-town high-school chemistry teacher. George himself had spent his years in the RCAF as an enlisted man—had not sought to be an officer. Jamie Reid came from a single-parent family headed by his mother, who was a senior nurse and nursing supervisor—but again was from a family, like George's, that had a history of literacy and education. Her people had come to Nova Scotia from Scotland after Bonnie Prince Charles's defeat at Culloden. David Dawson's adoptive east-Vancouver father worked in a steel mill. Although as a café owner Fred Wah's father was technically a businessman, his class position was limited by both race and the fact that he worked in his business, sometimes both cooking and serving the food, rather than merely managing it. But he was certainly a man of considerable accomplishment.

*

Is there a contemporary creative culture? That question continued to puzzle me, at least within Canadian contexts. At UBC I found many signs of such a culture, but not really "in spades," as my father would have said. This time he really would have been looking for shovelfuls.

What there was was not always in the obvious places. It was in the basement art gallery of the UBC library, next to the yellowing washrooms beneath the central staircase. It was in the Tallmans' unfinished basement with borrowed or rented chairs arrayed on a stained concrete floor. Underground. It was in a physics building lecture theatre. It was in three creatively

conjoined army huts where student actors performed European plays. The painting scene of Vancouver had come to Abbotsford only in the recent newspaper fame of Emily Carr—and there was much more here in Vancouver than Carr. Shadbolt, Bert Binning, Gordon Smith, Joe Plaskett, Roy Kiyooka, Tak Tanabe, Molly and Bruno Bobak were all painting work that a writer could learn from—and could sometimes see at the Vancouver Art Gallery. Two black-and-white paintings by Tanabe hung in the main room at the Tallmans'. In fact

Verso of the title page of the copy of Robert Duncan's book *Letters*, 1958, which he signed and decorated for me at his February 1961 reading.

there was much more strong late modernist painting being done in Vancouver than poetry of any kind. Throughout most of the '40s and '50s no more than ten books of poetry per year were usually published in all of Canada.

Duncan had talked about the difficulty of publishing his own poetry in the U.S.—all of his books before the Allen anthology had been published by small or private presses. Olson's "Projective Verse" essay had been published in a New York little magazine in 1950 but came to general attention—and to Vancouver—only when included in the Allen anthology.

*

There have been numerous versions circulated of the story of how Duncan's lectures, and *Tish*, came to happen in that summer of 1961. Among them are Tallman's in his 1972 essay "Wonder-Merchants," mine in the introduction to the collected *Tish 1-19*, Gladys Hindmarch's in her 1971 interview by Brad Robinson, "Before Tish," Fred Wah's in a 2000 interview by Margery Fee and Sneja Gunew, and Pauline Butling's in both the essay "Robert Duncan in Vancouver" and her parts of the co-authored book *Writing in Our Time*. All of these have been limited by the circumstances of their making and the fact that all of the writers had a role in the events they recount. One could say, following Olson's field theory, that they all experienced the events of 1961 from vastly different positions in a complex field.

Wah and Butling knew very little about UBC student poetry before that spring and summer and may very well have idiosyncratically framed what they witnessed because they were familiar mainly with Tallman and themselves. Neither had attended the Writing Workshop meetings or the creative writing courses in which Glady, George, Lionel, David, Jamie, Carol and I had become close friends and writing buddies, nor been a part of the "literary table" in the UBC cafeteria. Wah had built on his high-school band experience to become a music major at UBC—a training that would be evident in the metaphors of his *Tish* writing and in later poems such as "Music at the Heart of Thinking." Music was very likely already at the heart of his poetry thinking. Butling was an academic English student whose choice of courses had not yet intersected my own. Much as they were strangers to me that spring, many of us Writing Workshop regulars were probably strangers to them. Or so it seemed.

In the 2000 interview, Wah is trying to distance himself from *Tish* and strengthen his credentials as a Chinese-Canadian poet— although in terms of actual genetic heritage he would have twice as much call to construct himself as Swedish-Canadian. Bowering has liked to tease him about this—"Come on Wah, you've never been Chinese," Wah quotes him to Fee and Gunew as having said (Fee interview). Butling in her work is attempting to sever both Wah and Marlatt from *Tish*, and to confine *Tish* itself to the two years of its first editorial period—and thus define it as a two-year male-poet phenomenon. She would prefer *Tish* to be merely a warm-up act for a 1970s-to-2005 main event of multicultural and feminist poetry. In her book chapters, Bowering's writing life and mine end around 1970, while Wah and Marlatt after this time triumphantly transcend their *Tish* beginnings. I've been told that such snubs have pained George, much as they have annoyed me, although I'm sure he also recognizes that these are merely part of the hurly-burly violence of French theorist Pierre Bourdieu's "field of cultural production"—a violence that most critics, including Butling, like to pretend to be outside of. Duncan never did.

Tallman was writing his history of *Tish* for the U.S. journal *Boundary 2*, guest co-editing a Canadian edition of that journal with Margaret Atwood. I sense whenever I reread this romantic account that he was both competing with what he imagined Atwood's pre-sentation of eastern-Canadian poetry would be, and attempting to exceed the expectations of what he anticipated might be a skeptical and poorly informed U.S. audience. Tallman also had to imagine the undergraduate lives of many of the student writers he talks about—for me, for example, he was only one of a large number of professors I knew in my first three years at university. He had at best a general impression of my Abbotsford community, of Bowering's air force days or of Fred's life in Nelson and the Diamond Grill café. The student he knew best is the one who lived for several years in his house, Gladys Hindmarch. With the unconscious sexism of someone close to my parents' generation, he constructs her not as a writer but as the principal mysterious force behind *Tish*—"On still spring evenings, not a whisper of wind, when she walked out through the door the leaves on nearby trees would flutter into a welcoming dance" (*Godawful* 195). "She was a living metaphor for the numinous around, the most distinct single human form of the wonder of the place" (196).

In her essay "Robert Duncan in Vancouver," Butling romanticizes Duncan almost as much as Tallman romanticized Hindmarch. She quotes Tallman's remark in "Wondermerchants" that he resembled "a pinball machine firing on all circuits" and adds "i.e. with all the coloured balls bouncing up and down at once." She says that "he talked in ever widening circles, rarely in 'complete' sentences, with his already high-pitched voice going even higher when he really got excited." The tapes of the event don't confirm this—his sentences may contain digressions, but they always arrive at a meaning. His voice is a fairly rich tenor for which "high-pitched" seems something of a caricature. Perhaps Butling had a poor-quality copy of the tapes, or a poor-quality tape machine. When she recounts the reading that the students gave for Duncan, she attributes to him the comment: "Ask yourselves how many of you will be writing when you are forty." I doubt he phrased the comment quite this way—it sounds too much like Kennedy's inauguration speech later that year. She characterizes the students' reaction: "Eager/apprehensive faces turned thoughtful to ponder Duncan's challenge." Perhaps some did, but some also would have heard and remembered his declaration five nights earlier that we had "damn well better find a form of poetics that permits enough development that you're still doing something interesting to yourself when you're eighty-two." George, I know, was already committed to a possible lifetime of writing. Myself, I had begun to see—mainly through my association with Daphne—that writing would be the only future I wanted.

Butling gives her summary of the reception of Wah's first proposal to start a magazine in a note in *Writing in our Time*: "The idea of starting a magazine apparently began when Fred Wah went to see his high-school friend Lionel Kearns (they had both played in a jazz band in Nelson, BC) and said 'Let's start a magazine so we can read each other's work.' Kearns said, 'we should talk to my friend George Bowering.' Bowering said 'We need to talk to Frank Davey.' Davey said, 'let's go see Warren Tallman.' Tallman said, 'you don't know enough yet, let's form a summer study group.'" The daisy-chain effect Butling creates here suggests that there was an under-lying, if qualified, agreement with Wah's proposal. It doesn't convey the lack of enthusiasm for the idea that some of us had, or our hopes that Warren would at least delay any concrete moves. I'm pretty sure that both George and I already believed that we didn't yet know enough. It also suggests that Fred and Lionel were contem-poraries during high school, rather than two years apart.

Interviewed by Margery Fee and Sneja Gunew in 2000, Wah has the sense that Tallman's summer workshops, the July 1961 Duncan lectures and *Tish* all came out of the poetry course he had taken with Tallman in 1960–1961: "[B]y the end of that year, that 406 course, we had a pretty solid group of people who were inter-ested in starting a magazine, you know, we were going to move ahead. *Tish* started out of that group. . . ." He tells Fee and Gunew that he only took the course because he needed an elective for his music degree and his wife, Pauline Butling, had recommended Tallman's among various other English courses. Of the writers who would eventually be associated with *Tish*, he says he had met only Lionel Kearns, and in Tallman's class would meet Jamie Reid (I wonder whether he actually did—first-year students such as Reid could not register in 400-level courses). When he tells Fee and Gunew about the beginning of the 1961 summer meetings, he implies that several writers had already agreed on the magazine project, and telescopes the summer meeting idea and the Duncan visit: "[S]everal of us who wanted to start it went to Warren and said, 'Hey Warren, we want to start a magazine—how do you do that? Can you help us out?' He said—this was in the winter—'Just hold on. Don't be in such a rush. Maybe we should talk to some of these poets you're interested in.' That's when he suggested bring-ing Duncan up." Perhaps this is indeed what happened when Fred talked to Warren—but I was not there and did not hear such a story. I still hadn't heard of Fred. Certainly no one from that "solid group" in Tallman's 1960–1961 class except Wah himself stepped forward to be a *Tish* editor. Wah also tells Fee and Gunew,

> . . . we felt we were being excluded, we were outside; the centre wasn't interested in us—it never is—so we're going to fight our own battles, start our own magazine. "You're not going to publish this? We have to start our own magazine? You're not interested in us, so we'll read Americans."

I don't recall Wah attempting to publish at this time, or having much work that he wanted to publish, or having much awareness of eastern-Canadian poetry magazines. But that may only reflect how little we knew each other. I definitely hadn't yet thought of trying to publish anywhere. It would be another year before I thought of sending poems east, where they were quickly accepted—in *Mountain, Delta, The Canadian Forum* and *Evidence.*

Jamie Reid also does not appear to have heard such stories. In a 2008 interview by Sam MacDonald, he offers this recollection of first hearing the idea of a new magazine at Tallman's summer meetings:

> The first time I ever heard anything about the possibility of a magazine that we might ourselves create was when Fred Wah raised the idea with Warren Tallman at one of the meetings of the group of young writers that met at the home of English professors Warren and Ellen Tallman. In those days, we met under Warren's mentorship with the general aim of developing our own knowledge as writers and poets by discussing the work of various modernist writers, from Ezra Pound to Charles Olson, Robert Creeley, Robert Duncan and the poets of the so-called Beat Generation. Warren Tallman, as I remember, openly opposed the idea of the magazine, saying that we didn't know enough to start a magazine on our own. Whether this was an

attempt on the part of Warren to stir us up to the rebellion of launching the magazine, I'll never know. (Samael)

*

Sometimes I wonder whether *Tish* would have happened, or at least happened in the various precise ways it is said to have happened, had Tony Friedson not urged Daphne Buckle to attend the Writers Workshop in the fall of 1960, and had I not so intemperately pursued her. The "Projective Verse" party Bill and I held that January, with Lionel's quickly legendary visit to the emergency ward, did sharply raise the profile of Olson's essay within our circle of UBC student writers, even if it didn't sharply increase its understanding—and made more likely Warren's offer to hold Sunday meetings later that spring. I would not have been the same person at those meetings, or at the Duncan lectures that followed—if they had followed—without the long conversations Daphne and I had about poetics or my discovery while writing so intensely "for" her that I was a poet. I should thank her—I know I never have. Perhaps the *Tish* community, such as it is, should thank her. For me, my choice of genre when first hearing that she was about to join the Workshop turned out to be crucial. Before that week I had seen myself almost equally as a possible fiction writer, playwright and poet. When the founding of a poetry magazine happened, I might have hung back like fiction-writer Gladys or playwright-to-be Carol Johnson.

That is, I can't separate in my own mind my attraction to Daphne from the appearance of the Allen anthology, the enormous local interest in Olson's "Projective Verse," Duncan's lectures and the founding of *Tish*. Without her there would have at least been very few Bowering–Davey twin-poem pages in *Tish*, no Tishbook titled *D-Day and After* (with its audaciously punning epigraph from Hopkins, "Buckle! AND the fire that breaks from thee then"), no Contact Press book titled "bridge force." The bridge of that series—prominent in the twin-poems and in those two books—was in part the Lions Gate Bridge over which I had driven to North

Vancouver and Daphne's home, and in part the attempted bridge of my desire. The "bridge force" series had come about through my efforts to follow Duncan's advice to cease self-expression and instead explore and follow the images that one's field of experience was proposing, to move from personal plaint toward attention to the objects and histories one lived among. *Among* as Fred would write. Without Daphne I might never have felt the need to make that effort. One of the first things I read after that March of 1961, and before the Tallman Sunday meetings began, was Durrell's *Justine*, and then *Balthazar, Mountolive* and *Clea*. I was on much too familiar ground while reading *Justine*, and then read Balthazar's "interlinear" with enormous relief—because it demonstrated that if one could expand what one knew, alternate readings of one's own life would become possible. *Mountolive* and *Clea* further expanded the quartet's perspectives and dismantled the initial novel's romantic claustrophobia. There was a way out, and onward.

So that Hopkins epigraph—which no critic has ever attempted to read—is not perhaps all that outrageous—the "thee" that was the humbled falcon/Christ in Hopkins's poem could be me, the "fire" could be the poems I contributed to *Tish*, "Buckle" does operate satisfactorily as both a noun and a verb, the line could be speaking of Duncan's move from "path poem" to "field poem." It even could be read as a gloss on how *Justine* was "buckled" into the splendour, and wisdom, of the full quartet. Interestingly, Hopkins's "The Windhover" would be a poem that also otherwise haunted the *Tish* poets. Both Bowering and Dawson would greet people around the *Tish* office with a "Hi there, in your riding" or a "Hi there, in your riding of the rolling" or a "Hi there, in your riding of the rolling level underneath you." I, of course, would never stoop to such puns.

PART 3 A *TISH* STORY

Going Public, Finding Friends, Making Enemies (1961–1963)

August 1961 . . .

Like Ray Souster's girl at the corner of Elizabeth and Dundas, we are young and think we have no time to waste. Possibly we don't. We want to be up there riding—on steady or unsteady air. George and I are both nervous about teaching for the first time—his initial response when offered a teaching assistantship for a section of English 100 was "I'd be too scared, I'll just be a marker" (*Magpie* 32). If we don't use what's left of the summer to get our first issue out, he and I may get bogged down in preparation, marking and course work. The five of us meet and quickly decide that we want to put most of our energy into writing and producing the magazine— and none into finding and keeping subscribers. We'll work up a list of addresses and give the magazine away—and solicit donations. That's the way *The Floating Bear* and *Origin* are distributed. We'll each contribute a short statement on poetics and a group of poems for the first issue. We'll produce our copies by mimeograph, again like the *Bear* does. What return address will we use? We could use Warren's, but I worry that we are already too closely linked to him.

We could use one of our own, but we all rent and could need to move. We settle on Tony Friedson's—nine blocks downhill from where Bill and I room.

Someone contacts LeRoi Jones and Diane de Prima, the editors of *The Floating Bear*, and gets a copy of their mailing list. George and Lionel dig up a bunch of addresses of Canadian magazines and writers. I copy them all to three-by-five-inch index cards, which we can divvy up when we have to address copies of an issue. We have approximately 350 names. Warren thinks that he can cajole one of the English department secretaries to print the first issue on the department mimeo machine. He gives me a small boxful of stencils that he's already purloined. Even though most of us are still working at summer jobs, we are all also trying to collect enough donations to cover postage.

By the last week of August my summer meter-reading job is over, and Jamie, David and Fred have given me their contributions. George is in Oliver, so I pack my camping gear, manuscripts and typewriter and drive to the south Okanagan and the Inkaneep Provincial Park three miles south of the town. I sit at one of the familiar shiny varnished picnic tables and begin cutting stencils for the first issue. On a break I drive up to the site of the late-nineteenth-century town of Fairview and am surprised by how much recognizable rubble remains. I write a few lines toward a poem.

. . .

My opening editorial can be as long only as the six inches available below the centrefold of the first page. Some of the editors have been concerned that our readers will perceive our magazine's title as a woman's nickname, so I try to use as many scatalogical puns in the editorial as I can think of—several allusions to "sound" and "movement" and a concluding request for financial support: "*Tish* will be always on the bum." Our title will be rarely misperceived. But just to make sure, I will add a line to the issue's last page—"*Tish* is a fine kettle of fecis." Maybe we *should* have simply called it *Shit*.

Or maybe *Shit: a Magazine of Vancouver Poetry*. Less than a year from now a poet named Ed Sanders will launch a magazine in New York titled *Fuck You: A Magazine of the Arts*. For displaying it, the police will charge him and his bookstore with obscenity, but we will still be wistful.

. . .

Jamie has given us a poetics statement in the form of a poem. George in his statement has invoked the bogeymen of "teachers of freshman English"—apparently forgetting that he is about to become one. In mine I similarly invoke the bogeyman of "the scholar." Fred's word of the month is "mellisma"—he uses it in a poem and in his statement, where he calls for "vowels carrying mellismatic colour." He will also be "Fredric" Wah in these pages—he is taking publication and new career very seriously. All of the five statements argue that poets should be part of the "energy" field in which they are writing—as "interaction" (Wah), "instant response" (Dawson), "sensation" (me), as writers who "participate" with "things" (Bowering), who produce poems that are "a total response to what is happening" (Reid). Olson's insistence on a "kinetic" dimension to poetry is more or less visible—the least perhaps in Jamie's statement, which strikes me as I type as the most interesting and least mannered of the five. But of course to write a kind of "field" poetry from a position of openness to surrounding context is indeed what we all aspire to.

September 1961 . . .

Back at UBC George and I are inspecting the office space the department has assigned to us teaching assistants. It's in one of the old army huts—"B-6"—the name sounds like that of a new military plane. Until this summer the hut was laboratory space for the faculty of medicine, and seems to have housed at least a few ill-fated monkeys. Very few of the rooms are laid out as offices. The room George and I have been given is about thirty-five feet by fifteen feet, with a counter and lab sinks all along the window side. At the far end are

two nine-foot-square rooms, one a darkroom with a sink. Neither is large enough for a desk. The ceiling throughout is high. There are glass panels over the main doorway, and built-in shelves along the inside wall. Three desks and four or five chairs have been moved in—we have an officemate, who we discover is Bill New, whom we have distantly known when undergraduates. We would have preferred Lionel, but he has been assigned a single room directly across the corridor, which he has to enter through yet another small office. We suggest to Lionel that he switch with Bill, but he likes his cubbyhole. His staying there is a lot like his attitude to *Tish*. There are several other TAs and part-time faculty in little rooms down the corridor, but the only one I recognize is Betty Lambert.

George and I immediately move two of the desks so that they are front-to-front and we are facing each other when we sit at them. A makeshift "partners desk." We plan to write poems every day and shove them across the desks at each other, shouting "So there!" and "Take that!" When Bill New arrives, he settles himself in the far corner by the entrance to the two small rooms. Overall, the rooms are none too clean. The lab sinks have multicoloured sediment up their sides, and the counters, shelves and venetian blinds are dusty and stained. Some of the stains could be blood, or something that relates to tish. But the counters will be useful for collating pages—once we clean them up a little. There is staff and faculty parking on the street across from the hut—for which as TAs we qualify.

I have taken the cut stencils to Warren, and told him that we will need four hundred copies. I've dated the issue September 14. He calls a few days later to say that we can pick the copies up at his office. He has talked to Roy Daniells who doesn't want the magazine to be printed in the department again, but wouldn't mind slipping Warren a few packages of paper for future issues.

Once we have the copies, David, Jamie and Fred arrive and we begin addressing, folding and stapling the issues shut. We don't need envelopes because I've left a space for the address when I designed the first page. Then we lick and attach the required two-cents stamp. Bill New, who in a few years will present himself publicly as the Commonwealth Literature scholar "W.H. New," watches us with reserved bemusement. Postage will be our biggest expense—about seven dollars. We deliver about thirty copies on campus to students we know and to supportive faculty. Warren is going to host one of his Sunday meetings next weekend so that people can assess the issue and make suggestions for the next one. I am planning to take ten copies to the Duthie's Bookstore downtown on Georgia Street—the manager of the paperback and magazine section, an older man who everyone knows as "Binky," has offered to give us twenty-five cents each for them.

Back in Abbotsford for a weekend, I discover a grimy used mimeograph machine in the local second-hand store. It's a hand-crank model, made in Holland. It's not a Gestetner, but the price is right—fifteen dollars. After I get some solvent and remove layers of old ink, I discover it has a non-standard mount for the stencils, but that I can cut them and punch new mounting holes to make them fit.

October 1961 . . .

George and I are both overwhelmed and exhilarated by the classes we are teaching. Each of us has approximately forty students. The department has sent us class lists, copies of the textbooks and general instructions on how much writing our students are expected to do, but no advice on how we might teach. Jan de Bruyn is nominally in charge of the one hundred or more sections of the course, but there have been no meetings of instructors. No wonder George was nervous. Our hut is three blocks from the department offices but could as easily be a hundred miles. But my class is amazingly lively—I've discovered that it contains fifteen winners of major scholarships. At least two of the students are likely to deserve A+ grades. I am getting by in part by remembering how much I appreciated Ruth Humphrey's openness—and how well she knew the texts we were reading.

I am also busy with my own courses—I'm taking Elliott Gose's "Early Modern British"—it's actually a fin de siècle course—the Pre-Raphaelites, George Eliot, Hardy, Conrad, Wilde, Kipling, the Georgians. Not very "modern." Gose is a friend of Tallman's and a *Tish* supporter, so at least I will feel acknowledged there. Sam Perry is in the class too. I'm taking Hunter Lewis's twentieth-century literary criticism course. He is near retirement and frequently ill because of a long-term drinking problem and associated ailments, but enormously respected by students for his grouchy candour and up-to-date curricula—the very things for which many of his gentlemanly older colleagues disrespect him. I have enrolled as well in a cross-listed fine arts course with Walter Cragg—"Art and Humanism" it is called, but it is more accurately a course in existentialism, a course that the philosophy department has so far refused to offer or cross-list—they are not sure that Sartre will have the staying power of Aquinas. We are beginning a study of the impact on twentieth-century art and literature of thinkers such as Kierkegaard, Buber, Jaspers, Unamuno, Heidegger, Sartre and Merleau-Ponty. Plus I have a compulsory bibliography course with the dreaded Pre-Raphaelite scholar Dick Fredeman—dreaded because of both his womanizing and lack of humour. His practice seems to be to "sponsor" a new young woman partner to an M.A. every couple of years. I worry that I may have taken on too much— there's no charming young woman professor here to "sponsor" me! But at least I learned last year, I hope, not to let any one part of my life obsess me. But *Tish* could. My first-year class could.

Not too much came of the Sunday meeting at Warren's except a sense of excitement that we'd actually published an issue. The fact that twenty or twenty-five people turned up, and talked about the poems, seems to have stimulated all of us to write more.

We buy mimeograph ink and teach ourselves to print on our little Dutch machine. Fred is good at turning the crank and starts being perceived by the rest of us as the *Tish* printer. I have started leaving my office key on a ledge above the door so that Jamie, David and Fred can do work when George and I aren't around. The second issue is going to be much like the first, except the lead editorial will be by George, and we will have poems not only by the five editors but also by David Cull and Lionel Kearns. There are some interesting things here—my "D-Day and After" poem, George's "Sunday Poem," Fred's "Landscale" (his first "continuing" poem)—and Jamie's essay on Philip Whalen. We have decided to rotate the task of writing a lead editorial among the five of us. Fred will write the one for the third issue. I continue to write the various excited interpolations—in this issue they mainly urge readers to write back. So far *Tish* has received no mail. It feels as if we had tossed a boulder into a pond yet caused no splash or ripple. But there is an internal controversy stirring. This second issue contains the first part of a poem by Bowering called "The Meatgrinder"—a poem that he projects could ultimately be book-length. The second part is announced as forthcoming in *Tish* 3. But Fred and Jamie dislike what they see as its easy and derivative rhetoric. We had not foreseen that we might have such a fundamental dislike for a text one of the others had written, and so have no mechanism for resolving vetos and volos. We had imagined we would at least admire what was being attempted in a text—that our reservations about each others' work would assist us all in reaching what we aspired to. However, Fred and Jamie both see "The Meatgrinder" as contrary to the poetics George—and *Tish*—espouse—as being not worthy of him.

November 1961 . . .

I buy a new manual typewriter, made in Germany, to replace my old Royal portable—it has a wide carriage into which one could put a stencil sideways, and ten-point type rather than the twelve point of the Royal. We'll be able to have longer lines of poetry, and get more prose text on a page. My grandmother is volunteering to pay for it "to help with grad school." And I've received a note from George Woodcock, the founder and editor of *Canadian Literature*, a prof here as well as self-trained writer and Orwell scholar, asking me to write an article on Canadian little magazines. That's a surprise. I've never taken a course from him, or even met him. It must have something to do with what he's heard—or seen?—of *Tish*.

Warren hosts another post-issue gathering, and the "Meatgrinder" question takes up a lot of it. But Warren is giving us an essay for our next issue that partly addresses the question, an essay entitled "'When a New Music Is Heard the Walls of the City Tremble.'" It's also a kind of pep talk for all us—suggesting that our poems could indeed make the walls of a city tremble. Here he talks about listening for and projecting an inner music, rather than allowing intellect and wit to be "in control." It's a kind of position paper for the magazine—and more smoothly articulated than anything the editors might write. We also have our first short story— from Carol Johnson.

Now George has withdrawn "Meatgrinder 2," though he still jokes about liking it. He keeps threatening to declaim new parts of it if we aren't nice to him. But I hear strong hints here that we've persuaded him that it's a show-off piece. A piece of "closed" verse. And we've received some mail—including a thoughtful letter from Elliott Gose that describes "Meatgrinder 1" as mostly "overstylized rhetoric." I picked the letters up at Tony's and came back to the office shouting "Call me *Tish* mail!" There are encouraging letters from Canadian found-poet John Robert Colombo and Jon Edgar Webb, editor of the well-known U.S. "underground" literary magazine *The Outsider*, and one from Seymour Mayne, a young poet who edits the magazine *Cataract* in Montreal, a letter that criticizes the poems but praises the magazine as "more exciting reading than Reaney's kindergarten *Alphabet*." Mayne's friend K.V. Hertz has sent poems. We know all these people by reputation and are pretty happy to hear from them. We are split, however, about publishing poems by non-Vancouver writers. We don't want to be an eclectic magazine like *Prism*—we don't want to publish poems simply because, by one of numerous imaginable measures, they are arguably "good"—we want only to publish writing that in some ways furthers our own nascent understandings of what is needed in contemporary poetry.

George and I are also including in the issue our first "shared page," or page of "twin poems"—one poem each that we've written in response to the same object or event. The page is in a way the textual correlative of the shared writing space of our front-to-front desks. We had both been reflecting on the recent history of our office as a neuroscience laboratory, and on the stains on its sinks and counters, and have now sat at our desks and both written a poem about the ironies of writing poetry here. We are titling the page "Two Poems for the Critic."

One thing that did come out of the meeting at Warren's was that people think the *Tish* cover has been visually dull. So I have ordered a rubber stamp to say "TISH," and purchased a bright red stamp pad. We'll hand-stamp each copy as we address it. But when I go back to pick up the stamp, it reads "PISH." Whoever produced it is not, evidently, a follower of local literature. The stationery store has now given us a corrected one, and we are keeping the other— Jamie's suggestion—as our rejection stamp. PISH!!! David quips that this stamp should have read "SHIP" or "SSIP."

Many of the parties where some of us meet now are held at an old grey stucco house in the 4600 block on West Tenth, a few doors east of the university gates. A group of students has rented it from a landlord who is waiting to tear it down and build a large apartment building. Peter Jensen, a law student, Mike Valpy, who hopes to be a journalist, young poet David Cull, Lori Jasper who's from Germany and has the front main-floor bedroom. I think Jamie knows Lori from some writing classes, and George may know Mike from visiting the *Ubyssey* office—though I seldom see George here. Or Fred. Most of the students in our circle now refer to the place as

"The House." Parties seem to be its normal condition—if enough drop by there is a party. There are other young women living here,

and sometimes sleeping with the men, but there are no couples. Mike and Peter often joke—or warn—that one of them has a dry vagina. They don't say "vagina." No one suggests that perhaps the guys who've noted this condition haven't been great lovers. The big "House" news this month involves an older woman, a schoolteacher, who has come back for a postgrad qualifying year, and last weekend came to a "House" party, met one of the young guys and spent the night with him in an upstairs bedroom. Everyone is surprised that she still likes sex. People keep asking him what it was like. "The same," he laughs, "the same."

December 1961 . . .

Bill and I have continued to visit Carol and Mo for day-long games of Monopoly, sake and pizza. We are all good friends and companions whose main interaction is competitive punning and teasing. Bill's outings with Mo don't seem to have had any romantic dimension. I have written a mischievous Creeleyesque poem for her, "The Ballad of the Blue Mumu," which I plan to keep for a book that Warren now has me planning—a Tishbook. I give her a copy, and she asks me matter-of-factly, "Are you in love with me?" Possibly I am, somewhat, but how do you answer such a blunt question about love? What answer did she hope for—or did she care what answer? Or perhaps she assumed that if someone wrote a poem for her, it could only be a declaration of love? A cautious declaration of love. I don't do well with such questions.

That *Tish* become a book publisher is entirely Warren's idea, and also the idea that the first volume be mine. I'm not so sure— George and Lionel both seem to have more "solid" work—but

Warren seems to prefer my flakiness and recklessness—my willingness to write and risk publishing lines that will be deeply embarrassingly a month later if it also means that some poems will do things I didn't know I could enable to happen. He likes my dogged pursuit of a quick perceptual movement from line to line in new poems such as "For One of Them" and "The Guitar Girls"—from my readings of Merleau-Ponty this year I have begun conceiving such poems as phenomenological as much as Olsonian. He has been helping me sort and select poems—we lay the typescripts out in rows on his living-room floor beneath the two Tanabe paintings. He's also volunteered to write an introduction, in which he is already making clear that he sees these poems as "projective"— poems that "project the body of [the poet's] responses into the body of the poem." In pushing for this book Warren may be teaching me something that Duncan also stressed—to prefer the process of surprise creation over the deliberate creation of a polished product.

Surely George would have expected, if there is to be a Tish-book, that his work would be in it. But no, he is extremely supportive, and has volunteered immediately to see if his newspaper contacts in Oliver can do low-cost typesetting and printing. We didn't know each other all that well before Warren began his Sunday meetings last spring, but now after three months of creating and sharing a common desk space, we seem to understand and trust each other far beyond common-sense expectation. I feel similarly about Fred, Jamie and David but at a lower intensity, probably because I see them less often. As for them, they trust me but not George. Instead of trusting him they like, enjoy and indulge him. They smile or giggle or smirk when they say his name.

In the December issue, *Tish* 4, Jamie's editorial is forceful and cogent—the best-written one yet. Fred's essay on margins and his new "Landscale" poems seem important at least in his own progress. And George and I are presenting our second shared page, "Two Poems for a Bicycle Rider." This time, George had pushed a newly written poem at me from across his desk, but instead of responding by "pushing back" with one of my own I had responded to his. Both poems address the synecdoche offered by the bicycle of his girl-friend, Joan Huberman, or is she now his ex-girlfriend? There's a hint of ex-ness in George's poem, and in two other rather quiet George poems in the issue, "A Vigil of Sorts" and "Driving Past." Joan has visited the *Tish* office, as we've come to call it, a number of times this fall, not a lot, usually arriving on her bicycle. She hasn't seemed at ease here, or much interested in George's *Tish* friends. Sometimes she's seemed impatient to leave. Her step-mother is the well-known musician and composer Barbara Pent-land, and her father an engineer. They live nearby in a wealthy area of West Point Grey—the kind of wealth that doesn't necessarily need to display itself—the bicycle seems shabby, poorly maintained, despite having its own remembered shelter in George's poem. Sometime this fall George and Joan were supposed to be getting affianced. There was an engagement party at her house. During the party she discovered him embracing Carol de Ange-lis—much as he had at my "Projective Verse" party—and brought both the event and the engagement to an indignant end. A number of George's friends are saying this is a good thing, that Joan is too changeable, too protean for him, and some are even saying that he must have unconsciously wanted the engagement to fail. George doesn't believe in the unconscious but, these people say, it may have rescued him anyway. Friends in the *Tish* circle talk this way about each other—matchmaking and anti-matchmaking and knowing what is "best" for someone. I find this insulting and intru-sive—it reminds me again of Abbotsford. Although it may just mean that they care. George and I exchange these poems but we don't talk about Joan. We have never talked about Joan.

January 1962 . . .

Both George and I have attractive young women in our classes and sometimes tease each other about them. One of my attractive female students who has difficulty with English composition comes in to consult me about her recent essay. "Oh Mr. Davey," she says,

"I'd do *any*thing to get a pass in this course." George looks up and with a gesture indicates that he'd leave if I want him to. "There was your chance, Frank," he jokes, after she has left. "You let her get away! You'd better make sure you fail her again." George's favourite student—the one who he says makes his heart melt—is called Kristi Krug. Kristy *"Kroooog,"* George insistently croons when I tease him about his weakness for "Kristi Krugg." But his real attraction is to a third-year student he has encountered and who now occasionally comes to our office, Angela Luoma. She's blonde like Joan, and much more cheerful and confident. But she seems skeptical about George's seriousness. George is also still seeing Joan.

Over the holidays we have had another community meeting at Warren's, during which we came to the decision to rename *Tish* a poetry newsletter, rather than a magazine. It's partly my idea—it's been looking like a newsletter—it's been sending out mostly news of our current writing and thinking, and poems in process, rather than finished "product." *The Floating Bear* calls itself a newsletter. But we had got sidetracked into "magazine" by Fred's initial exhortation—"Let's start a magazine!" Of course "Let's start a newsletter!" might not have stirred things up as much.

One of the letters we will be printing in the next issue is from Marian Zazeela in New York City—a painter, musician and experimental artist who is our age—accusing us of feeding on our own "derivative little drippings" with particular reference to my essay on margins in *Tish* 3 and Fred's "Margins into Lines" in *Tish* 4. But along with the letter we will print at least three poems by George that build on a "margin" metaphor and promise a kind of serial poem. They are a new kind of poem for George—"Metaphor I" and "Telephone Metaphysic." Feeding off each other's energies and ideas is a big part of the *Tish* project—it's what got us started. George and I are also publishing in *Tish* 5 our third "twin poem" page: "Two Poems for a Girl with Guitar." The young woman of these poems is Diane Laloge, a friend of David Dawson who occasionally comes with him and Jamie and her guitar to the *Tish* office. I feel pretty good about my part of this page, and also about Lionel's poem "Top Coat." Another poem I feel fortunate to be including is Larry Eigner's "history"—which the other four editors do not care for, and insist that if I must publish it that I also publish their disapproval. Eigner is one of the poets of Donald Allen's *New American Poetry*; the other editors worry that I want to include his poem mostly to attach our newsletter to his celebrity.

February 1962 . . .

A repeated message in the letters that we had been receiving has been that we should stop publishing our reflections on poetic theory and just publish poems. That message has kept coming up in the post-publication meetings at Warren's as well, although not from him, and has now become part of our editorial debates. Fred and I have been the most engaged with poetics, and George and I the most aware that it is people with a romantic view of poetry as mysteriously inspired utterance who are the most dismissive of theory. But George is not entirely free of romantic views himself. He resists having to talk about his own creativity in case talking may make it vanish, or to talk about a poem before it is "finished," in case talking may prevent its completion. Shades of Coleridge and the butcher's boy, I think. He's having a similar problem in making a decisive choice between Joan and Angela. It's a kind of negative Freudianism—a fear that if you make the unconscious conscious it may go "poof" and disappear. At any rate we decide to cool it for now on the theory, at least in terms of editorials. All five of us have had a chance to write a lead editorial on a poetics issue. The editorials will now be for mundane news. I'm not sure I like this. It feels like we're backing down. We're also backing down on the "one guest poet per issue" principle. The issue we're preparing has poems by Padraig O Broin, David McFadden and Larry Eigner—almost a third of the issue—and none by Jamie.

By default, I end up writing *Tish* 6's unsigned "Editorial Notes," talking about myself in the third person. I'm reluctant to officially take on the job. Fred contributes a somewhat puzzling poem about a ming tree and a boy named "Hong" but when you get to the end it's a Canadian poem about snow. George and I have another pair of poems—"Two Dialectics for Bridges." I'm already thinking about another book, one I'd call "Bridge Force." My poem "To the Lions Gate Bridge" is a small step toward enlarging the field of my post-Daphne disappointment—something that I haven't done consistently well so far. I've also contributed a poem, "Intentions," that is simultaneously about process poetics and a female friend who midway through I realize is both girl and woman. I am startled, but the poem has it right. Most of the "girls" of our poems are women—although many would not appreciate being called that. And often we are reckless "boys."

We were certainly that earlier this month. Lawrence Ferlinghetti was in town to read, and at the last minute was moved from a small classroom to the eleven-hundred-seat auditorium where even at 4:00 p.m. he had an overflow audience. As usual there is to be a party for him a night or two later, underwritten by the English department—at the Friedsons' house, the *Tish* return address. But only faculty members are invited. Fred, Jamie and I are astonished—outraged. The English department faculty have mostly scoffed at Beat poetry, with some members joking that sociology would be the appropriate department to teach it. Which of them could possibly benefit from meeting Ferlinghetti? Tony explains that because of the unexpected turnout at the reading the department fears that the party could be overwhelmed by crashers. We are not placated, and at my suggestion we tell Tony that we'll organize a student picket of his house, and alert the local media, if we are not invited. Later that day, we and half a dozen other students get our invitations. We don't spread the word to others. At the party we are exceptionally well-behaved. I had enjoyed Ferlinghetti's laconic, often satirical reading, in which he skillfully "played" the audience for laughs and applause, but at the party he seems tired and rather ordinary. He talks to us mostly about running his publishing house and his bookstore. Or maybe that's what we ask him about.

. . .

Robert Creeley reads in the mathematics building—another 4:00 p.m. reading. Gladys tells me that Duncan had urged him to come. Several hundred of us are there, though nothing like the overflow audience that greeted Ferlinghetti. But we stay longer. He is reading the terse understated poems gathered in *For Love*—still in press at Scribner. I know many of the poems, but not how precisely he will speak them. At the end of the hour we applaud so much that he reads for another half hour, and talks to us for yet another. That evening there's a party at Warren's—where he appears to be staying. All the conversation is about poetry.

March 1962 . . .

We hear that poet Cid Corman, the editor of *Origin* and one of the first to publish Olson and Creeley, is giving a lecture on Noh drama at the University of Washington in Seattle—Thursday evening, March first. We wish it were a reading, but we can't pass up a chance to meet him. He's spending the next few years in Kyoto. That afternoon George, Gladys, Fred, Bill and I pile into my Ford and head south. February is usually the end of winter in BC, so I've had my service station install my summer tires last weekend in preparation for the trip. There's no interstate yet along the west coast—we are driving the old two-lane Highway 99. We keep stopping because someone has to pee or because a tavern looks inviting. Bill buys a bottle of his favorite wine—a fortified white called "Thunderbird." When we get to the outskirts of Seattle, Gladys has to pee and complains several times because I have passed a grocery or tavern that probably has a washroom. I eventually pull into an empty parking lot and us guys go and pee against a wall—"Private souls at a public wall!" George shouts—but Gladys has to go almost a block to find cover between two buildings. After the lecture we introduce ourselves to Corman and have a short, not-terribly-interesting talk with him, and then head back toward Vancouver. Fred's disappointed. Creeley was so much more open to his audience.

By the time we get to Everett it has started to rain. When we get to the Chuckanut Drive junction the rain has turned to snow. There are fairly steep hills around Alger and Lake Samish south of Bellingham, and I start having trouble keeping the summer tires gripping the road and the car moving. I need to carry some speed on the hills just to keep going. With some difficulty we get to the top of the last big hill, but just over the crest a truck, a tractor-trailer, has jackknifed across both lanes. We are doing about forty mph, and the front bumper of the truck is at windshield height about fifty feet ahead. I slam on the brakes and cut the wheels sharply to the right, expecting merely to keep heading forward under the truck. But the car spins to the right, skids inches past the bumper and rolls onto its roof in the ditch—then lurches back onto its driver's side. As the car rolls Bill's bottle of Thunderbird soars from the back window ledge and past my head toward the windshield—I reach up with my left hand and catch it. "What a move!" I hear Fred say. Someone's calling that I have to turn off the ignition—so we don't catch fire.

Warren and Ellen Tallman's Tish salon.

Bill and Fred are in back, Gladys and George in the front. I am the only one who has fastened a seat belt, so George and Gladys are now on top of me, and there's a similar heap behind. I can hear people outside—"Are you okay?" several voices calling. Most likely they've come from cars that were blocked behind the truck. Despite the snow it is quite dark. Then I hear people climbing on the top side of the car—they surprise us by managing to get the coupe's heavy passenger door open. We scramble up like we are exiting the hatch of a submarine—Glady stepping on George as if he were the conning-tower ladder—and then jump down and away as if we do such things everyday. Once we are out and our rescuers think we are okay, we are left alone. They are understandably preoccupied by their own predicaments. Gladys has a small cut on one knee from where she hit the extra switch I'd installed below the dashboard to "fade" the volume of the rear speakers. We each do little self-assessments and suddenly I discover a patch of warm stickiness all down my right abdomen and leg. But it's too dark to see it.

"I think I'm bleeding," I call out, and Gladys and Fred quickly try to check me out. I'm trying not to panic. "It's oil," they say. "Engine oil," says Fred, and starts laughing. I'm not so sure it's funny. It's soon going to be wet and cold. Other northbound cars that have snow tires are coming up the hill slowly and managing to pass the truck on the right shoulder that we skidded across. Within an hour several wrecking trucks have arrived, and a police car. Two of the trucks are working to get the truck off the highway. Another pulls my Ford roughly back onto its wheels and then onto the road. The driver wants $35, and tells me where I can find and pay the all-night garage that dispatched him. They have sets of chains for sale. The cop thinks the car is driveable despite the damage to the roof and driver's side, and tells me I can get an accident report for my insurance company from the police station in Bellingham. It's near the garage. I drive to the garage, get chains put on, check the engine oil level—which mysteriously is okay—and then head to the police station. The unplowed snow is now so deep that it is over the top of the Ford's front bumper. I decide to drive to Abbotsford, which is only twenty very familiar—and level—miles north, rather than the forty-five miles to Vancouver. The others would prefer to head toward Vancouver, I'm sure.

The engine starts to overheat—it's because the snow is far above the bumper and blocking the grill. We have to keep stopping to clear it. Sometimes George, Bill and Fred have to get out and push. The rural highway is totally snow-covered—virgin snow, untrammelled ways. We see no other vehicles. When we get to the Sumas–Huntingdon customs, we are told we are the only ones to have crossed in the last ten hours. In Abbotsford I take Gladys to the medical clinic where she gets her cut stitched up, and then drop everyone at my parents' house. I stop at my insurance agent, and then at Russell's Body Shop, a couple of blocks from the house. The bus to Vancouver doesn't leave until late in the afternoon, so we guys go down to the pool hall and shoot a few games. On the bus I study for a bibliography exam I have on Monday. The others sleep.

. . .

I am slowly getting to know some of the "downtown" poets that some people now think of as *Tish* rivals. I met bill bissett back in 1959 when he sat in the front row of Warren's poetry course and Lionel, Gladys and I sat in the back—but I didn't pay much attention because bill was just one of several inarticulate nameless students in the front row. But bill and John Newlove, Gerry Gilbert and Fred Douglas have been coming to some of Warren's parties and meetings, and to Jamie's parties now that Jamie has a place of his own downtown. Warren's parties are brightly lit, and people come to drink and talk. Jamie's are dark and shadowy, with Miles Davis's *Kind of Blue* seemingly always being played, and the tobacco and marijuana smog so thick one's eyes start to sting. Uptown and downtown. The downtown poets are centred on the art school where Roy Kiyooka and Takao Tanabe teach—both Douglas and bissett are painters as well as writers. Those with a little money make sure that Newlove, who is chronically without, gets at least subsistence food rations—one of them has joked to us about giving him a potato a day. There is indeed some rivalry between us and "them"—but it is good-natured. Newlove and Gilbert have recently sent us, or Fred at least, a book—*How to Increase your Word-Power.* I am mentioning this in my March editorial. I admire John's control of tone and rhythm, although Warren tells me that his poems, while polished, are also closed—that while they may move toward surprisingly precise wordings they rarely move surprisingly far from their initial perceptions. John will be a successful poet, he expects, but not an astonishing one.

John's first book, *Grave Sirs*, printed by "the private press of Robert Reid and Takao Tanabe," has just

been published in a large format and hand-set type. They have explored his poems as an occasion for their own artistry as printers and typographers. Reid is already a celebrated local book designer who is about to leave his position at the art school to practise typographic design at McGill. My own book, *D-Day and After*, Linotyped and designed by George's friend in Oliver whose previous book experience has been the printing of the catalogues of fall fairs, is supposed to arrive at the end of the month. Uptown and downtown doesn't quite account for us all—both scenes are academic ones, with different focuses; both have areas of wealth, limitation and useful connection.

The clever back cover of Newlove's *Grave Sirs*.

. . .

In the new *Tish* George includes the short poem "Back from Seattle" but doesn't mention Corman, the accident or the snow. Just the foreign match folders he's collected. At least he kept quiet about my panicked "bleeding"! In my editorial I mention what Corman had told us about his projected stay in Kyoto and plans for *Origin*. Elsewhere in the issue is an essay by Warren on Creeley's short stories. He's working at bringing Creeley to Vancouver to teach, but I don't think we're supposed to know that yet.

April 1962 . . .

The latest story at "The House" is that an attractive young lesbian student most of us know came to a party last weekend and went upstairs with a guy—"Oz" I think he's called. No one thought much about it until Peter went upstairs to his room and discovered them on his bed. He came back down describing with great humour how Oz's "white bum" was slowly bouncing up and down above Karen. When she and Oz came down, much later, she told people that she wasn't really sure she was a lesbian and thought she should try to find out. I'm not sure what she discovered. There's quite a few young women, especially around "The House," openly and thoughtfully enjoying different sexual possibilities. Most seem to have managed to get the new birth-control pill. Like me, Peter finds all this both fascinating and a little strange.

. . .

The new issue of *Prism* is out, with poems by Wah, Hindmarch, Bowering, Davey and Kearns. This is good, but not as exciting as it once might have been. They will publish something quite different in the next issue, and in the ones after. Out as well is my *D-Day and After.* We unpack the copies, divide them among us and begin hand numbering them in the space the printer has left for that on the inside back cover. At sixty-five cents a copy, we sell about fifty on the campus in the first week. I take ten down to Binky at Duthie's. People want to know if the cover image is supposed to be me. I say no, that any resemblance is an accident. A clean-shaven male face with hair. Some think it is a book about the war. I'm not sure what I think about being the author of a

Me, whom the cover artist hasn't seen.

book—with all that is going on it seems like a small step in a much larger process.

. . .

For our April issue I've written an anti-nationalist editorial, which some will probably read as anti-Canadian. I think I am still stinging from the smug British and U.S. nationalisms that I encountered when younger—and from the racial nationalisms of wartime Japan and Germany. If I had a word like "essentialism" I would use it. Instead I am stumbling around in search of words. It is poets, people, who make countries noteworthy, I try to write, not countries that make people noteworthy. "Place is no more than a man does with it," I write—using the convention that we all unthinkingly believe at this time, that "man" is an ungendered word that stands in as a short form for "humanity" and "mankind." *As a Man Thinks* is the title of the English department's standard essay anthology. *Man in the Modern Age* is the title of one of my Karl Jaspers collections. I'm now writing every editorial—nobody else wants to write them. None of the others care whether or not there is an editorial, I suspect. Just me.

. . .

Fred is arguing that we should get a higher quality printing device—perhaps a small offset press—particularly now that we are thinking of publishing a series of Tishbooks. There will be a book by George, one by Lionel and one by Francis Grady, an American who has been sending us new poems every month. Rather than paying a printer two hundred dollars to print a book, as we have with mine, why not spend two hundred dollars on a used offset press and print our books ourselves, he asks, for the cost of ink and paper. He has looked into offset technology—you can type or draw directly on an offset "master." The press is motorized so there's no more "cranking out an issue." For a little more money you can get a print shop that has an electric plate maker to burn type and visual images directly onto a metal master.

We gather some money together from ourselves and some sup-
porters and start answering newspaper ads for small offset presses. I
worry that we don't know enough to buy a good one—and perhaps
we don't. We buy a used Addressograph-Multilith Model 80 and
install it in the small room near Bill New's desk. Now we have to
buy masters, special inks, special wipes and the base for a wetting
solution that is applied to the master along with the ink. The principle of the printing method is that ink sticks to the typed or drawn
surfaces of a master while the wet solution sticks to the other areas.
The master transfers or "offsets" a reverse ink image to a rubber
drum, which then transfers a printed positive image to the paper.
Fred is sure that he can make all this work.

May 1962 . . .

Warren and Elliott Gose have been continuing to try to find me a
literary-minded girlfriend. Like my mother—but for different reasons—they don't think much of the Catholic high-school girls
they've seen me with. Elliott has been bringing his latest find, from
his last first-year class, to the Sunday *Tish* meetings and Warren's
parties, and I finally ask her out. Slim, shy and auburn-haired. Most
of the time I go to pick her up, however, a girlfriend of hers just
happens to be visiting, and invites herself along with us. I am puzzled. I don't know whether Elliott's protégée has asked her to do
this, or whether something else is going on. David Cull, however,
has a Triumph TR2—a two-seat sports car. So one Sunday David
and I swap cars, and I drive off with the young woman leaving her
friend beside the curb. Nothing much ever develops between me
and her, but I do like the TR2. I look around for one similar—test
driving an Austin-Healey 3000 at Fred Deeley's before buying a
new bright red TR4 somewhere else. It costs me only $1,100 plus
the trade-in on my Ford.

. . .

Fred has now printed the first offset *Tish*—# 9. It's a clean print job, nice dark ink, and with drawn images from my *D-Day and After* on the back page—something we could never have done in mimeo.

The only defects are the occasional hollow letter and ink loss on the centre of some pages. One problem with typing directly on an offset master is that the typewriter indents the letter image into the surface so that only the carbon around the indentation attracts ink for transfer to the paper. On one page we have to ink in the faint words by hand. Fred prints the issue on eleven-inch paper rather than the fourteen-inch paper we have used previously. We have an editorial disagreement about this—

David, Fred and our Model 80.

some of us are eleven-inchers, some are fourteen-inchers, we joke, making a sly allusion to Samuel Butler. I'm a fourteen-incher, myself. The long pages are easier for me, the typist and layout guy, to make look good.

The issue is notable for its letter from Vincent Ferrini criticizing Warren's essay on Creeley. He tells us that he read the essay at Olson's house—and then consciously or unconsciously mimics Olson's stern letter to him in *The Maximus Poems* by declaiming to Warren, "it is accuracy or nothing." We all laugh. Maybe he forgot to use quotes. The issue also has our first poem by Red Lane ("R.S. Lane")—possibly his first publication—and two poems by Earle Birney's latest discovery, a high-school student named Avo Erisalu. Birney tends to often make such "discoveries" of young not-too-confident writers who will easily accept his advice. However, he has had no interest in putting himself forward as having discovered George or Lionel—although he easily could have. He has also recently discovered Sonny Choy. But when Fred went to him in early 1961 for advice on his new poems—Lionel having told him that he should—Birney told him, "Oh I just don't have time for this." Fred was disappointed—and somewhat disgusted, as he had been at Corman's clear lack of curiosity about Vancouver and *Tish*. I guess Earle hadn't noticed he was part Chinese. I've never talked to Birney myself about writing poetry, and now probably never will— he has a Canada Council fellowship to go on leave next year.

The first issue of *Motion*.

My editorial announces the launching of a prose companion to *Tish*—the prose newsletter *Motion*, edited by Bob Hogg and David Cull. I don't find the title very interesting, although I suppose it is theoretically sound. I imagine readers talking about "going through the *Motions*." The first issue has contributions by Lori Jasper from "The House," Bob, David, myself and Jamie. Fred has printed it very nicely on the new *Tish* offset.

I've got news that I've won UBC's Macmillan Prize in creative writing—not bad considering all the accomplished writers here. But the biggest news is that it's official now that Creeley has been hired by UBC. Birney has been furious about this since early spring, and is now manoeuvring to have Irving Layton hired as a "counterbalance." Jake Zilber is going around saying to anyone who will listen, "In the country of the blind the one-eyed man is king"—his jest alluding to Creeley's lost left eye. And in a possibly related development, Roy Daniells has offered me a section of a 300-level faculty of education English to teach this coming summer. The offer astonishes me—this is a linguistic grammar course for education students, one required by a provincial ministry decision to replace the prescriptive grammar taught in provincial schools with a descriptive one. All would-be English teachers and present ones who are working on degrees are required to take it. Most of those who currently teach this course are graduate students who have taken Ron Baker's linguistics course—because almost none of the regular faculty feel qualified to teach it. But I am one of very few who haven't taken Baker's course. Has Warren whispered in Roy's ear about more than just the Creeley hiring? For me it will be a bit like taking Baker's course without having to write the exam. Pauline has just taken it—I borrow her class notes and textbooks.

Almost lost in the controversy over Creeley's coming and Birney's attempts to have Layton hired is the news that Louis Dudek will be here for the summer session to teach Birney's senior poetry workshop. Birney is said to have had a hand in the hiring, and I wonder at once whether this is a ploy to prevent the workshop from being offered in the regular term—and thus prevent Creeley from teaching it. I'd take that course from Creeley—particularly when as a 400-level course it qualifies for graduate credit.

June 1962 . . .

Jamie and Carol Johnson are in love. Whenever I see them they are together. Bill is back in Abbotsford working at PM Radio. It is two doors north of a Marshall-Wells hardware franchise operated by an elderly couple with two comely grown daughters. He often goes there if he needs something mundane—a knob or a bolt—for repairing a TV or fridge. The younger daughter, Helen, is going into third-year education at UBC, and is home helping out in the store between the regular and summer sessions. A few times when I visit Bill we take some cold pop out of one of the being-repaired fridges and go to the hardware store to share them. Helen needs to go to Vancouver in the next week or so to complete her summer-school enrolment, so I offer her a ride. I've decided to enrol in the summer session myself, in Dudek's poetry workshop—its schedule fits with that of the grammar course I will be teaching. On the way back from Vancouver, with the convertible roof of my TR4 folded down, a large bumble bee strikes the top of the windshield, bounces over it and settles inside the top of Helen's low-cut sundress. She is distressed, and so I pull over to the side, reach in with a bare hand and remove the unconscious bee. We then look into whether she has suffered harm.

. . .

The masthead of the June *Tish* is printed on an IBM Electric type-writer that has type-emulating fonts and proportional spacing—a kind of VariTyper. We have rented it to prepare the masters for George's book *Sticks & Stones*. Fred wants the book to look as professional as possible, but as is evident in the masthead, the electric typewriter makes even deeper indentations into the master than a manual one, exaggerating the "hollow letter" problem.

. . .

James Reaney has reviewed *D-Day* in his magazine *Alphabet*. And reviewed its author, of whom he worries that instead of "projecting himself through his typewriter" (as he assumes Olson recommended) "his typewriter isn't projecting itself through him."

. . .

I get to vote for the first time—there's a federal election. I find I am still a kind of civic nationalist, much as I wrote in our April issue—a nation is the aggregate of what we do for our fellow citizens. I am still angry at Diefenbaker's cancellation of the Avro Arrow, at his purchase of Bomarc missiles and F-104 jets from the U.S. to replace them. Then we discover that the Bomarcs don't work without nuclear warheads. I vote for the Liberal because he has the best chance of defeating the Diefenbaker candidate.

. . .

I decide to enjoy my new car by driving up to the Okanagan and visiting George. Bob Hogg comes with me. While we are there, Red Lane turns up with a hitchhiker who's been recently released from jail. George's mother comes out and takes colour photos of us with my camera. Bob and I then take a quick tour of the Krestova region

where last fall various "Sons of Freedom" Doukhobor families
burned their own homes, bombed power lines and paraded in the

nude to demonstrate their
disdain for material things
and laws that require children to attend school.
Twenty were convicted of
"violence" this past March
and imprisoned, and an-
other nine last month. Bob
and I are sympathetic be-
cause our understanding is
that these extreme Anabap-
tists came to Canada be-

Hogg, Bowering, Lane, me, my TR4, and unknown hitchhiker
in Oliver, summer 1962. Bowering's 1951 Pontiac is on the
left.

lieving that they had guarantees that they would be able to live
outside the public-school system. The little farms along the gravel
roads are strange: the orchards and pastures are overgrown, the
barns—most made of logs—are intact but empty, and where there
once was a house is a small rectangle of charred earth with the remains of iron stoves and bedsprings. We pick up a young hitchhiker
ourselves. He's not a Doukhobor. He sells his banjo-uke to me for
twenty dollars.

July 1962 . . .

I am back in Vancouver to begin Dudek's poetry workshop and
teaching the linguistic grammar course. The grammar class takes
place in the education building where Helen is taking her summer
course. One of her girlfriends is among my students, although most
are schoolteachers who are upgrading their credentials and are
between thirty and sixty years of age. Many are angry at being
required to take the course, and regard me and descriptive grammar much the way creationists view Charles Darwin. The oldest
student, a very pleasant silver-haired woman, was teaching the old
"a noun is the name of a person, place or thing" grammar twenty

years before I was born. The second-oldest is a somewhat cynical veteran of the Canadian Army's First Division in Holland. It's a lively class. Almost all the students are both diligent and resistant. They don't know that this is mostly new material for me too, except for the general principles. Of course it's the general principles they have the most trouble with.

Dudek's workshop is held in a room in the old Arts building—a quiet and pleasant space in the summer. Lionel is here most days, auditing, and sometimes George. I immediately like Louis—he is serious, curious, humourous, earnest and respectful to his students. He doesn't play games to try to impress us. His personal experiences in modernism are in many ways parallel to Duncan's, and some moments in his classes evoke memories of Duncan's far-ranging lectures. Bill should be here to tape them. He's also read most of the issues of *Tish*, and seems really glad to see me in the workshop.

. . .

The English department gossip lines have been flooded with stories about Birney's rage over Roy Daniells's refusal to hire Layton—even as a one-year replacement for Birney. He has apparently threatened to resign—although people say he would likely be required to teach one year following his leave. And Creeley and his wife, Bobby, have arrived, and rented a house just two blocks north of Warren and Ellen's—it has the same house number, 2527. He tells us that he has been going all through the house testing various rooms to see if he can write in them. It's an arresting idea, that some rooms may be more hospitable to creativity than others—particularly to students who have never had more than one room. I tell Bill, who's now back in Abbotsford for the summer, that I'm going to try writing on his side of our room. He suggests that I could also try the bathroom.

. . .

With Bill away, Helen and I spend a lot of time in that basement room. To my surprise, she is one of those young women who enjoys her sexuality, and has been, covertly, for some time. It is an old story but increasingly a public story. Helen doesn't much like the women at the usually messy "House," but in some ways is also much like them.

. . .

In my editorial in this month's issue I display my own rage at some writers in Montreal and Toronto who have written about an "olson-jones" (that's LeRoi, not D.G.) school and about the "Beats" as if these include all U.S. non-academic poets. The remarks aren't worth even a quarter the ink I expend on them. But I do go on expending. I am pissed. Fulminating even though I know I shouldn't. Well, my previous poorly thought-out editorial has at least attracted sub-stantial letters from Kearns and from Denise Levertov. This issue, *Tish* 11, also has our first poem by a student who was in George's first-year class, Dan McLeod. "Keep-a-movin'-Dan" McLeod, George calls him.

August 1962 . . .

Roy Daniells has now offered me a second section of English to teach in the fall-winter session, and a double teaching assistant-ship—$3,200. What with the $1,600 he's given me for the summer course I'm currently teaching, I'll be earning about the same as an assistant prof. What he's offering me for the fall is a section of first-year English and one of the third-year linguistic grammar course I'm currently teaching. George has been offered an extra course too but he tells me the combined money offer is only $2,400. I don't understand. I also don't understand how Daniells can have confi-dence in us—perhaps he's just happy that he's received no com-plaints. There have been no teaching evaluations and no classroom visits by faculty members in either of my sections or in George's. Of course the department has an enormous number of course sections being taught by part-timers and grad students—fifty sections perhaps?—seventy-five? The overall undergrad enrolment at UBC is now up to eighteen thousand from the eleven thousand it was when I arrived in 1957. Even the department's paperwork for these sections must be difficult. I've never taken a course from Daniells, or visited his office. We know each other by sight in the corridors and say a polite "hello" as we pass. He's a large, craggy man. I think of him as a friendly buffalo. I wonder whether he really likes me, or is he just desperate for warm bodies to put in front of classes?

My linguistic grammar course has been going reasonably well. I've presented it as a meta-grammar course—a course about how grammar can be taught rather than one in grammar per se. I've stressed that they don't have to believe in the "new grammar," as if a grammar system were a religion (which for many of them the old prescriptive grammar seems to be)—stressed that they only have to see its utility—how it clarifies how our language works better than prescriptive grammar did. I've taken them through old, middle and Renaissance English, to demonstrate how alive, open, inventive, adventurous and changeable English has been. Like a projective poem. I've persuaded them that most children learn most of the complexities of grammar before they attend grade school—that their job as grammar teachers is to raise to consciousness a grammatical system their young students have already, amazingly, learned and learned to use—so that those students can even better use that knowledge. And in class after class I have demonstrated the utility of a descriptive grammar, challenging them to give me a sentence it cannot parse. Most of them have become grudgingly receptive. I have too—I like this group for the ordeal it put up with. I've also raised my own consciousness of English sentence structure. As readers of my editorials will know, I needed that. I still need that. I need to write prose as carefully as I write poetry. But I don't. And I often don't listen with enough care to the poems I write. Last week the summer *Canadian Literature* came out, with it my article on little magazines—"Anything But Reluctant" I had called it. I'd written many drafts of it, a long first draft and then a bunch of shorter and shorter ones, each time trying to cut out wordiness, sarcasm, irrelevancies, awkward metaphors, pretentious value judgments—all those things I've learned not to like in what I've written in *Tish*. Woodcock has done very little editing of it—I guess that's good.

. . .

In Dudek's workshop I've been working mainly on developing a sequence or serial. I like Dudek's *En Mexico*, much as I like Dawson's current continuing poem "tentative coastlines." I like the way the continuing form enables one to focus outside oneself—on the images, rhythms and sounds the parts of the poem are proposing—and to locate a larger context and thus different meanings for one's personal obsessions. Dudek is a very perceptive reader, as well as a non-prescriptive teacher—he tries both to enlarge what his students know is possible and to help them realize the poems they want to write. You will never find out what you are personally capable of doing, or doing in poetry, until you get glimpses of what it may be possible to do. Dudek and Duncan are both teachers who can show a student numerous open doorways. Not every student can walk through them however, or be taught to.

One peculiarity of Dudek's workshop is a final examination—the first creative-writing exam I have encountered. The exam doesn't require one to write a poem. It is almost all historical and technical—how many syllables in a traditional sonnet or a haiku, what was asserted in the Imagist manifesto, what's the difference between a Shakespearean and a Spenserian sonnet, which periods and poets have used a ballad stanza, and why, what is blank verse, what is an example of a modernist prose poem, what is *terza rima*? For an ex-English honours student such as myself, this is not a huge challenge, but for some of the other students, ones who still believe in romantic theories of inspiration, it is a useless imposition, a scandal.

Before the workshop ends, Dudek asks me if I will guest-edit a special Vancouver issue of his magazine *Delta*—not a *Tish* issue but a Vancouver issue.

. . .

I've been working hard on assembling *Tish* 12—but without a lot of help. George is now in San Francisco and has been incommunicado, so I leave him off the masthead. I think he may have gone down there with David Bromige and be having second thoughts about both romantic commitments and an academic career—and about how the two may be connected. People say there's a possibility he won't be back. Fred has his usual summer job driving a tractor in the peat bogs on Lulu Island, and is weary by the workday's end. I'm rather embarrassed by my last two editorials and so for this issue have written only a brief and factual one, mostly about our having completed a full year of monthly publication. The four of us are impressed by that. The community that meets each month at Warren's is impressed—many have predicted that *Tish* would become at best an intermittent publication. And we have a poem in this issue by Daphne—despite all the mean-spirited things I have allowed my understanding of "projective" verse to enable me to publish about her. Actually, she had offered other poems as early as last fall—offered them to me, at any rate. We exchanged letters about them. I thought them too romantic, not sufficiently grounded in detail. She protested from her own evolving sense of what poetry was.

There is also a new poem by Red Lane, an "open letter to George Bowering," in which he openly aligns himself with the professed anti-academicism of Vancouver's art-school poets. He warns George that he may be about to make two mistakes, each of which would "kill" him. "The first mistake will be made," he writes, "If you go back to the university / In the fall / Or ever again." He's probably alluding to his absence in San Francisco, and how completing an M.A. could propel him into academic employment. These are questions I haven't tried to think through for myself. I seem just to go through whatever doors happen to open—like writing an open-field poem.

There is also Dawson's fascinating new poem on BC history— "tentative coastlines." I continue to like it a lot and hope I can learn from it. I've been feeling similarly about Fred's "Landscale" poems. There's a short poem by Michael McClure that we're very pleased to have, and one by Patricia Smith, who was the outstanding student of the exceptionally strong first-year class I taught. There's also a short poem by the anglophile Bromige, who has usually presented himself around UBC as better and more civilized than the *Tish* rabble. He went south to enrol at Berkeley. Now that's academic. I'm surprised that he wanted to publish with us. I'm surprised as well that John Newlove has sent us a poem, which I put prominently on the back outside page. It's anti-romantic, of course, as much of John's writing is, and perhaps sent to us because of its refusal to see any beauty in the British Columbia landscape—"it's summer in british / columbia / again shimmering / lakes, oh yeah, green / forests" it begins.

. . .

George is back, for three evenings of lectures that Creeley is giving at the Tallmans'. It's almost a reprise of the Duncan lectures of slightly more than a year ago—the same place, the same number of lectures. But a very different voice, cautious rather than expansive, repeatedly retreating and qualifying, or offering alternatives, rather than pushing forward and amplifying. "I want to say," he begins partway through the first evening,

> that perhaps the route back to magic senses was that in language one can possess or state or define relationships which otherwise can only be experienced, y'know. I can say I'm going to hit you, and propose all the activity of that y'know relationship, before I've ever got out of the chair.

It's a revealing example, I think. There is an aggressive defensive-
ness in his poems. He repeatedly emphasizes that the writing of
poetry is an activity that takes place within language and is thus
larger than any personal intention. Including hitting. "The problem of poetry is stylistic and linguistic, in other words, the form you
give the thing and the means whereby you gain that form are the
problems of poetry and not specifically what you have to say." This
emphasis leads him on the third night to totally separate the poem
from its author: "The poem means what it means," he says, "it has
nothing to do with the man who wrote it." The poet is merely "the
instrument by which the language writes the poem." A few words
later, however, he makes one of his characteristic qualifications.
"But he equally has to be conscious to what he's doing in order not
to mar it, not to object, or not to go to sleep at some point when all
of his intelligence is needed, y'know, for a recognition of what he's
doing, to allow more to occur."

There's not as much electricity in the room these evenings as
there was a year ago. Duncan's lectures opened things up; Creeley's
now offer caveats—"Men become tongue-tied when they think
overly about the problems of speech"—and rules—"there must
be a constant activity of a perceptive nature in the poem; you must
be constantly aware of what you are saying as you are saying it." As
if recognizing this, he concludes the third lecture by saying, "There
are no rules. The only rules that could possibly be said to exist in
this sort of business or activity are those which we could only recognize for ourselves, anyhow. In other words, the rules are inherent
in the nature of the act." Many of the questions he is asked concern
Duncan—as if the questioner may be unconsciously comparing the
two sets of lectures. One concerns how Duncan often begins poems
with a statement, as if he is "saying something." "You begin by
thinking you're saying something," Creeley responds.

You begin as Duncan suggests, or perhaps there are many other
means by which the same occurrence or occasion can be arrived
at—in any case, you begin and, as you write, each word that you

choose, from all the possibilities that exist for you, gives shape to that which you think you are seeing, or as you write—I'm using "seeing" here as "understanding"—you see the thing which is to represent your statement or rather, to take on the issue of your statement, going into place as you speak. Now as these words begin to go, then you find that other, perhaps other things, are occurring, which do not have really much to do with your statement at all.

These are not inspiring lectures but they are useful ones to those whose writing is ongoing. Creeley is addressing very private moments, those moments in which poems are being written, decisions about words being made, caveats remembered. It's as if we had asked Duncan last July, "How do we do all this, Robert?" And a year later he had sent Creeley to tell us just that.

September 1962 . . .

It's like a reunion here now as well as an anniversary. We're all back on campus and in or close to the *Tish* office. I don't talk to George about his absence, or about Red's poem. Even Bobby Hogg is back—he had gone to Calgary in June intending to get a permanent job. Most of us are caught up in excitement about how the thirteenth issue is shaping up. Robert Duncan has sent us an extraordinary and generous article that he wrote just last week, "For the Novices of Vancouver." He's clearly read every one of our issues closely. And Creeley has given us a short essay as well, "Why Bother." "A magazine not interested in being either the last word apropos some function, or taste, or simply a reflection of what is already 'valued,'" he writes, "such a magazine may define a new possibility by being, quite literally, the place where it can be formulated."

Creeley seems to be aware of *Tish*'s troubled Canadian reception. His piece addresses the question of its allegedly "non-Canadian" emphasis on the BC local—art "happens somewhere, not everywhere," he says. "When it does so happen everywhere, it has become a consequence of taste purely. . . ." He addresses the question of derivativeness—"[n]o man can work free of the influence of those whom he may respect in his own art" and then elaborates—"The light moves, so to speak, and those who see it have acquired an originality far beyond that qualified by terms of personality or intent." George Hitchcock, poet and editor of *Kayak* magazine, has sent us the poem "Advice," which we are reading as directly intended for us: "Cultivate your lunacy: / harrowed & turned / god knows what / it will grow," it begins.

We have received no similar anniversary words from any senior Canadian poets. None of the other editors comments to me about this—possibly they expected none. Over the past twelve issues it has been largely Canadian poets of our generation who have implicitly, if conditionally, welcomed us by offering poems to be published in our pages—Newlove, Gwendolyn MacEwen, K.V. Hertz, David McFadden, bill bissett. Is this because we are writing from Vancouver?

Duncan's essay, with its numerous quotations from our own work, is one that I will read and reread in search of clues for how I can extend and expand the few things he thinks I have accomplished. I imagine Fred and David will respond to it similarly. The title "For the Novices" keeps our youth and relative inexperience very much in view, but still, with its allusion to the German philosopher and poet Novalis—and to the extraordinarily high cultural role Novalis believed poetry to have—takes what we have managed to write extremely seriously. He gives an embarrassing amount of attention to my poems (not my editorials, fortunately), and to David's "tentative coastlines." He cites six Davey poems, not always favourably, but at the end writes that "'To the Lions Gate Bridge' is a poem without lapse, and the achievement crosses a line, for Davey now belongs to, has committed himself to, the major responsibilities of a poet." I want to believe him but I am not sure I do. But his argument that I have been evolving from a smart-ass poet eager to show off his wit, to a more "straightforward voice" and "poetic intelligence" attentive to what the poem at hand is proposing, makes a lot of sense to me. The only things in *Tish* that I painfully regret publishing are those poems and editorials in which I was straining for wit and one-upmanship. Why is he writing so much about me? Is it perhaps because my work has changed the most—and has illustrated most the advantages of committing oneself to a process and community without knowing the outcome? *Tish* has been a lot like a Duncan serial poem—with each issue bringing forth new complexities that we have had either to attend and respond to, or let ourselves fall by the way.

I am also thinking that Duncan writes mostly about me and David because we are the closest to his poetic; we do not write as many of the one-page "magazine poems" that Kearns, Reid and Bowering have been tending to write—the terse anecdote or description that is concluded with a hopefully pointed and clever aperçu. Our poems have been looser, more visibly "open." I'm surprised that Fred's "Landscale" poems haven't engaged him—although land, earth, Gaia, continent are more Olson's preoccupation than Duncan's.

Then there's his interest in the "twin poems" that George and I began publishing in *Tish* 2, and his distinction between cooperation and collaboration—"the collaborative is a form of wit; the cooperative is a form of magic." Duncan is the first to have remarked on these—which hasn't discouraged George and me from continuing to create them. They have been important to me at least through the way they have led me to focus outside my own preoccupations—to look at what someone else is seeing—not through their eyes but in the company of their eyes. It is perhaps no accident, I am thinking, that the poem of mine he likes the best is one I wrote within this cooperation. I don't know what George thinks about Duncan's comments—except that he thinks it's a great article, a huge gift and compliment to us. But I don't know what he thinks in terms of what openings it may be creating for him. Or what Fred or David or Jamie are seeing in it. Of course they don't know my anxious thoughts about it either.

. . .

Fred and I lay out the issue on fourteen-inch masters—a return to the format of the first issue. Caroline Friedson's son, Phil Morgan, a down-on-his-luck U.S. painter who has come "home" and is

living in the Friedson basement, draws an image of the Lions Gate Bridge for our cover—our first really graphic cover. Red Lane has given us some new and interestingly different poems. I write a short blurb about them—visibly derivative of what Duncan has written

Phil Morgan's drawing on the cover of *Tish* 13.

about my poems as well as derivative of Olson on Ferrini. *Tish*, however, has been causing Red to take his own writing interests more seriously—another consequence of our year's work. Who would have thunk? We are all in vastly different places in our lives than we were a year ago—and not because we intended to be. All we've done is work together to see what working together might bring. Fred says this several times, as if he worries that some of us might not know it. He says it with grinning self-amazement. The parts of Fred I like best are his innocent enthusiasms—"Let's start a magazine!"

October 1962 . . .

John Newlove comes to campus and gives a reading from his book, *Grave Sirs*, so spectacularly printed by Robert Reid and Takao Tanabe. There is a pile of about sixty copies on the table by the door. I buy one for $1.50. John signs it for me, illegibly.

. . .

George has broken his right hand. He was coming to a party downtown at Jamie's smoke-filled apartment and having a disagreement with Angela. She was teed-off about something George had said or done and wanted to break off with him. To both vent and display his unhappiness, George punched the burlap-covered wall of the staircase that leads up to Jamie's. He expected merely to smash some plaster. But the wall is solid concrete beneath the burlap.

Later that weekend he is getting drunk to dull the pain and accidentally locks himself out of the rooms he shares with his old Oliver buddy, Willy Trump. It is raining, he is miserable, and scales the building's roof to break and climb through a window. He sits down at a table and writes a very witty poem, "Grandfather," which is going be in our October issue. It's a bit like his old "Meatgrinder" poems in its rhythm and rhetoric, but more personal.

He tells me Angela and he are now back together. She is worried about his hand—she helped him get to hospital. She didn't realize how important she was to him. Actually George has often punched through walls when he is upset—sometimes he has done it just for show, or to pretend to be upset. But it's true that he didn't punch any resistant walls when breaking up with Joan. None that I know of.

David Dawson is on a tear. The new *Tish* 14 features two and a half pages from his ongoing "tentative coastlines" series—fourteen-inch pages—Fred and I are staying with the longer format. Fred and I both have new longish multi-section poems—mine, a contemporary "Morte d'Arthur," reflects the Renaissance prose narrative course I am taking—my only course except for my master's thesis. The poem is okay, it doesn't do much that is wrong, it doesn't seem especially indebted prosodically, but it also doesn't open up and go anywhere surprising. It feels mostly like a stepping stone to somewhere. I like Fred's Duncanesque poem much better.

But our stapling and mailing of the issue are interrupted. It's October 11, and there is a huge tropical cyclone approaching. There are warnings to stay inside. The winds the next day hit 130 mph in Oregon, and destroy weather stations in Corvallis and Portland. In Bellingham the gusts reach 98 mph. In Vancouver, the trees and power lines are crashing together across the streets. The Yanks are calling this the Columbus Day storm; the radio here is calling it Hurricane Frieda. Bill and I are among the few who still have electric power. I drive circuitously around blocked streets to visit the apartment Helen and her sister Margaret share. They load me up with perishables from their dark fridge—there is little chance that power will be restored for several days. The cover of our new issue has a map of the BC coastline and rivers. A similar one with isobars and wind-gust numbers is on the front pages of the Vancouver newspapers.

But this crisis, such as it is, is quickly overtaken by another. Forty nuclear-armed Soviet ballistic missiles have been discovered newly installed in Cuba. Most are operational. The U.S. is threatening to remove them by force, while also expecting any attack to cause the missiles to be fired. The U.S. navy is blockading the shipment of additional missiles and warheads. Soviet premier Khrushchev is threatening a nuclear response. George has brought a small radio to our office so we can know when the bombs are likely to start falling.

Our world seems to be in the control of idiots and madmen. Meanwhile an issue of the Cuban English-language newspaper *Granma* arrives—it was on *The Floating Bear* mailing list to which we've been sending our newsletter. Tucked inside is the iconic poster of a visionary Che Guevara.

November 1962 . . .

We are all still alive, even Che Guevara. It's almost a surprise. The newspapers are now running photos of Soviet ships heading back to Russia with enormous missiles strapped to their decks. In exchange, we are told, the U.S. has guaranteed to the UN that it will not invade Cuba, or sponsor an invasion. So they damn well should have, George, Lionel, Jamie and I are thinking. If not for the Bay of Pigs stupidity, none of this might have happened. We put our new Che poster up above the stained counter.

Helen and I have become engaged. No engagement party fortunately. My poems however feel potentially compromised, as if I may be writing for audiences with conflicting expectations. I like only one of the four poems I've put into this issue, "Bridge Force ix." I don't think much of George's two poems in this issue either. "Two Deifications" he has entitled them, as if to frame and foreground his own reservations about them. They are good magazine poems, concise, smart and heavily rhetorical. We are both perhaps taking steps backward.

Meanwhile Fred has been having trouble trying to print the new Tishbooks, George's *Sticks & Stones* and Lionel's *Songs of Circumstance*, and Grady's *On Walking*. Despite expensive repairs we commissioned a few months ago on the Model 80, there's a problem with controlling the ink flow. There are a dozen or more little black knobs across the rear of the machine that can be adjusted. We seem either to have too much ink and thus black smudges on the pages or too little so that the centre of the page is illegible. The problem is evident in the current *Tish*—we've had to go over some pages by hand again and ink in missing letters. But he has managed to print a separate edition of Sam Perry's essay on Olson, "Personal Locus." It was in *Tish* 10 and we've had so many requests for it that all of that issue is gone.

Both the classes that I teach have been going well. But neither is as interesting as they were the first time I taught them. There are not nearly as many outstanding students in my first-year class. The students in the 300-level grammar course are all young education undergrads, for whom the course is just another requirement and not a revolutionary life change. They had never liked the traditional grammar that they had been force-fed in school, and so at least a descriptive grammar is no worse. For some there is nothing they have to unlearn. George has a similar view of his class. But we still mark essays together at our twin desks, and exchange groans and imprecations. "Arrrgghhh," I will say. "Pish!" George will shout— "Give me the stamp, Frank."

Across the hall Lionel is having his own crisis. His wife, Dolly, claims she has found some pubic hairs on his desk. He protests that these hairs are from his beard, and that the desk would be too uncomfortable. George says, "Oh yeah?" Lionel thinks maybe one of us has been there with a girlfriend. Or maybe one of our visitors. His office doesn't lock, and Temple Maynard, who has the office that Lionel's opens from, often doesn't lock the outer door. "Oh, we wouldn't do that," we say to him, grinning. "Your desk is too uncomfortable."

From Gladys I hear that some people in our poetry community are upset about me and Helen—including Warren. They are hoping that we won't marry, and are wondering how they can prevent it.

December 1962 . . .

One of the fundamentals of the descriptive grammar I have been teaching is that English has not two degrees of stress, heavy and weak, but a gradation of stress from the least stressed to most heavily accented. I teach my classes to identify at least four degrees of stress, giving them the word "elevator-operator," which has its heaviest stress on the first syllable, and its weakest on each "tor." Most linguists now describe English utterances as being composed of linguistic phrases, each with one heavy or "primary" stress, and beginning and ending with an audible pause or "juncture." I sometimes entertain my students by showing them how one can take a sentence and, by speaking it with a different number of heavy stresses, inadvertently and necessarily introduce a new pause after each new heavy stress—and also, of course, introduce different implied meanings. It was the linguists George Trager and Henry Lee Smith who first noticed this—although stand-up comedians have known it intuitively for much longer.

Lionel has been working out of Trager and Smith in an attempt to refine Olson's "breath" notation of poetry. Each line of a poem, he is proposing, should have one primary stress, and begin and end with a pause or juncture. But he has been worried that readers may not give the primary stress to the same syllable that the poet gives it to. His solution this month is to arrange the lines so that all the heavily stressed syllables appear directly below the previous one, creating a "stack" of them. "Stacked verse" he is calling this. To make the location of the stress especially clear, he is drawing a vertical line—a "stress axis"—through the stack of stressed syllables.

Of course typewriters can't produce such a line. It has to be drawn by hand. Moreover, to determine where a line of the poem should begin on the page, one has to begin by typing—or writing—the heavily stressed syllable, and then working backward and forward. It's a labour-intensive system of notation. Lionel has three "stacked" poems in the December issue—the first two handwritten on the inside front page, and the third in type on page nine. He is following these with a two-page essay, "Notes on the Stack," in which he cites various poets and linguists including Trager and Smith.

We've been surprised to receive a poem about the recent Cuban missile crisis from Paul Blackburn: "The Crisis—a few notes." It has many wry moments that recall our own feelings at the time:

Walking into a bar at 3:30 in the morning
and a man buys me a drink because that's
maybe the last nice thing he can do for anyone on earth—
. . .

    'To be or not to be, that is the
    question: whether 'tis nobler in the mind to bear
    the slings and arrows of outrageous fortune, or
    taking nuclear arms against a sea of troubles,
    and by opposing

             /

                end them and ourselves—'
is not a question.

This is the first issue in which I don't have any poems. George has contributed a very strong self-referential process poem, "Points on the Grid." There are no poems by Fred, Jamie or David either. December is a busy time. Pauline and Fred are planning to get married in Nelson. George and Angela are considering a quick private wedding here in Vancouver. Warren and several others, I hear, have been having meetings to try to figure out how they can separate me from Helen. They think she has little understanding of how significant *Tish* has been or even of the things I "do." I am annoyed. I wonder who buys the beer for their meetings. On December 27 Helen and I get married by a Unitarian minister in Bellingham. The minister is Robert Fulghum. In a few years, as author of *All I Really Need to Know I Learned in Kindergarten*, he will be the most famous of us all. Wish Abbotsford had offered kindergarten.

January 1963 . . .

George is the only one of us who had any patience with David Bromige, and has kept in touch with him now that David is at Berkeley. We're including one of his new poems in the January issue—it's quite different from what he wrote in Vancouver. George, Fred and I all have contributed "married" poems of one sort or another. Mine ("Totems") concerns shopping, George's ("Husband") the role of a husband with a sick wife, Fred's ("The Transference") the pleasures of shared memories. There's still nothing from Jamie or David Dawson. Approximately half the issue is made up of solid poems from Diane Wakoski and Carol Bergé—two of the "Four Young Lady Poets" whose collection Fred reviewed cautiously but positively in issue 14. There are some big transitional things happening. Both George and I have rented and moved into new apartments—him an old, drafty and spacious one in Kitsilano, me a newer two-bedroom near First Ave. in Point Grey. Ninety dollars a month including parking. George is also casting about for a post-graduation job. Universities across the country are expanding, and new ones are being founded. Most M.A. grads are receiving three or four job offers without being interviewed. I'm not sure what I can do. Being between third and fourth years, Helen can complete her B.Ed. only at UBC or its affiliate campus in Victoria. I could get clerical work at the UBC library, but at the moment nothing else seems possible. The new Simon Fraser University is hiring, but Ron Baker, the chair, is taking on only students he once taught in his linguistics course. Lionel seems to have lined up a future job there.

On the shelves of the *Tish* office are sitting the unbound pages of the three projected Tishbooks. Fred has tried to print them, but is very unhappy with the results. They look like the pages of *Tish*. The shabby printing is acceptable for a newsletter, he thinks, but not for a book. We consider buying more paper and trying again, but Fred expects that the result would be no better. Another complication is that Grady sent us money to help buy the now apparently wasted paper.

. . .

My relationship with Creeley is much smaller than I've expected. The students who are in his classes see him often enough, but I've seen him only a couple of times about my thesis, on which he is advising. Otherwise I'd hardly know that he was in Vancouver. I think he may be holed up in his house working on his novel. So people say. He doesn't often come to the gatherings at Warren's, doesn't host gatherings himself, doesn't invite students to his house. When I have taken my thesis pages to him, he's been encouraging but not very specific. He's glad I'm getting it done. Of course he hardly knows me. Perhaps I'm being unfair to compare him to Warren.

February 1963 . . .

No Dawson in this month's issue but work for the first time from Peter Auxier—also poems again by Dan McLeod, David Cull and Gerry Gilbert. It's as if the future of *Tish* is already beginning to emerge. "Fredric Wah" has abruptly become the guy we all knew, "Fred Wah." About time. Creeley has received a generous offer to teach at the University of New Mexico—one that UBC is unlikely to try to match. He's in a strong position—Scribners is about to release his collected poems, *For Love*. And he's almost completed his novel, "The Island," his main writing project here in Vancouver.

The "New Vancouver Poetry" issue of Louis Dudek's *Delta* has arrived a scant seven months after Louis asked me to help edit it.

Several of the items—including George's "Sunday Poem," Lionel's "Stacked Verse" essay and my "A Vancouver History"— were first published in *Tish*. My part in the project diminished slightly after Louis left. He contacted several poets himself that he wanted to include—Sonny Choy, Avo Erisalu, Connie Irvine, Roger Prentice—and then asked me to include them in my introduction. But it's a good publication for us all.

The back page of *Tish* 18 announces a summer-session poetry cluster that features Creeley, Ginsberg, Olson, Duncan, Levertov and Margaret Avison 1) teaching, in a lecture-workshop format, the full-credit poetry writing workshop (English 410) that I took last summer from Dudek, 2) giving a series of evening readings and 3) staffing an Extension Department non-credit course in contemporary poetry. A limited number of auditors can pay to attend the poetry-writing lectures. The announcement almost makes me wish I hadn't taken the course with Dudek— although I would then be graduating next fall rather than this spring. And I'd have no summer income.

The announcement is stirring up a lot of excitement. Fred has never taken 410 and so is definitely planning to enrol. Jamie and David too. George and Lionel, who have like me already taken it, think that they can register as auditors and then crash the workshop sessions. I have just received a ruling from the department's senior committee on the reading list on which my oral defence of my M.A.

thesis will be based. It will be the department's first creative-writing M.A.—George and Lionel are planning to defend somewhat later. What we have each agreed to do is present a sixty-page manuscript of poetry accompanied by a sixty-page essay that examines the place of those poems in the history of twentieth-century poetry. I have expected the exam to be based on twentieth-century Canadian and U.S. poetry, but the senior committee has decided that it will be based on twentieth-century British and U.S. literature. The list of

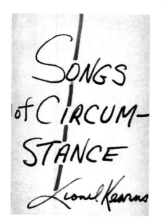

texts goes on for numerous pages. I calculate that there would not be enough time in a year to read them all. The senior committee is made up of older professors, including Akrigg. I wonder why I couldn't have been told sooner. The only course I'm taking this year is one on Elizabethan prose narrative. I could have been doing one on something in modern British or U.S.

Lionel has bound up about a dozen copies of *Songs of Circumstance*, making hand-drawn covers for them. He gives one each to me and George. We plan to throw the rest of the pages into the garbage. Both George and I consider his book and Grady's unsalvageable. I could bind up any number of barely readable copies for myself, but I don't bother.

March 1963 . . .

I am spending most of my time reading for this damn oral defence. I've never done any coursework in the twentieth century, except for Warren's seven-poem poetry course and the Georgian poems of Elliott Gose's "early modern" course. I've divided up the list and assigned particular days and hours to reading the various parts of it. I hardly notice *Tish* 19 being printed. All the editors have something in the issue, but George, Lionel and Fred are doing most of the work. *Tish* has a new address—my address on First Ave. Tony and Caroline Friedson are going to be away next year. If I'm still in Vancouver myself I'll probably still be the managing editor

However, George and Lionel and I have to vacate our offices sometime in May after we finish marking final exams. The Model 80 will have to find a new home.

April 1963 . . .

There's no resolution about my plans for next year. George has accepted a job at the University of Calgary. I've taken a permanent job in the acquisitions department of the library—I start at the end of this month. But it's not what I prefer to do.

The oral defence of my thesis is something of a farce. Like "practical art." Creeley spends much of the time trying to ask a soft-ball question only to discover the Faulkner text he thought I'd be familiar with is one I haven't found time to read—or better, wasn't on my list. Neither he nor Warren seem to know much about all the British texts I've been reading—Forster, Huxley, Auden, Sillitoe, Wain, Thomas—guess I should have expected that. Tony Friedson tries to look like he's asking tough questions and discovers he's addressing the few areas I'm overly familiar with. Warren and I both flounder. At the end I get the "A" that I need to maintain an "A" average but I am exhausted. I promise myself I'll never be underprepared for anything again. George and Lionel will both take a little longer to defend—I think they may have to officially graduate in the fall.

. . .

We've been slowly moving books and papers out of the office. I take the Model 80 to my apartment and store it in the basement locker. Fred and Pauline are probably going to follow Creeley and go to grad school in New Mexico. Without Fred, the Model 80 is even more useless than it has already proved to be. In hindsight, I wish we'd kept using our little mimeograph and paid to have the books printed. Fred and Pauline have also been hired by Warren to help with the summer workshop registrations and arrangement. I guess they have summer money problems too.

May 1963 . . .

Helen and I decide to go camping. We get her dad's account information and buy a tent and sleeping bags and other gear wholesale at Jones Tent and Awning. We drill the trunk lid of the TR4 to install a custom luggage rack, and head off to spend the twenty-fourth of May weekend in south-central Washington. It's raining when we leave late Thursday afternoon directly from campus after my work. The highways keep pointing toward a patch of blue sky that keeps receding until we have climbed over the coast mountains. We camp at Sun Lakes State Park for the weekend, and go hiking and horseback riding.

. . .

Warren seems preoccupied with the complex arrangements for the summer course. Who is going to stay where? How much is going to be tape-recorded? Can some of the official regulations around courses be evaded? People are starting to call it the "Vancouver Poetry Conference" but of course it's not a conference at all, it's a course, with tuition fees, admission requirements, visiting professors and students.

June 1963 . . .

My work at the library is mainly tracking down accurate bibliographical information for books faculty members have ordered. They circle items in catalogs, or scribble the approximations of titles on scraps of paper and send them to the library. It is more interesting and challenging work than one would expect—detective work. But the library has most of the necessary resources, the British Museum index, the Library of Congress catalog, *Canadiana* and numerous smaller aids that I am familiar with from Dick Fredeman's bibliography course.

At a lunch break I encounter Pauline. She tells me that there's a teaching job newly posted on the department bulletin board. The English department of the Canadian navy's military college in Victoria has a vacancy. She has remembered that Helen could complete her degree at the new University of Victoria because it has been, until this coming fall, a UBC-affiliated college. I hurry over to the department and check the posting. It's Royal Roads Military College. They are in a rush to fill the position, and are asking interested candidates to telephone them. I talk to the secretary who put the posting on the board—she says that Royal Roads phoned them and asked her whether UBC had anyone who might be able to do the job. Roads has had an unexpected resignation.

When I telephone Roads, the dean—the "Director of Studies"—asks me to come over for an interview early next week, and just bring my CV with me. I arrange two days off work, and off Helen and I go. I am hired within my first twenty minutes at the college—my interview is with Dr. Eric Graham, the "DOS"—Director of Studies. He is impressed that I have published a "book" and poems and articles in *Delta*, *Evidence*, *The Canadian Forum* and *Canadian Literature*, and edited a small magazine. I am naive—this is the first that I've seen my writing perceived as "publications." He likes Helen, too. This is a very polite middle-class all-male faculty—about twenty-four professors and instructors and their wives—and she will fit right in. He has no difficulty offering a good salary—my "publications" place me at a particular spot on the public-service salary scale. The regular teaching load here is seven hours a week—two two-hour courses and one three-hour one.

From here Helen and I go to UVic where she arranges her transfer from UBC, and then downtown to look for an apartment. Helen lived in Victoria for eight or nine years when her father owned the city's main hardware store downtown near Fort and Douglas. We easily find our way around.

Back in Vancouver I tell David and Jamie the news. We have a meeting at Warren's at which David, Daphne, Gladys, Dan McLeod, David Cull and Peter Auxier decide that they want to continue *Tish*. David Dawson is selected as the new managing editor. They want George, Fred and me to write retrospectives for their first issue, which they hope to get out by early August, while the summer "conference" is still underway. But they don't want the Model 80. It's not the best meeting we could have had—we talk a bit about the editing but not about the nuts and bolts of production. Warren had liked to joke that Fred and I were small-town hot-rodders who knew more about cars than about literature and universities. But it had been our rudimentary understandings of mechanics that had made first the Dutch mimeograph and then the Model 80 perform as well as they had, to meet those storied monthly deadlines. Except for Gladys, the new editors are city kids.

July 1963 . . .

It's a confusing time. I'm already missing George and Fred even though they are still in the city. I'm also excited about my move to Victoria and my new job, and eager to get started. Royal Roads will move our furniture and things to our new apartment at the end of August. Fred is looking forward mostly to the summer workshop— he's never taken writing courses before and in four intense weeks will have more instructors than most students get in four years. Daphne, David Dawson, David Cull and Peter Auxier are taking the workshop in the middle of their undergraduate degrees. For Lionel it's just another summer—albeit a particularly interesting one—in a city he is going to continue in. Me, I feel as if much of what I've done in Vancouver is completed, and much more needs to be worked through. I'm looking past the summer toward quiet moments for writing. Having already taken the workshop course number, 410, I don't think I could register for it even if I hadn't graduated. It also feels like part of the past rather than the future. So I continue working at the library and plan to attend as many events as I can register for or sneak into.

. . .

Hmmm. George and Lionel are registered for the workshop, even though they've already taken it. How'd they do that? I think I'm out of the loop these days.

August 1963 . . .

There are rumours that the writing workshop is less rich than people expected. Olson tends to speak in riddles, as I'd thought he might. Duncan is helpfully talkative but doesn't care for Ginsberg. Creeley seems uncertain and unusually low-key. Ginsberg is also quiet, still partly back in Japan and the Buddhist retreat that he had left to fly to Vancouver. None of the workshop faculty can figure out how they are supposed to jointly "teach" the morning "lectures." Usually they end up chatting among themselves, except for Creeley, who dislikes and resists small talk. So some students tell me. There are poets here no one expected—Phil Whalen, Clark Coolidge, Carol Bergé. Are they extra faculty or are they enrolled? No one I talk to is quite sure. Perhaps I could get time off and crash some daytime sessions. Some students I meet suggest that more happens outside the classroom than in, and that it is the atmosphere of being in the presence of so many creative people that they find valuable, not any specific comments on poems or writing. Some tell me they have been skipping the workshops and getting together themselves for discussions and informal readings.

. . .

Bobby Hogg has been arrested in the UBC caf, for having pot that the police found in someone else's possession at the "literary" table—the guy claimed it was Bob's, and on some days it might have been. Bob hadn't been able to attend many of the workshops anyway because of a summer job. Warren is trying to mortgage his house to bail him out. Olson reads for several hours, getting more into the poems the longer he reads. It is instructive just to watch him. Also demythologizing.

. . .

The first "new" *Tish* is out. *Tish* 20. The masthead doesn't say "monthly" or state the day of issue. It says that the next issue will focus on the summer workshop.

SUNDRY THOUGHTS FOR A SUNDAY MEETING

*

Why didn't we publish an April or May *Tish?* There is nothing in the March issue to indicate it will be the last one—in fact there's a note there that *Tish* is still looking for donations of two-cents stamps. Perhaps it's because the Model 80 wasn't working well— it probably needed $500 or more in parts and repairs. But we had managed to print several issues on it after the disastrous attempts to print the Bowering, Kearns and Grady Tishbooks. George and I are being evicted from the *Tish* office but not till early May and the end of the spring exam period. Were there enough poems available for two more issues? My own productivity had been declining over the past few issues. I didn't offer poems to the new editors for *Tish* 20. In some ways *Tish* 14 to 19 had been a kind of anticlimax for most of us, with not all of us contributing to every issue. My sense now is also that end-of-term rhythms of university life had begun playing a part. Things come to an end at the beginning of April— you begin to look forward to the next chapter, next fall. Many of us were looking forward to the summer workshop—and looking forward is nowhere as productive as attending to the present moment.

George was looking forward to his new job. His departure and Fred's meant that there would have to be a reorganization of the board. I don't believe that any of us were lobbying each other to do more issues.

The workshop itself was diverting energy and attention from *Tish*. First it absorbed Warren, and then Fred and Pauline. I don't recall now whether we even had a Sunday meeting after *Tish* 19. The Creeleys were leaving town in May—Bob would have to travel back from New Mexico to teach in the workshop. Creative writing was also winding down in the English department, and migrating to fine arts. Robert Harlow had been appointed its chair—a writer whom none of us knew. Birney was returning, but most likely not going to stay around for the workshops. It was almost time to be nostalgic.

*

It would be hard, however, to be nostalgic about Birney. In Elspeth Cameron's biography there is a page of testimonials that he gathered from ex-writing students throughout 1964 to help gain support for the new program. Most of the comments, including ones from Bowering, Marlatt and Lambert, address benefits of the program without mentioning Birney or his teaching. Marlatt manages to avoid mentioning any of the teaching—"What affected me a great deal was meeting others who were involved with writing." So too Rosemary Kent-Barber: "Excellent . . . [met] Marianne Moore" (Cameron 450).

Birney's response to the *Tish* writers still seems both curious and amusing. He was the "big" poet on the UBC campus, the senior professor and three-time Governor General's Award winner whose poetry workshop we all aspired to be accepted into, whose poem "David" I read in elementary school and whose novel *Down the Long Table* I read when I was fifteen. Its portrayal of Vancouver in the 1930s echoed stories that my parents had told me of the socialist rallies my father had attended, and of mayor Gerry McGeer "reading the riot act"—according to my mother—"on the City Hall steps." She always favoured graphic details. The Birney letters that Cameron cites in her biography show him to have had a surprising awareness of our newsletter—despite his never lifting a pen, coin or finger to assist it. *Tish* for him was a Warren Tallman and Roy Daniells project. Daniells was his enemy, and Tallman a peculiar foreigner. They had stolen and corrupted his students. In October of 1961 he writes to a friend that "followers of the Black Mountain Group are bringing out a poetry sheet which they have called TISH." Cameron reports that the tone of the comment suggests he fears he might be about to "become redundant" (Cameron 414). In the fall of 1962, however, he is including *Tish*, in a letter to Layton, as evidence that UBC may be about to become "a leading CW [creative writing] centre" in North America. The next fall he is complaining to Ron Everson that he won't want to bring out a selected poems as long as "the Franklin Davey's and the like are the critics in the influential journals" (446). Birney habitually in this period misspells my extended first name. But in 1965 he writes an excited letter to his wife, Esther, that "Frank Davey, who was the one student in the Tallman crowd who never said anything but bad about my work," has now written about "my 'regeneration'" (468). When I first read Cameron's account I was astonished—I had been barely out of my teens and had apparently had this enormous power over UBC's greatest writer. I should perhaps have mentioned his name more often. Birney's difficulty seems to have been that he didn't perceive himself as an accomplished and senior writer—as we perceived him. Instead he saw us as his equals—equals who could threaten him with our criticism and compete with him through our poetry. That we could was so bizarre an idea that I doubt any of us thought of it. But it was evidently real to him, and rendered him incapable of helping us. He even advised me not to offer a collection of poems as an M.A. thesis. Tallman's theory about him was slightly different—seeing him as "the isolato, the loner, and for this reason the wanderer. Able to draw on a wide range of influences, he is not inclined to join in" (*Godawful* 194). In turn, he theorizes, the *Tish* poets could not identify with him. "Because Birney is not a joiner, few of the poets were able to experience a Birney-in-themselves."

My relationship with Birney continued to be both close and fraught. At times we both were disturbed by the thought that I might be a younger version of him—him most clearly in 1965 in a now-comical three-way exchange with poet Gwladys Downes, which ended in my sending her a lock of my hair (Cameron reveals that Downes had been a Birney protegée), and me in 1972 when writing in my book *Earle Birney* about how he negotiated—poorly, I concluded—being both a poet and an academic (Cameron 505). However, even the praise I gave some of his writing there could not prevent him from feeling threatened by the book overall—deeply. Our relationship terminated with him calling me a "small and malicious twerp" (507) and making empty threats to sue, and me telling him to go screw himself. We did have some rhetoric in common.

*

Talk about *Tish* 1 to 19 has frequently raised a BC-alienation issue, an ignorance-of-the-rest-of-Canada issue, as well as an argument that north-south lines pull more strongly in BC than do the east-west. BC poets in 1960, apparently, needed someone in the east to build a CPR to Port Moody—a Canadian Poetry Railway.

Much of the credit—or blame— for this talk has to be given to George, who declared in the Bayard-David interview that the *Tish* editors "were people who had become deracinated—we didn't get any Canadian writing at school in BC. Most of the people in *Tish*—Fred Wah and Frank Davey—didn't know anything about Canadian poetry" (81).

As I recall, George never asked me what I knew about Canadian poetry. It wasn't true, however, that students didn't get "any Canadian writing" in BC schools. There was actually a considerable amount of Canadian writing in the 1940s and 1950s school textbooks—but it wasn't necessarily marked as "Canadian." It was printed "among" mostly British works, along with some American ones. Maybe young George thought all of it was British. But the Canadian writing I could have recalled for him included stories by Roberts and Seton, Pratt's poems "Dunkirk" and "The Ice-Floes," Birney's "David," William Henry Drummond's "Little Bateese" and Duncan Campbell Scott's "At the Cedars"—a poem I still recall when I pass the *Les Cèdres* exit on Quebec's Highway 20 east of Cornwall. There were probably more. I knew enough about Canadian poetry by 1955 to send one or two poems to the Ontario poet Anthony Frisch, who had invited contributions to an anthology he was assembling—*First Flowering: A Selection of Prose and Poetry by the Youth of Canada*, published the next year—without my poems—in Toronto by Kingswood House. In his gentle review of the collection, Northrop Frye suggested that, had it contained any writers of promise, it would have been "better entitled First Deflowering" (60). Wouldn't that "First" have been redundant, Norry?

I had also subscribed to *Tamarack Review* since 1956, and read numerous poems by James Reaney, Eli Mandel and Jay Macpherson without recognizing that these were important "names." In spring 1959 I had adapted that Kildare Dobbs story published in *Tamarack* into a play for Jake Zilber's writing class. It's possible that neither George nor Lionel knew about *Tamarack*, or of Kildare Dobbs. In his story about how little "we" knew about Canadian writing, George goes on to say:

> The only people that knew of Canadian poetry were Lionel Kearns and I, who got together before the *Tish* stuff happened anyway. Lionel had been an exchange student in Quebec and he brought back Contact Press books and I read them in one of the dorms. Souster, Layton, Dudek, D.G. Jones, Milton Acorn and all those guys. I hadn't even thought about Canadian poetry. I didn't even think about thinking about Canadian poetry. (Bayard & David 81)

It was Contact Press writers that Lionel and George had discovered as "Canadian poetry" (although not Milton Acorn, who wasn't published by Contact until 1963). I had discovered another fragment in a different city but was unimpressed, and never bothered to talk about it.

In two separate taped group discussions, one in 1980 and the other in 1985, Fred Wah adds to the story from the opposite point of view when he recalls his anger at eastern Canadian lack of interest in BC writing and his impression that young BC writers were expected to live outside of Canada's literary borders. In both discussions he cites a letter that he had seen published in a Canadian literary magazine in 1960 or 1961. In the 1980 interview it is from "an Eastern-Canadian writer" who announces he is, according to Fred, "more interested in New York" writing than he is in writing from western Canada. Fred suggests that his outrage at this comment contributed to Tallman's decision "to have Sunday afternoon meetings. . . . And that's how *Tish* started" ("Roots" 218). He thinks the writer was Seymour Mayne and the magazine *Evidence*, one to which he also believes he and other young BC writers had been unsuccessfully attempting to contribute. In the 1985 discussion, he again names *Evidence* and "a letter to the editor in there":

> I think it was from Kenneth McRobbie—to the effect that "We in the east" that is, in Montreal at that point—"aren't too interested in what's happening out west. We're more interested in what's going on with New York." I remember I was outraged at seeing this. . . .

evidence

Spring 1965 issue of *Evidence*.

He goes on to say that "for me that was one of the impetuses" for starting *Tish*.

However, *Evidence* was not all that unfriendly to *Tish* writers. I published four poems in *Evidence* 4 (Spring 1962), scant months after the launch of *Tish*, three more poems in *Evidence* 6 (1964) and essays in *Evidence* 9 (1966) and 10 (1967). Daphne and George published in *Evidence* 6, George in *Evidence* 7, Jamie and George in *Evidence* 8. And none of the issues contain the letter Fred describes. In fact, as I look through my old lists of publications from that period it is predominantly eastern Canadian magazines that are accepting my work—*Delta*, *The Canadian Forum*, *Mountain*, *Fiddlehead*, *Evidence*, *Island*, *Tamarack Review*. In 1963 George and I are included by John Robert Colombo in Ryerson Press's anthology *Poetry 64*.

There is also considerable irony in Fred's outrage that eastern Canadian poets were interested in writing being done in New York, when many of us were equally if not more interested in the poets of Allen's *The New American Poetry*—many of whom were also from New York. We were interested as well in many of the poets immediately south of us, in San Francisco—Ferlinghetti, Duncan, Spicer—much like eastern Canadians were said to be interested in the U.S. writers immediately south of them. Perhaps we had more in common with the writer of this letter than Fred wanted to admit.

Moreover, the letter Fred is remembering was not published in eastern Canada, although it was written by Kenneth McRobbie. It was published right on the UBC campus, in the second issue of *Prism*, in the winter of 1959, a full two years before Warren Tallman's Sunday meetings and two and a half before the founding of *Tish*. After saying that Birney's and Wilfred Watson's poems are "unexciting" McRobbie goes on to say that

> Some of us are going down to the YMHA Poetry Center, New York for a reading and general get-together soon. Point is, that we are establishing many links with American poets—especially those in New York and New England, and this is for us (apart from contemp. French, of course) more important than the fizzling out strands of things that pass for tradition here.
>
> When I say "we", I mean Toronto-Montreal; for we're very much in touch, solving the same problems . . . though they in Montreal don't go quite as far as looking to the US as Ray Souster and myself. I think they're wrong. Point is, I think there is this East-West split . . .

Fred's misreading, or misremembering, of this letter is thus in some ways hilarious. The U.S. poets to whom Souster was looking, and had already published in his little magazine *Contact*, included Paul Blackburn, Cid Corman, Robert Creeley, Larry Eigner, Vincent Ferrini, Denise Levertov, Charles Olson and William Carlos Williams—the very ones the *Tish* writers will soon be reading avidly. The "West" from which McRobbie thought himself "split" was not the Tallman-living-room west—it was the west of Birney and Wilfred Watson, which Fred was probably also split from. I know I was.

. . .

There are also, of course, those different responses of younger and older Canadian and U.S. poets to *Tish*. Fred thought he was being annoyed by the disdain of "Eastern-Canadian" poets of our own age—Seymour Mayne, Kenneth McRobbie, whichever. With *Tish* 13 I was most aware of the different responses of older poets in the two countries. The only older Canadian poet who took an interest in *Tish* was Al Purdy who, although older in years lived, had a career only three or four years in advance of ours. Not only had there been no supportive letters from Birney, but there had also been none at that time from Dudek, Gustafson, Reaney, Waddington, Page, Livesay, F.R. Scott, Smith or Layton. Our Canadian correspondence had come from writers of our own generation. Most of those, of course, hoped we would help them by publishing them. Most of the American responses were from writers like Blackburn, Eigner and McClure, who wanted to help us by giving us work to publish.

*

Warren Tallman—from the south—played the role for hopeful UBC writing students of the early 1960s that one might have expected someone like Earle Birney to play. Perhaps he could play it because he had no investment himself in being either a poet or a respected academic. The only respect he valued was that of the poets he hosted,

the students who came to his house to visit him, and the editors of
the largely non-academic journals and presses that published his
essays. His creating a scene or salon at his home for young writers
like ourselves was—along with writing those mostly unconven-
tional essays—his major project. He was never especially comfortable within the UBC department. The senior members often mocked
his teaching and preferences among contemporary writers—they
"snuffled" at "his aesthetic and open intelligence," Gladys would
tell the *Georgia Straight* in 1970. His marriage to Ellen was probably uneasy, despite their cheerful intellectual camaraderie; she
would eventually leave him for a woman partner. He had ambiguous relationships from time to time with much younger women
poets. He may have struggled with alcoholism in the *Tish* years;
he certainly did toward the end of his life. He welcomed gallon
after gallon of my sake; his house would be my first stop whenever I
brought more in from Abbotsford.

I don't recall any sibling rivalry among us to be his favourites—
mostly because he was always open about his opinion of each of us.
He would offer his personal assessment of George as both person
and poet in the same words whether George were in the room or
not. Or of Fred, or Daphne, or David Bromige, or me. If his assessment was critical, he would make his remarks humourous—teasing
George for hiding behind a smart-aleck persona, me for my knowledge of auto mechanics or Fred for usually wanting to start a magazine. We always knew he liked us, even when he did think us a little
weird or off-course.

My own relationship with him sometimes cooled—but not necessarily because of anything I was doing but because his own attention was occupied elsewhere. We were probably closest during the
summer and fall of 1961, when both *Tish* and my book *D-Day and
After* were conceived. It seems odd now that in the spring of '61
he opposed our founding of a magazine—because we didn't know
enough—but by the fall was encouraging us to start a press, and me
to assemble and publish its first book. The Duncan lectures of July
'61 and our response to them, and Duncan's response to us, likely

changed his mind about the magazine idea. We now knew something—although not a huge amount. The first few issues of *Tish* and our success in at least getting them "out" probably also changed his perceptions. As well, he and Ellen were in touch with Duncan that fall—by telephone and post. Things were undoubtedly said by Duncan.

I still believe that Warren was most interested in my poems that fall because, of all the *Tish* editors' poems, they were the most riskily processual, what Daphne would later call "writing as close as you can to what you are actually experiencing at any given point" (Bowering, "Given" 33). That is what he would emphasize in his introduction to *D-Day*—"each poem is, as it were, caught in the act." They "attempt to re-enact the weight and substance, the pace, feel and force of the response." The risk, of course, of such a poetics to the writer is the extent to which it exposes one's inner life—as in Daphne's *Rings* and *Touch to my Tongue*, or my *Weeds* and *King of Swords*—and the consequent risk of instability one must therefore accept in one's personal life. Poetic decisions—and publishing decisions—become private life decisions. I kept the poems of *Weeds* hidden from my first wife—together with the fact that I was writing them—because her distress at reading them would have consequences, which I wasn't sure I was ready to deal with. George was less willing to make the private public, as the process poem seemed to require. Carol Bergé notices this about him and his writing in her "report" on the 1963 poetry workshop—"the terribly skillful, almost masterful, work of George Bowering, who . . . revealed himself to be a man other than represented in his work, a disparity with which I carp, sharply" (10). It was a disparity with which a lot of people in the meetings at the Tallman house over the past two years had "carped"—and one which also lay behind Fred's and David's "sharp" objections in the fall of 1961 to George's "Meatgrinder" series. George would later dissolve some of this disparity by using various codes, quotations and constraints—"baffles" he calls them— which effectively allowed him to share the authorship of his work with both chance and literary inheritance—particularly in *Genève* and *Allophanes*. Distributing the responsibility. He would also avoid the problem by doing much of his writing as prose fiction in which he would include himself mainly as a self-reflecting narrator, so that the only "experiencing" he had to stay "close to" was that of writing a particular novel. These are much less personal—and less personally risky—fictions than what Daphne would write in *Ana Historic* and *Taken*. But they are all remarkable.

I was saying that my relationship with Warren sometimes cooled, which I think it did in the spring of 1963 as the big summer English 410 writing seminar a.k.a. "conference" was taking shape and I began feeling out of the loop. We were both extremely preoccupied, Warren with keeping on top of the ever-expanding complexities of the seminar and me with neutralizing the enormous reading list the department's senior committee had insisted upon as the basis of my thesis defence. This committee of older mostly British-trained profs was no friend of either Tallman or Birney— or of creative writing. When Birney's new program was established that fall it was effectively expelled from the English department; it was housed in the Faculty of Fine Arts, and Birney himself was in Toronto. My thesis and those of Bowering and Kearns were parts of the first and last three creative writing M.A.s the English department granted. And the committee was no friend of Warren's summer seminar/workshop. Adam Vidaver quotes a post-summer letter by Warren to Creeley: "The summer was entirely too successful, i.e. created amongst the many drones around here the firm if covert conviction that they mustn't let that happen again. So Vancouver as new frontier has closed up shop . . . I stay home and listen to tapes; for which, praise be" (7 December 1963).

But I think my relationship with Warren cooled also because of my marriage in December 1962 to Helen, whom Warren publically considered unworthy—philistine, I suppose. It brought him inadvertently closer to Fred and George with whose new wives he felt much more comfortable. They had already been part of the *Tish* writing and reading community. He may have also been uncomfortable with me because he knew that I'd been told about his efforts to separate us.

George alludes briefly to this discomfort when interviewed by Caroline Bayard and Jack David in their book *Out-Posts/Avant-Postes*—although he gives the false impression that my discomfort had literary grounds as well as personal ones. "What *Tish* mainly offered, to me," George says, "was two things: one, being taken seriously by people who I would take seriously, people in the group, and them saying, That's no good there. Frank really got upset with this after a while, like everybody looking over your shoulder. Doesn't upset me at all, I think it's wonderful." My "getting upset," however, was entirely with the way Warren and others offered themselves as authorities on my private life, and attempted to interfere in it.

But I could also understand why such interference seemed reasonable to them—it extended from *Tish* poetics, a poetics in which, at the moment of composition, there was no division between public and private—the poet's job was to embody all of his or her interwoven responses to a given moment, a moment that inevitably was constituted by similarly interwoven and interacting public and personal histories and events. I had let my personal responses to Daphne and the context in which I was obsessed by her be public in my poetry—"published." Those responses were now communal property. The people who cared about those responses had cared about both the poem and the persons. In fact it was difficult for readers to comment on such "projective" poems without commenting on both poem and person. I've had a similar experience with Daphne's later writing because of the ways in which she has marked works like *Ghost Works*, *Ana Historic*, *Taken* and *The Given* as autobiographical—thus making it almost impossible for a critic to comment on the characters in these texts without appearing to be commenting on the author's characterization of actual people, including herself. Many "polite" critics, however, have pretended not to notice the autobiographical markings. I guess I'm still one of Warren Tallman's "delinquents."

As for Warren and the others who feared for me in my relationship with Helen, there were many things they didn't know. Helen and I at the very least had fun together, and would for a number of years. Warren indeed liked to characterize me and the other editors as "delinquents"—"semi-delinquent young people" in a 1985 introduction (Niechoda 84) and "thoroughgoing literary delinquents" (Tallman, "A Brief Reintroduction" 115) and "conspicuously delinquent students" who "knew more about driving cars . . . than the ins and outs of university literature courses" in a taped discussion. Helen was a bratty and fun-loving kid in her own way—certainly much more so than Daphne in 1961 who wanted to be sure that I could write a sonnet. Helen too was from Abbotsford. Moreover, my time with her led me to Victoria where I met my second wife, of whom Warren and most of the others enthusiastically approved. I doubt I could have met her otherwise.

Out of the blue, however, in the spring 1965 issue of *Canadian Literature* comes an article by Warren Tallman on Frank Davey. It's the longest text he will write on a *Tish* poet. The opening sentence again conflates the textual and the personal: "Back of whatever skills a poet acquires stands the flesh and blood man, and all the skill in the world cannot eventuate in a distinctive poetry unless the man is himself distinctive—perhaps by reason of a superior nerve in the face of experience, a superior capacity for perception, or some personal quality which makes for inner magic" ("Poet in Progress" 23). But the article isn't quite out of the blue. It addresses my second book, *City of the Gulls and Sea*, which I had published the previous year in Victoria, and addresses perhaps more significantly my absence from that 1963 English 410 summer poetry seminar/workshop "conference." He's apparently brooded on that. He links the latter to the arrival the previous fall of Creeley and his resistance "to sham and sloppiness in all forms."

> Davey, who had been in the thick of the writing and talking, began to move toward the edge. His interest in *Tish* diminished markedly, as did his interest in discussions, as did the flow of poems. Of the *Tish* poets he was the only one who passed up the University of British Columbia poetry seminar conducted

in the summer of 1963 by Margaret Avison, Creeley, Duncan,
Allen Ginsberg, Denise Levertov and Charles Olson, although
he did attend their evening readings.

That this withdrawal was a going underground rather than
a running away becomes plain in *City of the Gulls and Sea* in
the form of [the] indwelling, margin-hugging line he practices
throughout. (26)

The difficulty with using the form of a poem to develop explanations of the poet's other actions is that there may have been more
in that field of events than was openly etched into those lines. As
well, Tallman himself was not especially happy with the 410 seminar
discussions I missed. In his unpublished account of the seminar, he
writes about how limited its achievements were, and concludes "By
now it must seem that with these notes I am loading the dice so that
most of the poets' attempts to discuss poetry turn up snake eyes
with the sevens and elevens reserved for their readings. Which is
true enough. The readings as a group were entirely superior to the
discussions as a group" ("Poets in Vancouver"). But I can't claim to
have been prescient.

*

Was *Tish* a cooperative? It's a question we never asked ourselves—
as Jamie Reid indicated a few years ago when an interviewer seemed
to presume that we were a sort of "collective": "I don't think we
TISH poets ever thought of ourselves as a 'collective' in the way
the term is used today, but maybe in fact we were a collective, and
maybe one of the first to appear in Canada of a kind of literary association which later became much more common, the 'literary collective.'" All we really considered, in terms of organization, was how
to get along—a bit like how those Hungarians in the Sumas Prairie
hop fields taught me to work for the pleasure of working. As I wrote
in the introduction to the collected *Tish 1–19*, "my election [as "editor"] was due to my appearing the least doctrinaire of the older editors (Bowering, Wah and myself) and thus being least threatening

to all." We did require a majority vote to accept material, but preferred a consensus.

Of course, the members of most editorial boards also try to get
along. What gave us a particularly "group" appearance was the stress
we placed on literary theory and aesthetics—our individual creative
theories also had to "get along." I suppose the only Canadian prece-
dent for this is the Automatistes and their 1948 "Refus Global."
That is, *Tish* wasn't just a shared project, it was a shared imagination
of what poetry and a place might be. It wasn't a "collective" in the
narrow Marxist sense of a formal assignment of responsibilities and
roles. It was much more ad hoc and spontaneous—more like a
jazz quintet. Stan Persky writes: ". . . this is the beginning of poetry
in this particular place. Suddenly the city has an imagination. It
didn't have one before, a collectivity. Suddenly people are writing
as Vancouver poets." In his article "For the Novices of Vancouver,"
Robert Duncan reads the interactions that produce *Tish* as "an exchange in changes" and writes that in issues one to twelve he sees
"everywhere an operating intelligence that is beyond the individual
poets, for me, embodying a mystery." He takes especial note of the
"twin poems" that George and I have written, calling these "hap-
penings of a cooperation. (Contrast with the collaborative poems
anthologized by Kenneth Koch in *Locus Solus 2*—the collaborative
is a form of wit; the cooperative is a form of magic.)"

It is true that groups of people can create more and differently
than what individuals can by themselves. But what Duncan was
pointing out was that the *Tish* interactions were also enlarging the
individual capabilities of the participants, that when they were working together the interaction inexplicably transformed them and
what they were individually capable of. Many people, of course—
many writers especially—do not wish to be transformed, or fear it.

George and I have written other "twin" texts since our UBC
years, although I suspect that only he and I have been aware of that.
I have not seen any published comments by others. In 1968 and
1969 we both began a series of poems based on Tarot cards that
partly intersected when I moved to Montreal that fall and to the

Sir George Williams English department where he was teaching. While I don't recall encountering his series *Genève* before he privately "published" a fifteen-copy mimeographed edition of it for his friends in February 1970, I know that he heard some of mine at a reading I gave at Sir George in August '69. He should have covered his ears. *Genève* was commercially published in 1971 by Coach House, and my *Arcana* also by Coach House in 1973. In 1992 when Greg Curnoe was killed, George came to London for the funeral, which I emceed, and stayed at my house. In the subsequent weeks we both began poems—his *The Moustache*, published in 1993, and my "Dead in Canada," completed in 1993 but not published until included in *Popular Narratives* in 1996. Like the poems in *Tish*, what has linked these has not been so much our reading of each others' poems as the overlaps in the fields of our lives.

*

Looking through my transcriptions now in 2009 of Creeley's August 1962 lectures, I am caught by the litany of "man" and "men" and "men's" that his remarks present—as in "there's more in the world than men know, than any one man can ever know." Indeed. Most people in 1962, as I noted earlier, experienced such words as "normal," accepting the prevailing assumption that they operated as synonyms of "mankind," "mankind's" and "humanity"—and thus contained references to women. Now we understand them as having merely contained—constrained—women. That prevailing assumption was accompanied by others. One of the UBC English profs of the early 1960s, Mo Steinberg, recalls that when it came to considering women job candidates, "we didn't question their intelligence [but] . . . we felt, they're going to get married or leave, going to have families" (quoted in Djwa, 299). Marlatt tells interviewer Brenda Carr in 1990 of being the recipient of a similar remark in 1963, probably by Birney, "What's the use of giving a woman an education? You'll just get married and stop writing," and of being "deeply shocked," it being "the first recognition that I had that women were not treated as equals to men in the seriousness of their engagement in writing. That's probably why I was so angry about it. I'm still angry about it, all these years later" (BT 101–102).

As early as her interview by Bowering in 1975 Marlatt had expressed unease with the gender and age relationships of the *Tish* years. Bowering asks her, "Did Creeley's work mean much to you during this time?" She replies, "Oh yeah, yes. All those guys, that huge overwhelming 1963 thing where all at once as a young writer you're faced with this literal and literary passing on of gods and demigods" (51). Freud would have something to say about that answer. Of the *Tish* community itself she tells George, "I always felt perilously on the edge. I never felt that I was part of even the *Tish* group." He asks, "Is that because you were a couple years younger?" She replies, "Yeah, & because the immigrant thing was very strong with me for years & years" (34–35.) She is more explicit with Carr, telling her that in "the early '60s"

> [A]ll my mentors and models were men, it was very easy to aspire to think like a man. After all, the writers we valued, the ones who seemed to have a large "take" on the world, a polit-ical edge combined with an historical-mythical, even spiritual breadth of vision, were all men: Duncan, Olson, Creeley, Sny-der, Ginsberg, Williams, Pound. (99)

Of "the second phase of *Tish*, which nobody remembers," and dur-ing which she was an editor, she says:

> . . . we were publishing Maxine's [Gadd's] poetry and Judy's [Copithorne]. So I didn't feel, at the time, like I was the only one, though I did feel a certain resistance to the dominance of the men. It was the men who really defined the terms of the prevailing aesthetic at the writing workshops, which was really the collective activity behind *Tish*.

She goes on to protest the exclusion of most women from the vari-ous histories of *Tish*.

It's only the filter of history that says that I'm the lone woman, and it overlooks the fact that Gladys [Hindmarch], who was actually involved right from the beginning, has continued to write, continued to publish. (102)

Pauline Butling makes a similar complaint in her essay "Hall of Fame Blocks Women":

Most magazines of the sixties were edited and produced by men. In some instances, however, women were "peripherally" involved: Martina Bissett and Maxine Gadd, for instance, with *blewointment magazine*, Daphne Marlatt and Gladys Hindmarch with the first editorial period of *Tish* (they also became official editors of the second *Tish* editorial group). . . . They participated informally in editorial discussions, perhaps helped with production and distribution. Gladys Hindmarch, for instance, recalls "that every time I went into the cafeteria (at UBC) I would join in a discussion or argument about some poem that was being submitted to *Tish*. By the time the next issue came out, I had seen at least half of it." (63)

However, whatever was "blocking" these women from participating officially was probably as much their own internalization of the assumptions of the time, and *Tish* magazine's declared focus on poetry, as it was any conscious attempt by the men to exclude them. With *Tish*, if Hindmarch and Johnson had stepped forward and asked to be part of the board, they most likely would have been. All of the women in the lives of the first five *Tish* editors were accomplished people with individual goals who taught, edited, published or, in the case of my second wife, practised law. On the other hand, it also didn't occur to any of us men to ask Hindmarch or Johnson to join the board, or to perceive anything abnormal in their reticence. "Her voice was ever soft, gentle and low, an excellent thing in a woman." This was a dynamic that we were all entangled in, much like we were with our portrayal of these young sexually independent university women as "girls"—something Duncan catches when he singles out my oxymoron "little grown-up girl" as newly "straight-forward" ("For the Novices").

The case of the somewhat younger Marlatt is a little different. She tells Carr that she felt toward *Tish* of 1961–63 much the way H.D. felt toward Pound when she would send him a poem saying, "Well, it might give you some pleasure to tear this apart." Marlatt explains, "I felt deeply involved with what they were all expounding, not only in terms of writing but in terms of ethics, a vision of how to live. [. . .] But at that age, late teens and early twenties, the change in aesthetics and values was pretty profound for me" (101).

For the record, I can recall none of Hindmarch, Johnson or Marlatt visiting the *Tish* office to help, as Butling suggests, "with production and distribution." If such help had been routine, I know I would remember. I would probably have written poems about it. In fact the only woman associated with *Tish* who I can remember helping in its production was my much-maligned Helen. It is her handwriting and hand-drawn heart that appear on the cover of *Tish* 14; she also assisted in addressing many of the copies of that issue and other later ones. I also don't recall the discussions in the cafeteria, mainly because I didn't like the cafeteria and bought food elsewhere, but I'm sure these did happen and quite possibly involved Bowering, Dawson and Reid, who used to claim part ownership of a "literary table" there. Similarly influential meetings of course happened Sunday afternoons at the Tallmans' house, and could have added a dozen people to the *Tish* masthead.

There's another small and probably inconsequential aspect to this history—the "naming" of Daphne. On the issues of *Tish* after her marriage she continued to be Daphne Buckle—as she was also when she published her novella "The Sea Haven" in *Evidence* 6 in 1964 and in Rimanelli and Ruberto's short story anthology in 1966. She is Daphne Buckle in *Open Letter* 1:2 and 1:4 in 1966 and in Bowering's *Imago* 8 in 1968. I don't think George or I ever thought to discuss with her what name she was going to publish under. We both assumed that it would be Buckle, much as Pauline Wah was

continuing to be Pauline Butling, and Gladys Hindmarch continued to use Hindmarch after marrying Cliff Andstein, and Margaret Atwood was continuing to be one of Lorraine York's "various
Atwoods." Were we "liberated"? Nah, probably not much, but we
were hip enough to know which way the cultural winds were blow-
ing. And despite the uncertainties, we wanted to keep our girl/
women companions.

Buckle/Marlatt is correct that Hindmarch has not been a large
part of *Tish* historiography. But then again neither have David Dawson or Jamie Reid, who were on the masthead and who published,
or have published, roughly the same number of books. bpNichol
used to theorize that the attention span of Canadian literary history
was incapable of dealing with more than one writer at a time from
any movement or region. He pointed out that for a while Grove
seemed to be the only prairie novelist, then it was Mitchell, then
both were forgotten and there was only Kroetsch. Margaret Atwood
was quickly designated as the big Canadian feminist writer—others
such as Marlatt, Marian Engel, Aritha Van Herk or Gail Scott have
been regarded as short poppies. bp himself struggled against being
regarded as the only "big" Canadian concrete and performance
poet—against Diana Ross–like billings such as "bpNichol and the
Horsemen." But indeed similar poets such as bissett, McCaffery,
Dutton and Riddell became lost in the large shadow critics allowed
bp to cast. bp's theory about *Tish* was that critics had awarded George
the role of its representative writer, and thus ridded themselves of
any obligation to write about the texts of the other four editors, or
of those of the later *Tish* periods—most likely, he thought, because
George's writing appeared to most closely approach Canadian literary norms. He accurately forecast that only by separating oneself
from *Tish*, and becoming the representative writer for something
else—such as postmodern criticism, or Chinese-Canadian poetry—
would any of the others get much literary-historical notice. I suspect he told all this to Fred and Pauline too.

*

Back to the war. In the spring of 1961 I received a for me unforget-table issue of *Evergreen Review* that had, in black and white on its cover, a tattered campaign poster of John F. Kennedy. The image

was eloquent in its declaration that the election that was supposed to have ended the "do-nothing" years of the ex-general president, Eisenhower, had been a fraud. Kennedy's presidency had become busi-ness-as-usual. The Cold War was being continued and being played, if anything, more dangerously. The U.S. war in Viet-nam—a continuation of post-colonial upheavals that the 1941 Japanese inva-sion had precipitated—was being con-tinued. Folksingers were celebrating Kennedy's "smoke and fire" torpedo-boat victories over "the hea-then gods of old Japan." Within two years a Cold War wanderer, Lee Harvey Oswald, will have killed him with a World War II rifle.

My *D-Day and After* of the next year was an allusion, of course, to Eisenhower's D-Day, and a metaphor, even though the "D" in that book's title poem was "destroy old poems day"—an attempt at a new post-D, post-Daphne, beginning. "Were my old poems the same brand as this?" it concluded. *Evergreen* had been asking a sim-ilar question about Kennedy.

Tish for the five of us, as cooperators and as individuals, was a project about moving on, moving onward, moving into the open. It's not that easy, as Kennedy was finding—or as Barack Obama is finding today. As a symbol the war for me meant the old ways of doing things, the old obsessions, the closed forms, the repeated conflicts, the sending of millions of people to die willingly on bat-tlefields by keeping boundaries around the information they were allowed to know. It meant arrogant humanistic assumptions about human capabilities to control both human society and the envi-ronment. The "Agent Orange" that was being dropped in Vietnam, along with napalm and other munitions, to help the U.S. control and shape Vietnamese society, was also a defoliant developed for weed "control" and crop "management." In her interview by Carr, Marlatt comments about her association with *Tish* and writers such as Olson, Creeley and Duncan:

> . . . I had the benefit of a poetic that, as you say, was open, that placed me, gender aside (well there's the problem), in an open field of composition and, in terms of ethics, set me within an environment I was interwoven with and responsible to. I think the ecological aspect of this poetic is very strong. The twinning of the language field, how you move within it, and the environmental field, how you move within that, and what your response-ability is in each case—that was a very important contribution. Now we have this notion of eco-feminism and this sense that women take responsibility for what's happening in strip-mining, in the clear-cutting of forests, the polluting of our waters—this sense that women are no longer confined to the old archetypes of enclosure within a domestic space. (100)

During the Cuban missile crisis of *Tish* 14 most of the world—including Cuba—was held hostage to the war games of the USSR and the U.S. There was no "middle ground," no "third way," no deconstructive analysis to be introduced to this binary standoff. No multiple possibilities in this park of literally "man"-made events. The ships carrying Russian missiles turned around, or they didn't; the nuclear missiles on the ground in Cuba were removed, or they were destroyed. The weapons were different but the military dialectic was much the same as it had been in 1914 at Verdun—mutually assured destruction.

*

In the spring of 1965 I made a return visit to the *Tish* office. One of the original editors had written me that he thought we were being ripped off—he wasn't sure by whom. Purported copies of George's book *Sticks & Stones* were appearing on the used-book market, most of them, he thought, on Bill Hoffer's book lists at inflated prices. Like me, he had thought that none existed, and also hadn't bothered to keep any copies of the badly printed pages. He didn't think George would appreciate unauthorized and inaccurate copies of his work being circulated. The printing of the book had been suspended partway through—there were still drawings by Gordon Payne to be printed and inserted, including one that was to be part of the title page. The copies on the market did not have the drawings, and only a rudimentary title page. The last time either of us had seen the pages was in the old office, on shelves to the right of Bill New's desk. We had no idea who—or even what university department—had occupied the hut since.

The building was unlocked, as it usually was in the daytime. And amazingly, on the ledge over the door was my old office key. I let myself in. On the shelves to the right of Bill New's old desk were all the ruined pages of Robert Grady's book and a few random badly printed pages from George's and Lionel's. I gathered them up and took them outside to be garbage. I returned and had one more look around. I opened each cupboard under the sinks. All I found was the little green Dutch mimeograph machine, on which we had printed issues 2 to 8. I took it out to my TR4 intending to keep it as a souvenir. That night I stored it in my parents' basement and—although I eventually cleared out that basement when my mother went to a nursing home—never again saw it.

It was not until 1989 and Roy Miki's *A Record of a Writing: An Annotated and Illustrated Bibliography of George Bowering* that I discovered the source of some of the mysterious books that I hadn't thought existed. George had stapled together approximately fifteen of them, using the incomplete title page as the cover, and taken them to Calgary. Fred had bound one for himself. Someone had also visited the hut and taken random pages to Bill Hoffer. The copies that Miki had managed to look at each had different poems missing.

I am still wondering whether we should have bought that Model 80, and what we might have accomplished if we hadn't. We could have done without maps and hand-drawn bridges and continued to print readable copies of the newsletter on that Dutch mimeograph. Or we could have printed all but the first page and had that page, replete with maps and bridges, printed commercially for ten or fifteen dollars. For the money we spent on buying the Model 80, on repairs to it and on wasted paper, we could have had both George's and Lionel's books printed and bound commercially. Where that might have led is impossible to know. Perhaps to Tishbooks that none of us got around to imagining? And to a more productive *Tish* second period? At least it's likely that in the spring of 1965 I wouldn't have been visiting the old *Tish* hut.

PART 4
SPREADING TISH

New Ecologies, Parties, Books, Children, Vendettas, Magazines (1963–1975, and here & there-after)

September 1963 . . .

Everything seems good. Helen and I have rented an apartment near Beacon Hill Park and downtown Victoria. Although on a large island just twenty-five miles offshore from Vancouver, that city feels almost a continent away. By car and ferry, it's four hours. I have a twenty-minute drive across the Johnson Street bridge and along a narrow waterway over to Colwood and the military college, where in the "castle" that serves as its administration building there is an underused library with a large collection of locally published histories and biographies, including at least one that has long been suppressed by a court order. The library windows overlook the college's elaborate gardens, the Strait of Juan de Fuca and the mountains of the Olympic Peninsula. I've resolved to try to follow Olson's advice to younger poet Ed Dorn to find out more than anyone else about at least one thing "whether it's Barbed Wire or Pemmican or Paterson or Iowa" (*A Bibliography* 13)—to find out all I can about Victoria. In that library I am in fact sitting at a hot spot of Victoria history. Its oak-panelled rooms centre the second floor of a Norman-towered stone mansion built by James Dunsmuir, once both premier—1900 to 1902—and lieutenant-governor—1906 to 1909—of BC. His father, Robert Dunsmuir, a coal miner who became a coal magnate, founded the up-island town of Ladysmith, where Gladys was born, and almost single-handedly underpinned the early economy of Victoria, getting a monopoly on supplying coal to San Francisco. He constructed both a railway from his mines to Victoria and a fleet of steam colliers to carry his coal down the coast. Although James had become estranged from his father—and barred from his extravagantly Gothic stone mansion "Craigdarroch" downtown—he had eventually inherited the family business. I've also resolved to meet Charles Morriss, the best-known book printer in the province, the printer who designs and prints both *Canadian Literature* magazine and *Prism*, and who operates a commercial printing company here that produces grocers' flyers alongside elegant volumes for literary presses.

Royal Roads offers the first two years of engineering, science and arts degrees. It's administered by the Canadian navy—as an imaginary ship. The senior officers and non-coms are mostly World War II vets. For the last two years, the students "go ashore" to the Royal Military College at Kingston in Ontario, and after graduation serve three years in Canada's armed forces. The English department at Roads is usually three or four people—at the moment it's three, and in some confusion. The resignation that created the vacancy I have filled was that of the chair, who has moved ashore and "up" to the college in Kingston. There are two junior members. The older of these, Vincent Sharman, is the more junior, having come to Roads from an M.A. at UBC only the year before. The younger, Barry Thorne, has a Ph.D. from Wisconsin and two years' service at Roads, and has been made acting chair while the college considers the department's future. The bread-and-butter course of the department is one in Utopian literature that is mandatory for all first-year engineering and science majors. There are also two arts courses, a first year and a second. There is only one section of the latter; it is traditionally taught by the chair. Among the students the English department's reputation is high. Its classes are among the few in which they feel free to express opinions, and its faculty among the few who do not invoke military punishments for lateness or falling asleep. Despite his faux British accent, Barry Thorne is savvy about this advantage, one that Vince and I also want to maintain. Apart from doing our seven hours each of weekly teaching, keeping minimal office hours, acknowledging the salutes of the cadets and enlisted men and having a twenty-cent beer and a game of skittles every noon in the officers' mess, not much is expected of us. I have two free days a week, a couple of other free afternoons and a lot of time to write.

October 1963 . . .

Even before leaving Vancouver I had sent the manuscript of the poems of my M.A. thesis to Louis Dudek in Montreal, for Contact Press. Not only have Louis, Ray Souster and Peter Miller accepted it for publication, under the title *Bridge Force*, but Louis has arranged a Canada-Council funded reading for me at the Montreal Museum of Fine Arts. Around the middle of October Helen and I catch flights from Victoria to Montreal. For both of us, it is our first venture east of the Rockies, and our first time aloft. The nearly new DC-8 lands briefly in Toronto at the old Malton airport in front of a decaying wooden World War II era terminal, before continuing to Montreal. Louis and Ron Everson meet us at Dorval with Ron's Cadillac convertible. The weather is unseasonably warm and sunny—eighty to eighty-five Fahrenheit every day. Louis and his wife, Stephanie, host us at their house on Vendôme. One day we spend with Louis and their little son, Gregory, in the park at St. Helen's Island, at that time still unmarred by Expo 67 planners. Another we spend with him and Ron in the Cadillac, with the top down and Helen perched on the rear deck, driving up and down the narrow streets of old Montreal while workmen hoot and whistle. Souster is the other reader at the museum—he comes in by train the afternoon of the reading, and vanishes almost immediately after.

Like a groundhog, says Louis. The audience is boisterous, and I enjoy the somewhat impolite exchanges I have with some of Layton's young disciples—Mayne and Moscovitch. There is cheering, jeering and laughter from different parts of the room each time any of us speak.

On the way back on the DC-8 I write the rough draft of a poem, "In Stereo." I hadn't encountered bilingualism before this visit to Montreal.

November 1963 . . .

I get another surprise note—this one from the editor of the *BC Library Quarterly*, a thin elegant magazine that's also produced by Morriss Printing. The editor has discovered—perhaps from Woodcock—that I am in Victoria, and wants me to write an article on Morriss Printing's role within BC publishing. Printing does interest me. The *Tish* office had been receiving an ever-increasing number of irregular publications printed in a variety of styles, from the hand-set pages and reclaimed fine papers of Jon Edgar Webb's *The Outsider* to the careful commercial typewriter-offset of David McFadden's *Mountain*. As the usual typist for the *Tish* issues, I had needed to think about rudimentary questions of layout and page design. Moreover, Olson's poetics had stressed how the visual appearance of a poem could represent its rhythmic or "breath" structures—the typewriter, he suggested, had given poets a means to precisely measure their lines. Typography has thus for me—and for George and Fred—become a part of poetics. It soon will be for Daphne, too. But it's a difficult part of poetics. Too elegant and it risks isolating the text from social impacts. Too rough and one is carrying pages from the *Tish* office to a dumpster. I have copies of Olson's gorgeously produced books from the Auerhahn Press—his collected essays *Human Universe* in an edition of 250 copies and his poem *Maximus of Dogtown* in an edition of 500. *Tish* may have so far reached more readers.

. . .

I decide that the best way to find out more about Charles Morriss and his print shop is to visit. He's a small, friendly older man with a muted British accent that I can't quite locate. He takes me around the building and shows me the equipment he and his dozen or more employees use, from large offset presses for the grocery flyers to a small proof press for hand-set type. It's high-quality machinery of various ages that he has personally selected. He was born in Winnipeg in 1907, he tells me, grew up in Victoria, and in his early years worked as a printer in numerous shops in the U.S. But out of a desire to know more about his craft, he went to England and studied at St. Bride's, "with Beatrice Warde," he adds. The names don't mean much to me, although the story does explain his accent. Because of the accent I'm not even sure whether he has said "Wand" or "Ward." My next stop is at the UVic library. Beatrice Warde, I discover, is an American whose early interest in calligraphy led to a self-education in type fonts and their history, and to a position in 1921 as assistant librarian for the American Type Founders Company. In 1925 she moved to England, and in 1927 began a thirty-three-year career with the Monotype Corporation. She published a collection of essays on typography, *The Crystal Goblet*, in 1955—the title refers to a modernist transparency that she had urged in typography—type that was to be a "polished window" to the text. St. Bride's Foundation Printing School was founded by the City of London in 1893, offered evening courses beginning in 1894 and full-time courses in 1919. Warde is still alive. There was a private-press exhibition at St. Bride's just this year, July 27 to August 2, at which she gave the opening address.

Morriss is much like us poets, caught between the commercial and career structures of the general culture and a desire to do work that transcends and alters its expectations. Giving up employment in mid-career to study at St. Bride's, he needs his commercial printing business so he can maintain his family and purchase the equipment and materials for his serious work. But the success of the former risks making a hobby of the latter.

At Munro's Bookstore I look for a copy of F.R. Scott's recently published translations, *St-Denys Garneau & Anne Hébert*, which I saw at the press. It's spacious and attractive, the original French printed in a mid-blue and the translations in black. But although printed by Morriss, the design and typography are by Takao Tanabe. I buy it anyway. There's also the Morriss-printed and designed book by George Nicholson, *Vancouver Island's West Coast*. Maybe I'll come back for it.

December 1963 . . .

Fred has started his own magazine. It's the first I've heard from him since leaving Vancouver. It's called SUM: *A Newsletter of Current Workings*. It has a bright yellow cover, a short Fred poem on the back and an Abraham Lincoln stamp. "Workings" is a real Fred word— he tends to look for words or usages that should exist and don't, but then becomes convinced they do and uses them "as if"—and suddenly they do. Workings—as at a gold or silver mine. Hmmm, I think they do have some of those in New Mexico—the closest I've been is Virginia City, Nevada, and there'd been a big silver mine there—Comstock? SUM has been very neatly offset-printed from electric typewriter copy—you can see ghost images from the offset "blanket" behind the text on several pages. Except for Fred and Gerry Gilbert, the contributors seem to be Americans. A much larger proportion than in *Tish*. It's also different in its professing an eclecticism: "Not propogating [sic] any particular dogma, the magazine depends upon the writer's own concern and responsibility for his writing," the title page says. American rugged individuals. Maybe that's the only way Fred could get the contributing editors, Ron Loewinsohn and Ken Irby and John Keys—all U.S. small-press writers that I know—to join in? Irby is with Fred in Albuquerque, Loewinsohn in San Francisco and Keys in New York. SUM also states that it has official institutional support from Fred's department— it looks like a secretary typed these neatly structured pages. I worry about Fred. I wouldn't want to have to make my way in U.S. poetry.

. . .

I've begun writing a series of poems of Victoria. It's such a self-contained place, surrounded on three sides by the sea, and inwardly focused. Helen has given me a copy of the Nicholson book for Christmas. As well as all the amateur histories like his that I'm finding, there are weekly articles in the newspaper—the *Colonist*, founded in 1858—many of which reprint or recall nineteenth-century stories. A self-announced "colonist." I write Fred to thank him for the mag, and enclose drafts of a few of these new poems.

February 1964 . . .

I get a long letter from Fred, apologizing for taking so long to respond. He says he's had a difficult first term. He and Pauline are about to have a baby. And the university has withdrawn its support for *SUM* because of some "four-letter words." But then he goes on to comment on the poems I've sent and his letter becomes strange, with numerous retreats, qualifications and more apologies for what it is saying or has said. "I'm not trying to tell you how to write yr stuf— I just feel that you are capable of more pushing energy from what I've known of you," he writes on the second page. He also writes,

> I tried this with George when he wrote me way back last fall but I don't think he was humble enough to take it from me—I trust its not exactly humility which is involved but awareness? comprehension? I've tried my damnedst to look at yr things more objectively than I cld have in the past—and possibly I've succeeded; who cares. What I want to do is demand more action from you than you've cared to give me here: come out of yrself quickly, you're trying too hard from what I see here (like George tried too hard at times, poem a day thing, you know what I mean) and rather than clarify yr poem I feel yr drive tends to make it hazy, vague (just like I am right now). I'm not trying to get to any one WAY, I just feel generally, that you cld

go so much further with what basics you do have. To push out, insist, against our boundaries, it's at the edge where it becomes exciting energy, at least for myself. I think I'm guilty of the same lethargic & static unmoving that you and George are. All 3 of us seem to have, at some point or other, stopped moving out on the risk.

To me Fred seems in the throes of things he was somehow unable to say during the face-to-face interactions of *Tish*. But he nevertheless wants to publish some of the poems I've sent. I have mixed feelings about that—despite the uneasy tone, Fred's comments have come close to some of my own misgivings. He writes, "Please don't take me wrongly. These poems are a hell of a lot better than some of the crap in *SUM*." I'm not sure about that.

. . .

Now George has started a magazine too, in Calgary. Again I'm looking at the typography. The cover looks a lot like that of *SUM*— the contributors' names listed in a tidy column down the left side— six Americans and a Brit. Not much of a Canadian scene in Calgary either, I guess. A wonderful small squared-off typeface—where did George find such a typewriter? His introductory note announces *Imago* as a magazine "for the long poem, the series or set, the sequence, swathes from giant work in progress, long life pains eased into print [. . . .] the cumbersome thing the ragbag mag won't have room for." Even a poem that "will use up the whole mag." So *Imago* does have a dogma—it doesn't particularly like those "ragbags" of single-page magazine verses—the short punchy lyrics that George is so very good at writing, and getting published. I like that announcement—I think of it as a kind of amusing self-critique. *Imago* looks in one way like a big attempt to extend *Tish*—swathes from works in progress, parts of sequences or series, such things that were a large part of our own contributions to it. "Eased" into print.

From Fred, *SUM* 2 also arrives. Except for Fred, this is also a nearly all-American issue, with Keys, Irby and Loewinsohn joined by Paul Blackburn, Judson Crews, James Koller, Robert Kelly and Robert Duncan, plus a few whose names I don't know. Lots of one-page poems but in too-relaxed a style to be "ragbag" verse. The issue has a mischievous "open this end" printed along its spine, but I don't get fooled. There's a note that the "institutional" support for *SUM* has ended. The production and the paper seem both a little cruder and more imaginative. Fred has been sightseeing—he has two short poems about a Navajo girl and three-legged dog. Somewhat Ray-Sousterish. No other news from him though—I still have no idea what program he's in or what he's studying. Or whether the baby has arrived.

March 1964 . . .

There's been a huge earthquake, a Richter 9.2, in Alaska. On Good Friday. I'm wondering if it's at all connected to the recent U.S. nuclear bomb testing on Johnston Atoll. The resulting tsunamis have completely wrecked Port Alberni, at the end of a long narrow inlet just to the north of us, as well as causing damage in Japan and Hawaii and deaths as well as damage in California.

May 1964 . . .

Helen is graduating from UVic, and her parents and sister, my parents and my grandmother and Bill, my UBC roommate who has married her sister, all come over and visit both campuses. I've finished a poetry manuscript focused on Victoria, its old Chinese cemetery, some local tribal myths, and at the end of the month take it to Charlie Morriss for suggestions about design and printing. I could send the manuscript elsewhere, but want to have a book printed by him and I don't know of any publisher who would both want my book and be able to afford him.

SUM 3 arrives, in the same beautifully crude papers as the previous issue. There's a Denise Levertov poem—the first poem by a woman that Fred has published. There are also poems by George, Bromige, Cull and me. Except for my poem, which in this context of mostly loose-lined poems seems overly controlled, and the Bromige and Levertov, they all read as if they could have been written by the same person.

July 1964 . . .

I'm busy sending out review copies of *City of the Gulls and Sea*. I like what Morriss has done, the tall slim shape that matches the shape of the poems, the pale green acid-free paper that he found left over from a larger job. He's set it in the same Baskerville as the Nicholson book, with uppercase titles in a bold sans. The only element I don't like is the small Viking ship he's put on the cover— I shouldn't have okayed that. He said it was the only ship casting that he had. It was $300 to have 400 copies printed. Thirty-four pages. I've priced it at $1.75—a lot for a book these days. The hardbound 356-page Nicholson is only $10.00. But the local Hudson's Bay store takes 15 copies.

. . .

Helen and I leave for a camping trip. We're going down to the Bend/Redmond volcanic area of Oregon, and then to Crater Lake. After that we may cut over to northern California and look at some of the tsunami damage from the Alaska earthquake. We won't be that far from Albuquerque, but except for *SUM* 3 I haven't heard much from Fred and Pauline.

August 1964 . . .

Jamie Reid has panned *City of the Gulls* on Co-op Radio in Vancouver—or so Gladys writes in a short note. I locate his new Cranbrook address and write to ask him what's up. It pisses me that his only "message" to me since I left Vancouver is so public. I tell him he's a "traitor." His review is the first I've heard from or about Jamie since I moved here—except for a few poems in *Tish*.

October 1964 . . .

Here's the second issue of *Imago*. It seems to be something of a crossover with the last SUM—there are four recent SUM contributors—me, John Keys, George Montgomery and Robert Duncan. It's set in the same attractively square typewriter font as the first issue. George and I have both been researching and writing about our new locations—his poem here considers parts of the history of Alberta.

. . .

I receive an angry and aggrieved letter from Jamie, along with his review copy of *City*, with black fountain-pen comments on pretty well every page. About four of the pages he really likes. Extravagantly likes. Of course there are about twenty-two others, and each time his complaint is about passages that I had misgivings about, and echoes some of Fred's comments. Dull, low-energy passages that also for me reflect this quiet, boundaried city.

. . .

The fall issue of the *BC Library Quarterly* is out with my article on Morriss. And right after has come a note in the mail from George Woodcock, asking whether I'd be interested in writing a short tribute to Morriss for *Canadian Literature*'s twenty-fourth issue. Of course I say yes.

. . .

I've started a couple of new poetry projects. I've been trying to
write some anti-Wreck-of-the-Hesperus narratives of the ship-
wrecks Nicholson recounts, poems that look into the economics
of nineteenth-century west coast shipping. And I've also written
a couple of pieces occasioned by the children Helen is teaching
in a "special ed" class at South Park School. It's a nineteenth-
century school on the edge of Beacon Hill Park. "Special ed"
classes here are a dumping spot for any child who can't "keep up"
in a regular class.

. . .

The Hudson's Bay has ordered another twenty copies of *City*. I
notice that they display them next to the imitation totem poles and
fake birchbark canoe models that they sell to tourists.

November 1964 . . .

I'm restless. I shouldn't be. It's pretty clear I could teach my seven
hours a week at Royal Roads indefinitely, as many of the older faculty here seem to be doing. The city has a Mediterranean climate,
only thirty inches of rain a year. I've been reading Creeley's *The
Island*, the novel he was writing in Vancouver, which was published
late last year. Victoria seems a lot like his Mallorca—comfortable,
inbred, a long way from everything.

I've been thinking I should maybe begin work on a doctorate.
With a Ph.D. you get paid almost twice as much for teaching the
same classes. Then I could travel more—at least to Vancouver! But
I also don't have any ambition to be a scholar or critic. That could
be a problem. I want to study only things that might help with
writing. But I write the GRE—the Graduate Record Exam—just in
case. I study by reading George Sampson's *Concise Cambridge History of English Literature*. I'm surprised that the exam seems easy—

probably geared to Americans? I rank in the seventy-sixth percentile in math, despite not having studied math since Grade 11,
and the ninety-eighth percentile in language, and the ninety-fifth
in English lit.

December 1964 . . .

I've been going through the stash of university calendars in the
library at UVic. The only Canadian literature doctoral programs
seem to be in Edmonton, or in Ontario at the University of Toronto
or Western. And they seem to expect two or three years of coursework. Berkeley interests me because it's just across the bay from San
Francisco, and Josephine Miles teaches there. At Duncan's recommendation I've been reading her astonishing book on poetic language, *Eras and Modes in English Poetry*. But Berkeley also requires
two or three years of coursework—about fifteen courses—and three
foreign languages. I check the calendars of the other UC campuses
and find much the same requirements. But Southern Cal, which is
independent, is different. It requires only six courses—followed
by sixteen hours of comprehensive examinations in four different
fields, all written in the same week. I recheck the calendars. There's
a pattern—the more years of coursework required, the fewer the
comprehensive exams. When I write to the Southern Cal department for additional information, I learn that most of their doctoral
students are required to take up to a year of courses after the comprehensives—courses prescribed by the department to address the
deficiencies revealed by the exams.

. . .

Red Lane has died—suddenly, from a brain aneurism, in Vancouver.
Red, who had prophecized that a return to academic work would
"kill" George.

January 1965 . . .

I apply for admission to Southern California—it's the only application I make. Helen applies to its special ed masters' program. We are
both accepted, as we expected. We are going to go down this coming
summer and do coursework and then come back to Victoria to our
ongoing teaching jobs. USC has a three-week session in June at which
one can take one course, and a seven-week session in July and August
at which one can take two. We can both do half our coursework. We
arrange to rent an apartment in the married-student housing on
campus for June through August.

February 1965 . . .

Royal Roads has announced a new cluster of "Arts Research
Grants" for faculty members. Our faculty association has successfully protested a long-standing military-college policy of offering
research grants only in the sciences and engineering. There's not
a lot of money available, but enough for a newsletter like *SUM* or
Imago. I don't want to do such a project on my own, however. Some
of the best things about *Tish* for me were the sustained dialogues it
opened for me with other writers. I've never talked as much about
writing and poetics as in the *Tish* years. Then there were the letters
to *Tish* that kept coming in. There are still occasional letters from
George in the new *Tish*, commenting candidly—although pater-
nally, I think sometimes—on what the younger editors are publishing. And a couple of times there've been ones from Jamie.

. . .

The entire cadet body and military staff have assembled for the
first raising of the new Canadian flag—February 15. The college
flagpole is a ship's mast in a circle beside the porte cochère of the
castle. I stand with the rest of the faculty on the marble staircase
between the classroom block and the castle—"Neptune Stairs."

There's a fountain with a statue of Neptune at the top. I know privately how unhappy the senior officers are about having to lower  the old flag—the flag they fought under in the North Atlantic and off the Korean coast. But the ceremony—the lowering and folding of the old, the raising of the maple leaf—the anthem playing of the college band—all is done efficiently and professionally. The younger officers are cheery—they link the new flag to the forces' new post-Suez peacekeeping mandate. I tend to link it to George Woodcock, Louis Dudek and the narrow streets of Montreal.

Raising the new Canadian flag at Royal Roads Military College, Feburary 15, 1965.

March 1965 . . .

I've got an idea for this grant program—a magazine in which writers "talk" publicly to each other about poetics and their writing projects. Write "open" letters. Might even be able to get Fred to write to me, and give him a different context than that hip U.S. one he's connected with in Albuquerque. And create a magazine that does the very thing—the talk and theorizing—that the writers in Toronto and Montreal complained about *Tish* doing.

. . .

The Hudson's Bay orders another twenty copies of *City*.

April 1965 . . .

Imago 3 arrives—with the first full-issue long poem, Lionel's *Listen, George*. I don't like it much. It's a long, witty and rhythmical soliloquy—reminds me a lot of George's "Meatgrinder." Everything in it is upfront—and when it's all upfront there ain't much out back.

Each part seems like one of Duncan's "single path" poems. But Lionel has always differed with us about that.

. . .

From what I hear the Vancouver arts scene is becoming more widely social, public and "psychedelic." The arts and underground left-wing politics have been publicly merging, and along with them writing and filmmaking and performance art. Sam Perry has been working at David Orcutt's studio at UBC at learning filmmaking and image projection. Lionel's book may be a new kind of entertaining performance poetry.

May 1965 . . .

Word is that I've secured an "Arts Research Grant" to start a magazine, and will have secretarial help and maybe even access to the local branch of the Queen's Printer. I write to Fred,

> The offer is this: if you, Jamie, George and David will simply provide two or more pages per issue, showing what are your concerns, what poems you are writing, what poems you like that others near you have written, and what reactions you are having to recent publications, I'll coordinate and publish whatever the four of you send me. Each person wd have own pages, own editorial autonomy, own right to blast any of the other four, and own address listed at the top of his pages so reader reaction cd come direct. Each could publish on his pages any of the letters he received. The need no longer exists for a TISH to reflect a group's activity—where's the group—the need now is for something to keep the five of us together to build on whatever we piled up in those first years. And individual autonomy—something that works both ways—is the only way on. I spoke to George and Dave at the Blaser/Spicer readings last week in Vanc., and they're with me. Can we count on you?

Jamie isn't interested. Fred agrees, but without much enthusiasm.

. . .

I finish a draft of my poems on unhappy children and historic ship-wrecks, "The Scarred Hull," and send a section to Gladys. She replies that the personal parts are glib, unworthy of the portraits of the children.

June 1965 . . .

It's off to Los Angeles. We go to Abbotsford for a day to see our par-ents, and then head south late Saturday morning. Interstate 5 still isn't completed, although large parts of it are now driveable. We take turns driving the TR4—a big leather suitcase strapped to the lug-gage rack, and the space behind the seats stuffed. It takes us nine-teen hours driving straight through. We naïvely didn't look ahead for a place to stay, and so steer down the Harbor Freeway to the Exposition Boulevard exit to the USC campus and start looking for a motel. There are a lot of them—each one advertising "clean sheets" and an hourly rate. We calculate how much that would cost, and then decide to look elsewhere—by the airport, we think. We drive south on Vermont Avenue past dozens of similar motels before turn-ing west toward Inglewood and finding a more familiar-looking one, indeed, near the airport. We are near the Watts Towers that Duncan spoke admiringly about during those 1961 lectures.

Meanwhile Jack Spicer has headed north. In two weeks' time he will be giving three of his own lectures in Vancouver. I have all of Spicer's scarce little books with me.

I begin a four-week course in American fiction. It meets every morning for three hours—usually in a pub on Jefferson Ave. near the Shrine Auditorium, because the assigned classroom isn't air-conditioned. I write a paper on *Winesburg, Ohio* that the prof thinks I should try to publish. But I don't want to be a published critic, so I file it away.

July 1965 . . .

The neighbourhood around the university is mainly small neat bungalows from the twenties and thirties. It looks a lot like a flat version of Vancouver. The residents are almost all black. Most of the people we meet in the married housing are white and they drive to Beverley Hills to shop and can't believe that we shop nearby. There we're usually the only white customers. In the supermarkets and drugstores are big displays of hair straighteners. Displays of *Ebony* magazine. Young men sell copies of Elijah Muhammad's newspaper *Muhammad Speaks* just outside the entrances. There are large posters of the late Malcolm X. There's also a lot of people our age just sitting on porches or leaning against buildings as if waiting for something to do. The smaller shops all have heavy black grills covering their windows. Some have grill work all around the cash desk, and your money and change have to pass back and forth on a sliding tray. The Americans we talk to say all this ironwork is normal but we've never seen such things.

. . .

The June issue of *Tish* has been forwarded—with two sections from the new book I've been working on. On the facing page there's a note about a "poetry conference" in Berkeley, but it gives no dates. There's a poem by Lionel with a note indicating he's in England. And four poems from Jamie that indicate he is still in Cranbrook. We seem to be spreading out.

. . .

Gladys writes again, somewhat angrily, about "The Scarred Hull" draft. She writes that "the child-shipwreck interplay with Helen as a kind of balance/ballast, was structurally beautiful, and the collision aspect was almost perfect in a <u>formal</u> sense. [But] the shift to the couple who weren't anything ruined this. Each child each object

in Helen's class is something-someone. There is a type of magic at work. The you-the-poet in those two pages could not possibly be in my eye (idealistic) the prick who focused on those petticalities [sic] so un-bitchily and so self-righteously." She hopes we can get together and talk in September. I rewrite one of the "couple" sections and delete the second.

Helen and I at USC.

August 1965 . . .

Fred writes briefly from Nelson where he and Pauline are spending the summer. They have left Albuquerque and are heading to Buffalo, to which Creeley is also moving. Fred sends me the titles of some linguistics books I've wanted. I write back urging him to send poems for the first *Open Letter* with a note "defending" them. I also suggest that we could publish part of Pauline's thesis on Duncan, which she's planning to finish at Buffalo.

. . .

We had bought a small cheap black-and-white TV at a nearby drugstore, and are watching the late evening news. There's some conflict involving the police some thirty blocks south of us. Passing cars have been stoned. Thursday morning before classes we check the TV news and the clashes are continuing. Some stores near the conflict have been looted and set afire. After classes we check again. From our third-floor balcony overlooking Exposition Boulevard we can see helicopters overhead to the south and large plumes of smoke. The TV station has a helicopter and is broadcasting live coverage, along with a map that shows where the conflicts are occurring. We drive out to a Ralph's supermarket nearby on Santa Barbara Avenue and stock up on bread, vegetables and some meat that we can freeze. Friday morning we hear that classes have been cancelled.

We stay inside watching fires that we can see simultaneously from our window and on television. The announced boundaries of the unrest keep expanding northward until by late afternoon the whole campus is inside them. There is only random traffic—mainly racing black-and-white police cars on the streets below. We can see smoke and some flame coming from the Ralph's where we shopped last night. We start hearing gunshots, but they don't seem close. Despite small fires even directly across the streets from its edges, the campus seems quiet. But around 10:00 p.m. some francophone friends from Quebec drop by and tell us that our building superintendent has been up on the roof of the building—he had to disarm three fraternity boys who had taken rifles there to "defend" the complex. Then we hear that the National Guard has been called out.

The next morning we begin seeing small convoys of military vehicles, but the fires outside and on the TV continue. By evening the announcers say we are under twenty-four-hour-a-day curfew. I have now heard more than thirty gunshots, although I wasn't counting while we slept. Sunday morning the National Guard soldiers begin sweeping the major streets on foot. They come down Exposition Boulevard from the west, with their Garand rifles pointed at our balconies and yelling up for us to stay inside. Later that day just down the street they kill a middle-aged black woman who doesn't stop her car at their checkpoint. With a fifty-calibre machine gun they've set to fire automatically. We can only hear the sounds but our TV interprets them. The curfew isn't lifted, and the campus reopened, until Tuesday. We drive out that evening to one of the few unburned markets, on Figueroa. On the way back we are following a National Guard truck full of troops when a nearby car backfires. The white soldiers all jump up and point their Garands.

Earlier in the day, in the poverty ward of San Francisco General Hospital, Jack Spicer died. His head gone up to the aether. But I won't hear about that until I get back to Victoria.

September 1965 . . .

There's been some changes in the Roads English department. Vince Sharman has left to begin doctoral studies in Edmonton. He had chafed under the military administration. I'll miss his sardonic comments about the fancy balls every December and June, about the walls that are "bulkheads," the floors that are "decks" and the washrooms "heads." And about the "bidding wars" at the college marks meetings when a cadet needed to be saved from failing out. "English will give Honeywell two." "French will give three." The military hates to lose an investment. "Five more?" "Very well, chemistry will give five." Another new M.A. has arrived from UBC to replace Vince—a tall young man who so far doesn't take the military aspects of the college very seriously: Ted Whittaker. Barry Thorne has left too—moved "up" to a position at Queen's. He was probably going to be replaced here as acting chair anyway. From Royal Roads' companion college, "CMR," the two-year Collège Militaire Royale at Saint-Jean, Gerald Morgan has arrived to be the permanent chair. He's a small man, British-born, I think, not far from retirement age, and quiet, cheerful and academically street smart—very different from Ted. He was once a merchant navy officer, became a Conrad scholar and of course married an attractive Polish woman—Janka. I'm not sure in what order. There's also a new librarian. It's a young woman. The first woman ever on the Royal Roads faculty.

. . .

A note from David Dawson that he has asked Dan McLeod, the current *Tish* editor, to send me and *The Open Letter* a copy of the current *Tish* mailing list. He writes that he assured Dan that "no usurpation was intended."

. . .

I write again to Fred, asking him for poems—"I'm taking anything in poetry, poetry commentary, language, or language for poetry, and still want for the first issue a letter from you to us all to tell us where your [sic] at and what's up." I write also that I'm still "inviting Pauline to publish the leading sections of her thesis on Duncan."

October 1965 . . .

There's an official letter in my mailbox from Eric Graham, the director of studies. It tells me that last July the college research grant committee approved a $250 grant for the academic year 1965–66 "to establish a small literary magazine, *The Open Letter*, which will be printed and distributed on a non-profit basis." Because the public will "inevitably" associate it with the college and Department of National Defence, the committee recommends that the magazine have "an attractive format" as well as "high intellectual quality." It also recommends that I "avoid publishing material which could prove to be embarrassing to the Crown," and that I remember "the laws affecting Federal Civil Servants with regard to certain restrictions on their political activities."

. . .

The older officers have secured a World War II Canadian tank—a Sherman—to be a campus monument. There are already fourteen-inch naval shells—deactivated I presume—lining most of the central roadways. The tank, which is presumed to have served in Italy or Holland, comes on a flatbed truck, and is lowered by a crane onto a cement pad to the east of the castle. The new flag flies about a hundred feet west of the old tank.

. . .

Imago 4 arrives. It's dedicated, without comment, to Jack Spicer, but one of its major pieces is a six-page poem by George recalling Red

Lane. I reflect that it is the first elegy any of us have had to write. George has sent me a copy of *The Man in the Yellow Boots* as well, which has also just been published, in Mexico City, as a full issue of *El Corno Emplumado*. It is dedicated to Red Lane, and has another elegy by George, for his father. So his father has died too.

. . .

I write to Fred, "Am daily awaiting your open letter for the first issue, and whatever else you find in poetry or articles that you'd like to see included."

. . .

Dan McLeod has sent me the *Tish* mailing list—the list that began four years ago from the *Floating Bear* list.

November 1965 . . .

I write again to Fred: "I sincerely hope that you are alive and well. . . . I'm still holding up the *Open Letter* for you, Fred."

. . .

I've done all I can on my new poem manuscript, "The Scarred Hull." George may publish it as an issue of *Imago*, but I've sent it first to Jamie with a curt letter asking him to suggest changes. I'd much rather see his comments this way than in a review.

. . .

Tish 31 has come in—the first issue since June, although the masthead has been saying it is "monthly." It indicates that Bob Hogg is now in Buffalo. I hear Dave Cull is there as well. Guess it's the new mecca. Bob has sent *Tish* some impressively precise poems, full of subtle surprises.

. . .

From the Hudson's Bay there's another order for copies of *City*.

. . .

I manage to get the first *OL* published. It's been a scramble to get things together, and I need to get at least three issues out within the fiscal year, which ends March 15. I write a brief introduction that characterizes the mag as "both a symposium and a debate" and implicitly names it an extension of *Tish*. David and George send strongly supportive letters. "[N]othing gets results like questioning, arguing, plain disputing, because only when a man [sic] can defend his position is he sure of it. . . . & I don't think the charge of 'in-group' activity holds here. [T]he mag will succeed on its own merits, as an open forum," David writes. George writes, "I like the idea of *The Open Letter*, and would urge the former *Tish* people to keep their noses in this new mag. For one thing, I want to know what you are all doing, even if it isn't what I'm doing." Fred sends some poems but declines to send a letter. As well, some parts of George's letter are defensive or defiant—I'm not sure which. He writes that during *Tish* he "would be jumped on with questions such as: why are you paying attention to those Canadian poets who are not writing out of our traditions? Answer: because I am a poet before I am anyone's monkey. . . . Question: why do you write those smart-aleck poems that sound like bad Ferlinghetti? Answer: because I am not satisfied that I can write good and better poetry by sticking with one process and trying to improve it." The answers don't really address the questions and make me wonder what the actual answers might be. And that word "traditions" sure seems loaded in the wrong direction. Aren't we too young to have traditions? Allen's anthology wasn't called "The Traditional American Poetry." But it's still a fascinating letter, that seems to anticipate—or invite?—more jumping on.

I create the cover by cutting by hand a large "O" from part of a lingerie ad, and pasting Letraset letters around it. I hope this is attractive enough. I closely supervise a college secretary who types the copy sideways on eight-and-a-half by fourteen paper in the correct sequence for "booklet" printing. I give her a paste-up of each double page to use as a model, and instruct her to make sure that the letter characters in poems line up vertically just as in the manuscripts. Afterward I use Letraset again to apply page numbers and the initials of each of the contributing editors to the bottoms of the pages they have contributed. At the top of Fred's section I sardonically note that "all" he has sent us is poems. I know the comment is ambiguous, but so too is my response to Fred.

Open Letter, issue 1.

December 1965 . . .

Responses to *OL* are starting to arrive, including one from Daphne, to whom I have not written since 1961. She had received a copy because her name and Bloomington address were on the *Tish* mailing list that Dan sent me. She writes to politely but firmly dispute a brief remark I made about *Tish* writers and the epic. I begin drafting an "open" reply for the next *OL*. But I also begin writing a cautious personal letter to her in which I ask whether she would like me to send her copies of my two recent books—despite the references to our history that she would find there.

January 1966 . . .

Jamie has sent "The Scarred Hull" ms back with numerous good suggestions. No letter, however.

February 1966 . . .

Imago 5 is here, with a stunning poem on the Vietnam War by Finnish poet Matti Rossi, translated by Anselm Hollo. The poem, which keeps switching viewpoints, seems to empathize with the landscape, the Vietnamese and the U.S. draftees. But there are also very weak and formally uninteresting poems by Purdy and Newlove who may have tried to write longish poems just to be in George's magazine. Talk about not writing "out of our traditions."

. . .

The Canada Council has come through with a doctoral fellowship for me. It's renewable, too, but I hope I won't need that. I've optimistically applied for one year's leave of absence from the college.

. . .

George writes to ask me to send him "The Scarred Hull"—"the revised manuscript you got back from Jamie."

March 1966 . . .

Daphne has written back—"I was happy to get your letter," she begins, "& am looking forward to *Open Letter* 2 which, if out, has not yet reached me." She says she bought a copy of *Bridge Force* on a recent visit to Vancouver—"[I] steep myself in the poems because they are so much located & the quality of your living (this isn't criticism, but appreciation) comes through clearly—West Coast! Those particularly lucid, insane states of falling between Things." But she also wishes that the writing was less from "outside, recounting." And adds, "Yes, please do send any other books, & forget or don't worry about the effects other than those of the poems themselves." Generously said, I think.

. . .

Open Letter 2. There's been a decent response to the first issue—so
many letters that there's not money to publish them all. There's a
letter from George that offers what are to me helpful criticisms
of the poem Dawson published in *OL* 1. Nothing from Dawson.
A letter from Fred which is mainly a long quotation from Olson's
"Apollonius of Tyana" about keeping silent and a comment that
he feels that anything he says these days is "small talk." He sends
poems by others, two of which—by young Olson scholars Glover
and Butterick—I publish. Privately I wonder whether Fred feels his
words are "small" because he's in Buffalo and with the very "large"
Olson and his growing crowd of students. But I publish a brief note
defending him in which I suggest that his restraint may be better
than the indiscriminate inclusiveness George has defended. There
are also strong letters from U.S. poet Gene Fowler, who offers a
long response to Dawson's work.

I do at least one thing in this issue that pushes the boundaries—
although not those of the Crown. I publish two poems by Gerard
Malanga but preface them in my "open letter" with harsh criticisms
of his work generally—calling it overrated—and even one about
the present poems. I wouldn't like this to be done to me, but then
it's a risk one takes in sending work to this *OL*. I have mixed feelings
about what I'm doing. My own poems here are open to similar
commentary—like Dawson's were by George and Gene Fowler,
or my *City* was open to public appraisal by Jamie. Malanga is indeed a seemingly highly rated young U.S. counterculture poet,
with several large collections published by the widely respected
small press Black Sparrow, and poems every month or so in a little
mag. Presumably someone will write back to *OL* to defend him. I
also make an innocent remark, I think, about visual poetry. bpNichol and David McFadden have both sent some, and I comment
that visual poems are "irrelevant to what I know as poetry" and
offer to send them on to George, David or Fred in case one of
them likes them. Indeed, visual poems were outside of the oral and

linguistically based poetries of *Tish* 1 to 19, as well as outside my own practice.

Daphne's open letter protests a comment about the epic that I also thought was innocent, or merely descriptive, in which I wrote that "from where I see all our writing from *TISH* 1 and onward, the epic—certainly no epic seen before this century—and at least epic size, epic vision, has been always our final goal." I had been thinking of "our" influence by Olson, who had converted the inherited celebratory epic into one of historical and geological process, an epic of both place and cultural protest—thinking too of Pound's *Cantos* and their sardonic opening invocation of the *Odyssey*. Daphne writes that my comment "smacks of heroics, of the ego, which is afterall uninteresting. The single point is the place." I write an unnecessarily long, equivocating reply. This is probably as much a moment in feminism—and in my personal nervousness around Daphne—as in *Tish* poetics, but neither of us may know that. I will later read her *Steveston* as an epic—at least from the viewpoint of the fish.

. . .

After I've mailed all the copies of the *OL* issue I write sarcastically to Fred—I'm still unhappy about his apparent vow of silence: "If you think *OL* would be just as useful with blank pages, let's hear about it."

April 1966 . . .

OL 3: George feels picked on, but is going to turn the other cheek. "I get the impression that everybody wants me to be snarky or something: and I am conscious that . . . there were rivalries and disagreeable talking among the poets inside the group in Vancouver yore. I didn't like that much; . . . so you see I aint going to put down Frank or Jamie or Fred et al, although I might from time to time try to say something nice." "Love to all you bastards," he signs off. And mean ol' Frank in a letter to George goes through *The Man*

in the Yellow Boots pointing out which poems he thinks are "bald,"
"obvious" or incidental and which ones he thinks outstanding. By
"obvious" I mean that these are the kind of poems Duncan was
describing in his 1961 lectures as relying on "the poet's own powers and the poet's own choice, and the poet's own cleverness." I
threaten to compare George's stylistic eclecticism with that of *Fiddlehead.* Dawson writes about the attractiveness of the serial poem
and the "correspondences" it can create, suggests that this is similar
to my understanding of the "epic," and that it explains "Warren
Tallman's dissatisfaction with incidental poems." And in another
letter I defend Dawson against George's claim in the last issue that
he overuses the definite article in order to create false archetypes.
The "disagreeable talking" is multiplying, and in yet another letter,
New Mexico poet Keith Wilson is cheering us on: "The concept
of *Open Letter* interests me greatly—and the more 'open' it can get,
frankly, the better. Certainly I will pass the word. . . ."

May 1966 . . .

A brief note from Daphne. She hasn't yet received #3. She men-
tions Mary Ellen Solt's "turning to concrete poems. She [Solt] says
she is so tired of verbiage. A risk run, like this letter. I never think
about the thinking/writing when writing—which is what counts.
All ways. Fred's probably right, you know."

June 1966 . . .

I've got *OL* 1:4 assembled and ready for printing—Ted Whittaker
is going to look after *OL* while I'm at usc. But I'm worried. The
magazine has done more than I had expected—the response to the
dialogue-and-exchange concept has involved more people, and
more enthusiasm. I worry that this energy will be dissipated while
I'm gone. Ted is gung-ho, but doesn't know the people very well,
and may not see the same value in the "open letter" idea as I do. He
may not enjoy pasting all those Letraset initials either.

In this issue there's a letter from William Harris responding positively to the "epic" discussion Daphne and I had, a good-humoured response from Gerard Malanga to the rough handling I gave his poems, an appreciative letter from Keith Wilson and an odd letter from bpNichol suggesting that I was pontificating when I wrote that I still saw visual poetry as "irrelevant to what I know as poetry." I was just describing a personal foible, beep, I should reply. Don't take it so darn seriously. There's a letter from George saying that all his poems—including his "little conscious poems"—are an "honest attempt" to know his soul. But he does prefer his longer, more searching ones. There's also a long May 9 letter from Sam Perry in which he outlines his past and current work with film, and how he fell into filmmaking through a peyote session in the fall of '63. He writes that after briefly turning away from creating image flows to recording "people reality" he has come back to making film that is "a communal hallucination," and that "I will have finished all I know by next year." I write three letters—that's a great thing about being editor, you can always get the last word. In two of them I write only about the good things in some of the Buckle, McFadden and Brigham poems I'm publishing. We could discuss those. George has also sent a poem by Chilean poet Raquel Jodorowsky that he has translated—I can't see why he's sent it, and begin a third letter to *OL* about it.

. . .

Helen and I leave for our year, we hope, in Los Angeles. This time we aim to arrive when the married students apartments office is open. Around midnight, we stop at the Shakey's in Grant's Pass, Oregon, for pizza. More of the interstate has been built—the trip takes us only seventeen hours. I'm going to take the remaining two courses I need, and then write the comprehensives in November. With luck, my sixth required course will be called "Dissertation Research."

August 1966 . . .

It's a busy month. I've just passed my French language exam. Frank Zappa is playing at the Shrine Auditorium on the north side of campus. The *Los Angeles Times* continues to publish on its front page daily lists of U.S. casualties in Vietnam. David Dawson tells me that Robin Blaser and his young partner Stan Persky have moved to Vancouver—Robin has a teaching job at Simon Fraser. That's big news—he'll be the most celebrated non-Canadian writer to move to Vancouver since Malcolm Lowry—and unlike Lowry most likely plans to stay. *Imago* 5 is here—a full issue of my new book, *The Scarred Hull*. George produced it just before leaving Calgary for London, Ontario, where he is going to start a Ph.D. And I've hired a tutor to help me prepare for a Latin exam.

. . .

We suspect that there's a key club operating among the young married undergrads with small children who occupy the townhouses that our tower overlooks. Helen's noticed early in the morning the wrong spouses coming out of several townhouses and waving to each other as they return to their own. Very interesting, she says. She makes discreet inquires among the longer-term residents on our floor and confirms what we've seen. The club apparently involves some of the residents on the ground floor of our tower too. It's "the Pill" that has made this possible. Sex can now be a community pastime.

September 1966 . . .

I've got two months and three weeks before my comprehensives— those four four-hour exams on four consecutive days—medieval, eighteenth-century, modern British, and lyric and narrative poetry from 1200 to the present, followed by a three-hour oral. I've chickened out on writing the American lit comp, even though that's

arguably the area of my proposed thesis. I'd argue however that the
area is poetry. I've studied each field for a month at a time during
my time back in Victoria. Now I am studying each field for two
weeks at a time during this month and next, and then it'll be each
for a week, and then each for a day. I'm remembering the promise I
made to myself after my M.A. defence.

. . .

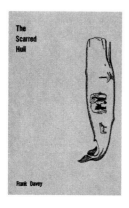

The Scarred Hull

Frank Davey

George writes from Toronto, although he's
recently been in BC. He says he has dropped
copies of *The Scarred Hull* off in Abbotsford
at Helen's father's hardware store. "Creeley
teaching at Buffalo for $17,000," he adds.
"Birney is going to Waterloo for more, then
going to Irvine, near you, in 1968 spring. . . .
I was accepted by Durham, but going to
Western." He means accepted for a Ph.D.
program.

October 1966 . . .

There's a small earthquake on the twenty-sixth—a 4.9. Our sixth-
floor apartment seems to sway a foot in each direction. We have
two six-foot-tall metal bookcases, which fortunately are side by
side, and I manage to keep them from falling over, although the
books on the top shelves come down.

November 1966 . . .

Daphne writes that she has received a copy of *The Scarred Hull*. She
wishes it were less "controlled" in its rhythms and perceptions. She
wants me to "risk more." That's much what she said about *City* and
Bridge Force.

. . .

Just before the middle of the month I write the four comprehensives. Between the last exam and the oral I get a painful eye infection—both my upper lids swell until my eyes are shut. I go to the sports medicine clinic where O.J. Simpson, Tom Seaver and the other USC Trojans go for physio, and which looks after the grad students after hours. The doctor says the infection is caused by the recent heavy smog, and gives me an antibiotic. Two days later I can see well enough to carry a football, and the examining committee has told me all four exams were impressive. I'm free to start writing my dissertation.

. . .

Helen and I take a break and drive to San Francisco for the Thanksgiving weekend. We visit Robert Duncan and his partner, the painter and graphic designer Jess. Duncan and I discuss my thesis plans. Helen has never known a gay couple and is astonished at how hospitably housewifely Jess's attention to us is.

When we get back there's a letter from George saying that Sam Perry killed himself last week—"complications of acid and Crease Clinic, and bailiff taking all his media equipment. I don't know much about it, but I feel awful." Sam really has finished all he knew.

. . .

OL 5 is also waiting in the mailbox. There's a roughly sketched female nude on the last page—I hope the Crown isn't embarrassed. The issue is as precisely laid out as I could hope—even Letraset initials in the corners of the pages. I'd seen some of the contents and had a chance to contribute a letter about them. My comments about visual poetry, and an aside I made about Bob Dylan, have continued to bring in letters—there are ones from David Cull, Jamie Reid, Victor Coleman, Albert Drake, Gene Fowler and another from William Harris. Some of these writers have also been engaged by George's soul—Victor seems to be snickering at it. Albert Drake is the one who drew the nude—he was illustrating some visual poem possibilities. Not bad.

December 1966 . . .

I've started a draft of my thesis. In San Francisco Duncan suggested a theory-practice structure—particularly since there's been almost

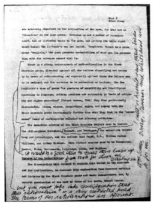

no scholarship on him, Olson or Creeley, and since my supervisory committee won't know much about them. All three poets have had to be scholars of their own work. I bought a few very new books from him—the stunningly printed *A Book of Resemblances*, the boxed *Six Prose Pieces*—hand-printed on hand-made paper in an edition of thirty copies—the locally published *Of the War* and the scarce *Writing Writing*, Duncan's Stein imitations, which Fred published from Sumbooks just after arriving in Buffalo. Duncan also gave me a lead on some tapes, including one of a Creeley lecture, which the language laboratory at Berkeley will sell copies of.

A page of an early draft of my dissertation proposal, annotated by Robert Duncan.

. . .

George has published *Imago* 7, the first issue from London. It looks much like the Calgary ones, with similar contributors—George, Lionel, Carol Bergé, Olson, Anselm Hollo. But it also looks like he's lost his old typewriter—the issue is set in a very ordinary font. The contributors' notes say that Lionel is back in Vancouver and that George has a new poetry book, *The Silver Wire*, published in Kingston. I don't have time to read the poems.

. . .

We drive back up the coast to spend Christmas in Abbotsford, leaving in the late afternoon after one of Helen's classes. We've recently bought a 1966 Mustang convertible, with a four-speed manual transmission, from the actor Wally Cox—"Mr. Peepers." He'd leased it for a new Hollywood wife from whom he's now separated, and was in a hurry to sell. It runs much more quietly than the TR. We drive in the midnight darkness through Oregon. Helen sleeps. There's almost no traffic. My head is full of Duncan's 1961 lectures, which I've been re-listening to. South of Portland I find myself writing a Christmas poem in my head—I "write" it and memorize it while driving. It's "A Christmas Song to Mary." We get safely to Helen's parents' house in time for breakfast—and while the French toast is cooking I write down the poem. It's great to be here—Helen always finds it transgressively erotic to make love in the bedroom of her teenage years.

January 1967 . . .

I hear that Fred has helped edit the third issue of *The Magazine of Further Studies* but I don't get a copy. "The magazine of far-out studies," George calls it. Neither Ted nor I heard from Fred for *OL* 5, nor now for *OL* 6, which he's almost got assembled. He doesn't think he can publish the four issues he's hoped to do, so number 6 is going to be a big one. Fifty-two pages. There's no time to send me what will be in it, but about a third will recall Sam Perry. I've sent him a poem I've written about Sam—a poem which I worry is probably too obviously based on Sam's favourite Olson poem, *Maximus from Dogtown I*. Merry with too much bull. I also wish I could break away from the tight-looking left margins I've used. Sam would have. But when people die they don't leave you time to become a better writer.

February 1967 . . .

I've finished the first draft of my thesis—on the German typewriter that my grandmother bought "to help with grad school."

. . .

And here comes *OL* 6. Ted has really pushed the limits this time. George—perhaps inspired by the Matti Rossi poems in *Imago*—has sent in three anti-Vietnam-War poems. Ted has partly covered them by writing a letter condemning them for having only a partial attitude toward violence—in a sense thus containing them within a possible debate about political poetry. "A small bloodbath is better than a big one but it isn't as good as no bloodbath at all," he writes. "Polemical poetry addressed to one side of the war is not only naive, it has a good chance of being bad poetry. Bowering's poems this time are damningly true and over-adroit; solipsistic and relying on the cute end line to make sure of their impact." Good old Ted, I think. George does rely on cute endings in his "conscious little poems." And a discussion about the ethics of anti-war poetry is usually an accepted part of a military college curriculum—*dulce et decorum est*, etc.

Gerald Morgan has contributed a fine letter that answers the puzzlement I had about the Raquel Jodorowsky and George's translation of it in the last issue—and also inadvertently answers George's comeback in this one. George has apparently misrecognized some of the subtleties in Jodorowsky's Spanish. The guy who published *"Esta Muy Caliente"* and later gave it the alternate title *"Hace Mucho Calor."* And the visual poem debate continues to simmer—there are letters from Douglas Barbour, Jack e Lorts, Gene Fowler, david dubbleyew and others. There's a nasty and impatient letter from me to Albert Drake. Today I can't remember why I wrote it like that. Maybe because I'm no longer finding some of the discussion personally useful.

. . .

Ted writes that they've lost a young member of the English department in the middle of the year. Another newly minted M.A. He went
to a mess dinner—a formal dinner in which the officers are required
to wear their dress uniforms and full medals—wearing a Nehru jacket
with small Christmas-tree balls hung on its left breast pocket. The
counterculture came to Roads, Ted says, and got quickly sent away.

March 1967 . . .

I've written to Gerald to apologize for George's maladroit poems.
He writes back that he thought *OL 6* was "acceptable" and that
"David Dawson continues to be brilliant."

. . .

There's a new letter from Gerald, dated "Easter Monday." It begins
by saying "your elegy is the best poem I've seen from you. . . .
Sam Perry in OL6 is first-class, and David Dawson brilliant." But
apparently the college administration, as I feared, has not considered *OL 6* "acceptable." He goes on to say that he has had to expend
much "time and wit" defending *OL 6* to the college grants committee because of the Bowering and Goldberg contributions, but
in vain. "B and G. have written <u>finis</u> to O.L. at Royal Roads." He
asks me to apologize to David, whose book, "Where the Orders
Are," was to be the next issue.
    In the same mail there's a letter from Daphne, saying, "I haven't
heard from you for a while." She likes my Sam Perry poem—"one
of the best things you've done"—and then surprises me with several
paragraphs about sound and concrete poetry—Ernst Jandl's work,
Ian Hamilton Finlay's.

April 1967 . . .

OL 7 is already here, David's "Where the Orders Are." Ted writes
that he won't be at Roads next year—I'm not sure whether he's

leaving voluntarily. Not sure also who has paid for the *OL* 7 printing—maybe Ted sneaked it through while the committee and Gerald were still arguing? He's done a superb job, I think, of keeping
OL going. But there's a new problem. Even if the committee could
be mollified, I can't apply for a grant for 1967–68 while I'm on
leave, and Ted can't apply now that he's leaving. So a year may have
to pass between the letters of #6 and whatever I can publish in #8.

July-August 1967 . . .

At USC a student can defend a doctoral thesis on the basis of the
penultimate draft. My defence has gone well. The next step is to
deposit the final manuscript at the USC thesis office in a format
acceptable to the university thesis officer and University Micro-
films in Ann Arbor. The female thesis officer is feared across the
university, and as a result one Robert Smith has established a typing
company whose only business is the preparation of USC theses.
His company employs several dozen typists, each with an electric
typewriter, and several editors who mark up one's manuscript in the
required formats before it is typed. Students who have lined up in
the thesis office to try to deposit their works frequently see a Robert
Smith employee walk directly to the back rooms with an armful of
theses that are instantly accepted. The company's price for my
thesis is $600. I hand over the manuscript and the money and head
back to my job in Victoria. Once I receive official notice that the
thesis has been filed, Royal Roads will give me a $1,000 raise. Helen
is graduating with her Masters this September. My official graduation won't be until January.

. . .

Helen's closest friend here in LA, a vivacious young Mormon
woman, is getting married, and would love to surprise her guests
with a "Canadian" wedding cake. Fruitcakes—the culinary kind—
are as unusual at U.S. weddings as they are commonplace in Canada.

Helen offers to bake one as our wedding present. Gail says she can use the kitchen at the Mormon centre, right beside the campus. Helen has baked single Christmas fruitcakes, but never anything this large. The almond-paste icing and the pedestals for the tiers are easy to find, but not the nuts and dried fruits. Wrong country, wrong time of year. But Helen has found a recipe that uses Cross and Blackwell's mincemeat, which is available. Except that the labels brag that the mincemeat contains real rum and brandy, and Mormons aren't allowed to drink. Small crisis while Gail and her fiancé, Pete, decide that the alcohol must have been long ago cooked off. The ingredients fill a two-foot-diameter bowl, which neither Gail nor Helen are strong enough to stir. Helen gets me to do the mixing, while she and Gail laughingly hustle the mincemeat jars out of the building and into a garbage can far down the alley. The four layers come out of the ovens as if professionally baked. My most creative day for some time. Three weeks later almost two hundred Mormons compliment Gail on her unusual and delicious cake. On their honeymoon Gail and Pete drive our TR4 up to Victoria. We will be driving up a week later in our Mustang.

. . .

Gerald writes to say that the college is "agog" at my imminent return. But he doesn't answer my questions about Ted's departure and the mysterious printing of the Dawson issue.

September 1967 . . .

The English department has changed again. There are two new faculty members—Geoff Aggeler, a new Ph.D. from somewhere in the California system, and Roger Tallentire, a reserve Navy lieutenant who has just finished an M.A. at UBC. Geoff and his wife, Sondra, and their children have settled into one of the townhouses in the Post Married Quarters—the "PMQS"—on a small plateau north of the "castle" and the academic buildings. Roger—who seems to have a private supply of money—has bought a lakefront house about a mile from the college. He's also caught people's attention by driving an E-type Jaguar roadster. He has a wife, he says, who's in Vancouver—he hasn't wanted to disrupt her career with the Mercantile Bank. He goes back to Vancouver on weekends. Some Mondays he reappears with a different Jaguar—an old Mark VII Saloon. It's his wife's—he's borrowed it for the week to carry lumber that can be leaned through its sunroof, lumber for renovations to his house.

. . .

George writes from Montreal to tell me he's now living there—writer-in-residence at Sir George Williams University. He's withdrawn from the doctoral program at Western. He says he usually knew more than the profs, and in the grad seminars often ended up doing most of the teaching. He reproaches me for having returned to Victoria: "I also have it from unimpeachable sorceresses that you have settled for life (is that possible in Vic?) in that city, wch I say is ok if that is what you think you want, but I wd take it as a Purdy terrible sentence." I also hear that Fred and Pauline have moved back to the Kootenays, to Castlegar.

. . .

I go to visit Charlie Morriss, taking with me the poem I "wrote" on the overnight drive last Christmas—the "Christmas Song for Mary." For $50 he will design and print a broadsheet for me, seventy copies in red ink on yellow-green paper, that I can send to my friends this December.

. . .

I visit Ted, who plays for me a couple of Bob Dylan albums that had come out while I was ignoring the world in LA. He tells me that some Roads faculty are now calling *Open Letter* "open sewer." A kingly title for a *Tish* mag he says. We teach that Blake serial poem in our Utopian Lit classes—*The Marriage of Heaven and Hell*. But he just laughs when I ask him how he got the Dawson issue out.

November 1967 . . .

Helen has had difficulty finding appropriate work in Victoria. She had delayed looking because she hoped to be pregnant. We had a lot of fun all spring and summer working at that. Her gynaecologist here thinks she could be allergic to my sperm—too bad we didn't know that when we were at UBC. She could go back to teaching a class similar to the ones she taught from 1963 to 1965, but all she'd be using her new degree for would be a higher salary. She finally accepts a job as a provincial social worker, dealing mostly with pregnant teenagers, many of whom have no idea who impregnated them. Despite the irony of her situation, Helen enjoys telling me their stories. One of the girls got pregnant during an exciting transatlantic voyage. "There was Tom, and Eddy, and a couple of the stewards," she apparently told Helen. "And then one night there was the band." The Pill has changed lifestyles, but not all young women have thought to take it. Because of her job commitment, Helen has gone back on it.

. . .

Helen and I have seen Roger now at Royal Roads events with several different young women. There's been no sign of his wife.

. . .

I've started work at reviving *OL*. Now that Ted is gone, it looks like the "research" grant will be restored. I've written to David expressing my unhappiness at how far from a four-person dialogue *OL* has strayed in the past year, and suggested that perhaps I should restrict its range of contributors. Part of that "straying" of course has been caused by Fred's silence and my preoccupation with my dissertation. He writes back saying that in his mind *OL* has been taken over by "aliens." He'd like it to go back to being a magazine of a "community"—with a "tight sense of relatedness." But now there's a letter from George suggesting that I should ask Victor Coleman and bpNichol to become contributing editors. Not sure that David would like that.

. . .

Daphne writes from Napa, where her husband, after some difficulty, has been able to arrange an internship. I've expressed to her the concerns about *OL* that I mentioned to David. She thinks *OL* should remain "open." She encloses four prose poems. They are fascinating, intriguing texts, made up of fragmentary images, sharp juxtapositions between sentences, quick shifts of viewpoint from impersonal to first-person singular to quotations to first-person plural. All bound together by recurring rhythms. I am not sure I fully understand them but then I don't believe I fully understand poems by Hopkins or Donne either. Daphne has been sending me prose poems for the past few years, possibly out of the work she has been doing on Francis Ponge for her thesis at Bloomington. I have never thought of prose poems as a solution to the formal stiffness I have sensed in many of my Victoria poems. But these prose poems seem to show some remarkable possibilities. I don't tell her all this—I worry that I may be misreading them—I don't want to appear stupid. But I start tinkering at the form for the first time, starting a sequence of texts that shift only slightly in tone between each section.

. . .

Robin Blaser and Stan Persky come to Victoria for a brief holiday and ask for my advice on bookstores. Helen invites them for dinner.

I spend an afternoon with them helping them find books. Because of its large retirement population, one that for decades has been dying thousands of miles from its nearest relatives, Victoria has several antiquarian bookstores packed with unusually rich holdings. Robin collects nineteenth-century folk-tale anthologies, both traditional and literary, anthologies often published with lavish Pre-Raphaelite or art-nouveau decorations. He finds almost a dozen rare examples. With great delight that evening, he shows them to Helen, calling them "fairy tales." Helen will later recount this to her mother and sister.

December 1967 . . .

As usual Royal Roads holds both its Christmas ball and administration New Year's party. The ball is held on the large "quarter-deck"—normally an indoor hardwood drill square—of the academic building, with a live orchestra. Formal dress is required. The officers and cadets wear their dress uniforms; the cadets' dates and other women are expected to have floor-length gowns; the civilian men black or white tie. The wives of the older officers and faculty often wear the same dress year after year. But Helen and some of the wives of the younger officers feverishly sew new dresses every December—and again every May for the graduating ball—from Vogue or McCall's patterns. Slim is in this year, and Helen has made a dress with a long slim brown velvet skirt with an attached top of cream and matching brown brocade. Roger Tallentire has hinted that his mysterious wife may make an appearance, but she doesn't. He tells me she's been involved with her bank manager, but expects that this soon will end. He thinks she will be at the New Year's party, with another couple from Vancouver. And

Linda's Mercantile Bank photo, 1967.

she is. We share a table together at the New Year's party in the "castle," where there is again a live band. His wife is called Linda, and
she is surprisingly articulate and widely read as well as attractive.
Roger is, as always, very social, and dances with their woman friend
from Vancouver, with Helen and with several of the young officers'
wives, but not with Linda. This seems odd and unfortunate, so I
invite her to dance.

January 1968 . . .

Coach House Press has sent me and *Open Letter* a review copy of
George's new little book, *Baseball.* It's an eye-catching shape—a
long green triangle—something I can't imagine Charlie Morriss or
Tak Tanabe attempting. It's dedicated to Jack Spicer, and has a lot
of Spicerish smart-ass lines and obscure literary allusions mixed in
with what is a structured, nine-inning serial poem. A closed serial
poem—no extra innings. It's the first extraordinary text I've seen
one of us publish. The first that I'm sure will outlive us. George is
so much better when he stops writing tidy consumable little one-
page products and writes poems in which the "meaning" is in the
process and flow of the language. Where you have to "read" all the
shifts and changes. I'm envious.

February 1968 . . .

Roger is throwing a small party at the lakeside house he has been
renovating. Linda is going be there to help host. It's a moonlit
night, so you can look out over the lake and at the surrounding fir
and cedar trees. He has renovated in Spanish style, installing faux
black-brown hand-hewn beams across the ceiling, and has even
made by hand octagonal black tables, with black steel trays built
into the centres. He worked in his earlier years as a part-time musician, and entertains everyone with five-string banjo renditions of
"My Old Man's a Dustman," "Seven Old Ladies Locked in a Lava-
tory" and off-colour lyrics to "Humoresque." Before the party

breaks up I chat briefly with Linda, who tells me that she used to read *Tish* back in 1961 to 1963, and sometimes go to readings. She was in high school—Britannia. I ask her where she got her copies and she says at Duthie's. She says that Binky would always give her one. I say she must have been a special customer, and she says no, that each month Binky gave away free all the copies of *Tish* that I had sold him.

. . .

There's a letter from Daphne. She and Alan will be returning to Vancouver, possibly permanently, in September.

April 1968 . . .

Robin Skelton gives a reading at Ivy's Bookshop in Oak Bay. He's the self-declared major poet in Victoria. He teaches at UVic, and tries to dress like a mediaeval Irish bard. I usually go to the readings at Ivy's, but I wouldn't cross the street to hear Skelton's narrow pomposities. Similarly, although I've seen him in the audience at various readings, I've never seen him at any of mine. In his audience tonight is Robert Sward, a U.S. poet from Chicago—and U.S. Navy vet—who has recently joined the UVic faculty. According to Ivy, Skelton takes exception to one of Sward's comments, and in the heated discussion that ensues unwisely pushes Sward, who quickly punches him in the face, knocking him down. A one-round knockout. A lot of people in this city would have wanted to see that, I tell Ivy. She laughs and agrees. We joke that Robert is now Victoria's new poet champion.

. . .

A fairly lively arts scene has been developing downtown in old buildings near lower Government Street. A couple of makeshift gallery/coffee houses have been holding impromptu readings. A lot of young people in their late teens and early twenties have been hanging out there, some of them also taking art courses at the old Victoria College building. I've given a couple of free readings for them. I hang out there too, often with a tall dark-haired young woman named Dorothy who wears tie-dyed clothes and likes to talk about art and aesthetics with a kind of desperate and breathless eagerness. She reminds me a bit of Daphne in 1961. Dorothy knows most of the people who come here, and introduces me to a talented but unformed young artist, Dennis James.

May 1968 . . .

I write to Daphne and to David about a poetry anthology that I'm thinking of assembling and trying to get published. A day later there's a letter from Daphne—she writes that she hasn't heard from me for some time. She's read my recent article in *Evidence*, "How to Use a University," and likes how I "stressed the value of the energy-atmosphere of likewise involved friends" and goes on to say how at *Tish* "we were simply lucky to have 'occurred' together" and been able to achieve "a tremendous give & take of influence, the magnetism of personalities as well as of ideas." A week later she replies to my letter about the anthology. She likes that our letters have crossed—"I don't think that this is the 1st time we've been writing more or less simultaneously after a silence (believe in thought-signalling?)" Her thoughts about an anthology are pretty well a continuation of her previous letter, and articulated much better than I could manage.

> I liked your idea of bringing forward that "magic" operative in early *Tish*, or at least a general shared sensitivity to it. The people who were central to that, & I don't mean necessarily their work, were Glady and Jamie, & it was bound up with a perceptiveness for environment which operated in all the work. I think what was consciously espoused, that geographic stress brought over from Olson (& the acuity of perception we learned from

Williams) were/was not foremost in personal values which
propelled the work—that letting things happen you spoke of,
which of course leads to a poetics. I was thinking about the geography: Point Grey surrounded by the sea, by woods, on the
north the mountains, & an aura of indian totems (Jamie the first
to clue into such values with his poem on Mungo (Martin?) . . .
things loom in the poems . . . The good work is built around:
lights, bridges, stones, gulls, sustained by them. The voice is
often a meditative calling on things, as if they had the power to
conjure (or more precisely, their names had, nouns important),
out of a certain absence, to cross a dimension: there is an aura
of 'lost loves', of historic personages CALLED UPON that
haunts early Tish (& even the tone of irony in yr, or George's,
or Bob's work doesn't mask it).

July 1968 . . .

I have been working on random poems that I wrote while I was in
Los Angeles. The most powerful book I read that year was John
Speirs's study of mediaeval English poetry, "the non-Chaucerian
tradition," a study of how much of pre-Christian nature consciousness was preserved in poems such as "Maiden in the Moor Lay"
and *Sir Gawain and the Green Knight.* The book connected with
my readings of Thomas Malory, and my growing apocalyptic fear
that humanity's abuse of the planet—in Vietnam, in the 1965 atomic
tests at Amchitka, in the Torrey Canyon oil-spill disaster—is reaching a crisis level. The U.S. Army's obsession with occupying Vietnamese hills has connected ironically for me with the Buddhist
veneration of hills. I think some of these poems—"Sentences of
Welcome," "The Mountain," "The Making," "When"—are the
best I have yet written, and might have been parts of a long series
had I not been in Los Angeles. But if I hadn't been in LA, I might
not have been reading Speirs. I should probably publish these
poems as fragments of a lost serial poem. As Duncan has said, revision of old writing is impossible because you are no longer living in

the field which helped forge it. The only revision can be new writing. My new writings are the tarot card poems I've started on—there's almost the same sense of impending apocalypse in my draft of "The World," which I've written after seeing *Planet of the Apes* at a local theatre, as there is in "When." Already they are diverting my attention from the anthology idea.

. . .

There's been an Ingmar Bergman festival at the Fox Theatre. More than a dozen of his movies, from popular ones such as *The Virgin Spring* and *Wild Strawberries* to obscure ones such as *Winter Light*. I go every night for two weeks, and see every film. Helen's not interested. That mediaeval sense that you find in *The Seventh Seal* and *Virgin Spring* that the bleak everyday world can also be magically spiritual seems to run through all the films. For me they hauntingly reinvoke both John Speirs's book and the Gawain poet's dark forests. It's a shock each time to come out of the movie house and onto a busy twentieth-century street.

August 1968 . . .

Roger's wife, Linda, has quit her job in Vancouver and is moving here. She's going to enrol at UVic. Helen is also going to be at UVic—she's decided to enrol in a new special-education doctoral program that the education and psychology departments are offering. Roger has decided to throw a large celebratory outdoor party, and has "borrowed" two gallons of the recent batch of sake I have made. Alas, Helen and I are away on the mainland that week, and miss the party, but Linda tells us afterward that the sake was amazing. She and Roger served it as if it were punch, and within ten minutes of arriving every guest was wobbling. She says she got into an animated discussion with the commandant, who was standing in the garden with his back to their fish pool. In the midst of delivering a particularly humourous line, she slapped him playfully on the chest, and he staggered backward and onto his back into the pool.

October 1968 . . .

Gerald is organizing a conference next month for the Victoria branch of the Humanities Association of Canada, and wants me to write and present a paper. I suspect he may be having a hard time getting material. I ask him what he'd like me to write on, and he smiles cryptically and says how about Leonard Cohen's songs, or maybe Bob Dylan. I can't imagine where Gerald has heard songs by either of them. Perhaps on the radio in his vintage diesel Mercedes? I buy Leonard Cohen and Bob Dylan songbooks at Munro's, and also write to Cohen's publisher about some songs I've heard that didn't make it into the book.

. . .

Helen has made friends very quickly among the faculty in her program. We go to parties at two different houses, and throw our own party, which the hosts of those parties attend, along with people from the military college. We also have been seeing Roger and Linda almost every week, either at Roads events or various parties. Helen is both impressed and intimidated by Linda's exuberance and apparent self-confidence. She phones her for advice on food and party plans. She tells me that Linda will still be slim, beautiful and vivacious when she is sixty—implying that she herself may not be. I'm not so sure.

. . .

Some days I wish I hadn't agreed to write this paper on Cohen and Dylan—turn off the music and you're left with magazine-verse lyrics close to the ones I wish George wouldn't write. Plus a self-satisfied anti-romanticism that recalls those similarly "cavalier" lyricists

Lovelace and Suckling. I'm finding little to discuss except their themes, which—making things worse—seem disturbingly attractive. "Babe, I'm gonna leave you," Dylan keeps singing. "So long, Mary Ann," Cohen joins him.

. . .

Daphne sends me a copy of her new book *Frames*—from Vancouver. She urges me to write her, or come to a new series of Sunday afternoon meetings that Warren and Glady are organizing.

November 1968 . . .

I finally get another *OL* published. Indeed, the momentum of the first six issues has been lost. But I do have a beautiful art-nouveau cover by Dennis James, some poems by another local young man that Dorothy has brought to my attention, an essay on folk rock by my new colleague Geoff Aggeler, the four extraordinary-to-me prose poems by Daphne, letters about the old *OL 6* from Douglas Barbour and Gene Fowler, and poems from several others including George. I haven't been able to raise a word from Fred, and so I've dropped him from the masthead. With nothing from David, and only George's poems from him, I haven't bothered putting initials at the bottom of the pages. Except for George's two pages, the initials would all be mine.

Open Letter, issue 8.

I've also written more of my prose poem series, tentatively titling it "Weeds." But it seems to be a surprisingly unhappy series, and I am keeping the pages just behind a small door in my study that leads into the attic.

. . .

Gerald likes the paper I have delivered on Leonard Cohen and Bob Dylan—"Poetry and the Popular Song" I have called it. I'm not entirely happy with it—it seems too personal, personal like my new prose poems. It has made me too aware how much Helen and I seem to be drifting apart—"You're the reason I'm travellin' on," Dylan keeps singing in my ear. But Gerald is suggesting that I now submit it to ACUTE—the association of Canadian university teachers— for its next annual conference, at York University in Toronto. Damn, he is determined to push my work in directions I haven't considered. He says I should write more articles about Canadian literature. I tell him I know only a small amount about Canadian literature. He replies, "But you write it, don't you?"

December 1968 . . .

Daphne replies to a letter I've sent her about *Frames*. She says she thinks of it more as an "initiation" than a narrative. She wants to see some of my new tarot poems. She hopes I'll be at Warren and Glady's next Sunday meeting, just before Christmas. It'll be held at Jim Brown's. I write back that I'll be there.

. . .

Helen tells me that most of the young faculty she is taking courses from and who have been inviting us to their parties are members of a campus key club that tries to meet at least once a week. They believe that this is a sane and structured way to contain their sexual temptations and prevent them from becoming marriage-threatening romances. I ask whether this means no hanky-panky allowed outside of the key club? She doesn't think so. "It don't matter anyhow?"

. . .

Helen doesn't want to attend the Royal Roads New Year's party this year. She wants to attend the party at the UVic faculty club, and has already arranged to get tickets. I insist that we go to Roads. She asks why am I so determined to go to Roads—and I joke that I want to kiss Linda a happy new year. It's a joke but also not quite a joke. Before the Christmas ball she phones Linda and asks what she will be wearing. She comes away from the phone complaining that Linda said she doesn't know—that she will be making up her mind at the last minute. Linda's lack of anxiety about what to wear appears to annoy her—she may even envy it. At the ball Helen is sure she has created the wrong dress—a mid-blue lamé. She tells everyone we talk to that I am unhappy not to be coming to the New Year's party, because I had wanted to kiss Linda a happy new year.

. . .

There's another letter from Daphne. I've sent her my "A Christmas Song for Mary" broadsheet. She says she reads it as a rosary. But she doesn't like my "More heat on Daedalus" in *OL*—says I'm "falling back on old ground rather than moving on." She's looking forward to seeing me at Jim Brown's—"2 pm Sunday."

Neptune Stairs.

January 1969 . . .

On New Year's Eve day there was a record thirty-five-inch snowfall and the UVic Faculty Club party was cancelled. Victoria apparently owns only one snowplow. We went to the Roads party in the "castle" after all. Had to walk in half a mile from the main road—one of the few that had been plowed. At midnight Linda astonished me by rushing over to the centre of the dance floor and embracing and kissing me. For more than a minute—while everyone else stood around us singing "Auld Lang

Syne." Helen was probably her intended audience. New Year's morning we returned to Roads to drink punch in the mess and to ride toboggans down Neptune Stairs between the academic building and the castle. Linda and I rode several times together.

. . .

Gerald now wants me to write a paper for the Humanities Associations' West Coast Conference, to be held here in April. He has been asked to organize it too. He suggests that because I have written *The Scarred Hull* I should write about Pratt. I tease him that Pratt is probably the only Canadian poet that Conrad scholars read. He grins—Pratt and Davey, he says.

. . .

Helen and I have agreed to separate. She's involved with one of her professors—one of the two whose parties we've been attending. Possibly with both, I suspect, although that may be unfair. She's worried that he could lose his job. She was hoping I wouldn't mind. Me, I'm more angry with her than I can express—although I'm not sure why. Maybe because sex was my main tie to her? Or is that unfair too. Also isn't this breakup what I had expected? and wanted?

. . .

I've written to Daphne and Gladys expressing—venting is more like it—rage and disappointment about how my marriage has suddenly collapsed. Daphne replies quickly that I must have contributed to the mess. She hopes I may still be coming to the Jackson Mac Low events on Tuesday, February 4th that she wrote me about last week, and says he may be also at Warren's on Sunday the 2nd. Tuesday's only four days away.

February 1969 . . .

I don't know Mac Low's work well, but I decide to go. When I arrive I learn that Mac Low needs a number of people to participate in his multi-voiced readings—I agree to be one of them. At the rehearsal I discover that he composes his works almost as a set of chance musical harmonies. He selects samples of distinctive discourses—scientific, sociological, right or left wing political, "true romance," detective, marriage counselling—and copies passages from these onto stacks of file cards. Each reader gets a stack of a particular discourse, a stack of playing cards and a stack of numbered cards. The numbers indicate the number of seconds to delay before reading. The colour of the playing card indicates loud (red) or soft (black). The value of the card indicates the degree of loudness or softness. The readers are told to shuffle each set of cards thoroughly, turn a card over from each stack and begin reading aloud accordingly. While the texts have been composed by others, Mac Low has designed and directed the particular textual event we are creating. I am stunned. The effect is to diminish or eliminate the "originality" of the individual composers—and to reveal that they to a large extent at least have been "written by" the discourses that they have employed. All of these texts are exposed as being at some level mere rhetoric. One could do this with other people's poems, I think—juxtaposing in a similar way random passages from Layton's poems, Cohen's, Newlove's, David Dawson's, bill bissett's—and create mild parodies by merely uttering the original texts. In the actual performances Mac Low's method gets another result—it shows how discursive conflict occurs and is conducted. Sometimes a whispered text is drowned out by a loudly declaimed one. Sometimes a matter-of-fact text is subverted by a mischievous one. Sometimes four or five texts read at similar volumes vie with each other to be heard, and none are. If you did this with poems, you could create simulacras of literary history.

. . .

Helen has moved out, taken an apartment, and I have put our house up for sale. I've been working on the *Weeds* sequence—there are now around twenty sections.

. . .

Gladys writes, as she said she would when I saw her in Vancouver. She sends me a long typewritten letter that she had written three years ago while I was in Los Angeles—about *The Scarred Hull*, which I'd sent her in manuscript—but which she didn't mail. There she had repeated her caustic observation that I had portrayed my relationship with Helen superficially—"Why back away," she had written. "Does marriage do that to people?" She had somehow caught on to how, with Helen, I had tried to repeat my father's story of marrying and protecting a vulnerable "little girl."

> She knows you think she is [weak] and continues to be that way with you. Or is it a habit? After all that's how it all started, didn't it, she told you her problems and you didn't tell her yours. And later you were expected to play the role of the strong bright young man who could apparently accomplish anything you wish.
>   And this is what annoys me about what is happening now. Everything comes too easy for you: money, grants, cars, jobs, publications, even degrees have become a habit. You slide through on your intelligence and ability and don't distinguish any more between who you actually are and what your image of you is. For instance that crap you wrote about creative writing courses [she is referring to my "How to Use a University" article that I'd written for Alan Bevan's *Evidence*, and which I'd also sent to her in manuscript] is simply a riding on a person-image-name and certainly doesn't hold by itself. You could say so much yet you ask so little of yourself.

"Still true," she adds now in ink in the margin. And then in type she adds a postscript:

I think several of the things I said three years ago still hold. I do care about you. I do get jealous (my remarks re Helen) (my snipes about yr sliding through which I can't, by nature, do) (sliding through in terms of university only, the publication thing doesn't make me angry, but there were times that your constant writing and my constant not writing made me jealous). I think I should place less blame on Helen and more on yr relationship to poetry which seems to me to be screwed up partially by yr relationship to her (for example missing the Vancouver conference was simply stupidity on your part).

She goes on to advise that I be cautious about recommitting myself to a woman and outgrow my "adolescent view" of them. It's a pretty astute letter except for one thing—my sliding through. That's mostly a self-created image too. Ever since I was in elementary school and discovered that the other children loathed young guys who worked for grades, I've been pretending that I can't help but succeed. But I'm not going to admit it.

. . .

Margaret Atwood is in town, and giving an evening reading from *The Circle Game* at Ivy's. It's the first time I've met her. Partway through the evening the phone rings, stopping the reading. Ivy apologizes for not having disconnected it. It's Helen, calling me. She says she has taken an overdose of tranquilizers. It's now my turn to apologize, *sotto voce*, to Atwood, who is very gracious and says she "understands." Gladys would indeed understand the whole drama—but I still have to play it out. I dash around the corner to a pay phone and call Helen's professor friend and his wife, who I think might have a key to her apartment. He does, and we meet there. She opens the door and is seemingly normal, but there is an empty pill bottle on the kitchen counter. "I flushed them down the toilet," she claims. We take her under protest to the Jubilee Hospital where they pump her stomach—whether they need to or not.

It's too late to return to Atwood's reading. I go home—Helen's friend can wait for her.

. . .

There's a card from Daphne reminding me of a reading by Duncan in Vancouver this coming weekend.

. . .

One morning at Roads, Roger announces that he has won a doctoral fellowship to study linguistics at Cambridge. He's already got a line on a rustic little cottage in the countryside nearby. Roger tends to find such things. Gerald and Geoff and I congratulate him. I comment that Linda must be looking forward to spending the next year in such interesting surroundings. Is she going to do an undergrad year there? Roger says she's "not going." He'll probably be there several years. He doesn't want to disrupt her life. It's much what he said when he first came here from Vancouver. He imagines that she will continue her studies at UVic.

March 1969 . . .

I get a phone call at home from Howard Fink at Sir George Williams. He's chair of a committee that wants me to come and be writer-in-residence there for the coming year. He says they will want me to be sure to spend time at the university, perhaps by teaching an upper-level writing class—Mordecai Richler is writer-in-res currently and is hardly ever there. Sounds amazingly good to me. Gladys would say almost too fortuitous. Sliding through. When Helen hears the news, she is even more depressed. She has always wanted to go back to Montreal.

. . .

Rowland Smith from the ACUTE organizing committee writes that my Cohen-Dylan paper is "first reserve" for a session at the Learneds. I'm not optimistic, but he thinks there's a good chance that they will need to move it onto the program.

. . .

I host a party—it'll be the last one in this house. It'll use up the sake. I invite everybody I know—the young people from downtown, Helen and her UVic friends, the younger officers and faculty and their wives from Roads. I make a four-hour reel-to-reel tape from Beatles and Creedence Clearwater Revival and Rolling Stones LPs. There are people all over the house including the bedrooms, the rec room and the basement garage. Around midnight I encounter Linda and ask her what her plans are for the next year. Not a good move. Roger hasn't told her about his fellowship or admission to Cambridge. I'm stunned, but also impressed by the calm resolve with which she goes off to confront him. He dislikes public displays of unhappiness and retreats to the driveway. Shortly after she returns for their coats and they leave.

April 1969 . . .

Daphne writes that her baby is due this coming week. She apologizes for not telling me that Allen Ginsberg and bpNichol were both in Vancouver last month to give readings. I think that she may have forgotten because I missed the Duncan reading. I've been so busy that I haven't yet told her that I'm heading to Montreal.

. . .

I've sold the house—on my own, without an agent—and will move out at the end of the month to one of the vacant PMQS. I only technically qualify—still barely being "married"—but the college is content with the arrangement since it's only for two months at most.

I've got *OL* 9 published, with another art-nouveau cover by Dennis James. It's got a complex letter from Larry Eigner who is responding to both #8 and Daphne's new book from Black Sparrow, *leaf leaf/s*. George, who has claimed to believe that her book is about hockey, has sent in a useful essay, "Serving or Filling Orders." It seems to implicitly comment on David's book *Where the Orders Are*. Two strong poems from him too, and another from Daphne.

. . .

I've telephoned Linda a couple of times. She's forgiven me for being the bearer of awkward news. She tells me that Roger gave her an even bigger surprise when he left Vancouver to teach at Roads. He hadn't told her about the job or about having bought the lakeside house. The first she knew about them was from a note she found on their kitchen table when she came home from work, a few hours after he had left for Victoria. She also tells me that Helen has hired her to do some of the field research that she needs to complete for one of her courses. I think of Glady's letter. . . .

. . .

I've finished my paper on Pratt for Gerald—I was surprised by all the emphasis on group solidarity in Pratt, which seemed admirable to this member of the *Tish* group—except that the ultimate groups seem often to be employees of capitalist ventures—the CPR, seal-hunting companies, steamship lines—and that this collective spirit not only helps build the wealth of oligarchs but extends the humanist exploitation of the planet. "E.J. Pratt: Apostle of Corporate Man," I title the paper. A *Tish* reading of Pratt. It's also an elaborate extension of my short essay in the last *Open Letter*, "More Heat on Daedalus." But few people will notice that, because those who know Pratt will seldom read contemporary arguments about poetics and ideology and those who read poetics will rarely have read any Pratt. The strange insularities of Canadian Lit. When I present the paper to the conference, Gerald responds warmly. He likes it because it offers plausible readings of the poems and an arguable position. He wants me to send it to Woodcock at *Canadian Literature*. He also wants me to bring Helen to a dinner party he is holding next month for his departing department members. He says that I "must" bring her, that Geoff and Sondra and Roger and Linda will be the other guests. Gerald likes order and symmetry— and may be hoping to do a little marriage mending too.

May 1969 . . .

First of the month—Rowland Smith from ACUTE calls—he catches me as I'm moving furniture into the PMQ townhouse. He wants to know whether I would come to Toronto next month—the tenth— and present my paper on Dylan and Cohen. He apologizes for the late notice, but one of the previously accepted papers has been withdrawn. I think quickly—I'm pretty footloose these days, and have to drive to Montreal anyway to begin the Sir George Williams gig. Sure, I say. I'll just leave a little earlier and stop at the Learneds on the way. He seems surprised as well as pleased. What luck. Gladys would be rolling her eyes.

. . .

Gerald's party is at the end of the week. He and his wife and law-student daughter Monika live in the old groundskeeper's house, near the college gates. It's a formal dinner, everything very correct. I've driven in to Victoria and collected Helen in the TR4. Roger and Linda have come in her big Mark VII rather than the E-type. Throughout the meal we are all very polite with each other, and have an enjoyable time. As we are rising from the table after a round of liqueurs, however, Linda impishly changes the mood. "What are we going to do next?" she asks "How about the all-night triple horror at the Tillicum Outdoor?" Geoff and Sondra excuse themselves, they have to get back to their babysitter. Roger exclaims that he hates horror movies. Linda probably knew that. Helen suggests that we all go back to her apartment and bake brownies. A few minutes later Linda and I are in her Mark VII heading off to the Tillicum, and Roger is getting ready to drive Helen in my TR4 to her apartment. Gerald and Janka are standing anxiously in their entrance hall.

. . .

There's another postcard from Daphne. Her son Christopher was born May third. Would I like to visit.

June 1969 . . .

I stay in Victoria for the college's Farewell Barbecue, an annual first-week-of-June event for the administration and faculty. About a third of the officers every year have new postings. Roger will soon be off to Cambridge. The next morning Linda and I drive off in the TR4 toward Toronto and Montreal—we know that they are somewhere to the east. The night of the seventh we have got as far as Winnipeg, and over a baked ham, pineapple and white wine dinner notice that Ontario is much wider than we had expected, and that we still have about fourteen hundred miles to go. Linda does more than half of the driving—aggressively, cheerfully making the TR move like a Jag. We roll into Toronto around 7:00 p.m. on the ninth.

. . .

At the Learneds on the new York University campus, there's George, and Victor Coleman, and James Reaney and Wynne Francis and Al Purdy and bunches of other people I know only as names in magazines. Reaney wants to publish my Cohen-Dylan paper in *Alphabet*—I guess it didn't sound like my typewriter wrote it. George and Victor want us to visit the Coach House Press. Tonight Oxford University

Press is throwing a house party down in the Annex somewhere, and everyone is welcome. We go to Coach House. We go to the party. One of the people we meet is Gary Geddes who is editing a series of monographs for Copp Clark. He brings Al over because Al has just backed out of writing the one on Earle Birney. Not my kind of thing, says Al. Gary and Al want me to take the book over. You can come down to Ameliasburgh and I'll give you my notes, says Al—from the interview I did. Linda says, "Sure, do it"—I think she wants to see Al and Eurithe's A-frame. She's already calling him "Al" and teasing him about his cigar. George says, "Do it Frank, I'm doing the one on Al." I don't want to be a critic, I'm going to be poet-in-residence, but I say yes.

. . .

Linda has had her period since our first leaving Victoria, but that hasn't slowed us down. Our last night in Toronto she tells me she is going to throw away her birth-control pills. She wants to make an irrevocable break from Roger. To make sure he divorces her. The day before the Farewell Barbecue we had gone to a lawyer and giddily made steamy depositions about the good times we'd been having together, when first, how often. Now she's laughing and undressing and saying I dare you.

We spend a couple of nights camping, and then head to Ameliasburgh. Al is in his Malbec period. He buys gallon jugs of Algerian Malbec wine in Montreal or Salaberry and brings them back to Ameliasburgh. He shows us a single bed up a ladder in the loft of the A-frame. Big enough for lovers, he jokes. He shows us a photo he says he got Eurithe to take of him looking at Angela sitting with her drawers down in their outhouse. Linda tells him she thinks George took it. We are impressed with his library. Walls of books from floor to ceiling. Not just poetry but history books, philosophy books. Behind that cigar he may be a lot more intellectual than he lets on. He gives me the tape he made of his interview with Birney—but it's more a chat than an interview.

August 1969 . . .

I give a reading at Sir George—all of the new series "Weeds" and several parts of my new tarot series. I've been getting settled at Sir

George—getting used to having to walk a city block to the library. George is apparently writing a tarot series too—he started it last month. We've been meeting more of the Sir George faculty. We've been up to Howard and Marty Fink's cottage in the Laurentians, where Linda cuts her left foot

Writer-in-Residence.

on their wharf and gets to practise her French at the nearby emergency ward. And to Clark Blaise and Bharati Mukherjee's house.

. . .

We're also spending a lot of time at George and Angela's long narrow apartment—it has a front door that opens onto a long hardwood corridor, with a series of six or seven rooms along the right wall. George has set up a hockey net at the far end of the hall, and with a hockey stick practises stickhandling their two chihuahuas down the hardwood and into the net. We exchange Beatles records and make party tapes from them.

. . .

Roger arrives, with a young woman from Ottawa in her Jaguar E-type coupe. Has he been drinking? Linda immediately insists that they stay over in our guest room. It's an awkward visit for them, particularly when he learns that Linda is pregnant. Afterward she feels a bit sorry for the young woman. Just a bit.

September 1969 . . .

We figure out that George has been having a fairly serious romance with the department's beautiful young blonde Swiss receptionist, Evelyn. But it doesn't seem to affect the Bowering household all that much. The repartee is a little more smart-ass sarcastic but there are still parties, visitors come and go, the chihuahuas, Frank and Small, keep landing in the net.

. . .

Daphne writes from Madison, Wisconsin, where she says she's living in an isolated rural house. Al's job at UBC didn't work out, and now he's at this university. Gladys and her husband, Cliff, are here too. Cliff has a Woodrow Wilson fellowship in economics; Glady has a Canada Council Arts "B" grant.

October 1969 . . .

Birney comes to give a reading at Sir George, and stays with Linda and me for a few extra days so that I can interview him for the book I've agreed to write.

November 1969 . . .

Victor Coleman visits the Bowerings, and then Glady does, travelling from Madison. George insists that they read my new "Weeds" manuscript. Glady says that she's amazed, that it's the best writing I've done. On the seventh Ginsberg reads at Sir George. Afterward a bunch of us go to dinner with him. Howard Fink, who is looking after the arrangements, sends Linda and me with Ginsberg in a taxi to the restaurant. He and Linda sit in the back, and I sit in the front beside the driver. Ginsberg is fascinated with Linda's slightly swollen belly, and rubs it gently as if it might be magical. He decides he must sing some of Blake's *Songs of Innocence and Experience* to

Part of the score of Ginsberg's Blake songs, from *Tish E*, April 1969.

our child—he's recently set them to music, and published the settings in *Tish*. The taxi driver, who has been accelerating to seventy mph between each red light, keeps casting worried looks into his rear-view mirror.

· · ·

I have a reading to give at the University of PEI in Charlottetown. Because of Linda's pregnancy, and the three-month wait to get a civil marriage in Quebec, we inquire about getting married there. The clerk says they would need an island property owner to post a $500 bond. Why, Linda asks—in case we frighten the cows?

November 20 . . .

Linda and I decide to slip down to Plattsburgh across the border in New York where there are no impediments to marriage. With the licence we receive a huge newlyweds' hamper—worth several times the cost of the licence and the gas to drive down. We go to the nearby farm of a part-time Justice of the Peace for the ceremony. He calls to his wife as he greets us—"Would you iron my shirt, honey?" Linda thinks it must be his marrying shirt—he's still in his barn clothes. There's a nervous young man here too, waiting to contest a speeding ticket. The JP thinks he's our witness, and only figures out after he's married us that the young guy hadn't intended to be. It's like we're all inside a projective poem. When we get back that night to Montreal, at Linda's suggestion we celebrate all this with lobster chow mein at a Chinese restaurant on Monkland Ave. PEI lobster.

. . .

The Christmas break is approaching. Evelyn bakes a large batch of hash brownies and hands them out to department members from her receptionist's desk—the desk that everyone has to pass on their way to their offices. There is a lot of bewildered and wondrous laughter in the classrooms that day.

December 1969 . . .

As the winter weather has set in, Angela has been dressing and behaving oddly in public. She's wearing only black—not hippie black, more the black of widows' weeds, and rarely smiling or speaking. Marty Fink thinks she's gone into a version of mourning.

. . .

George's new book, *The Gangs of Kosmos*, is out. The strongest poem in it, "The House," about being a routinely devoted husband, seems to be set in his Montreal apartment. A Charley Pachter sketch of Margaret Atwood takes up most of the front cover—how'd that happen? Is that because it's an Anansi book? Or is she one of the gang members? I ask George. This east is mysterious.

. . .

Daphne writes. Glady has told her about my "Weeds" poems and about Linda's pregnancy.

January 1970 . . .

Charles Olson has died. I had never really "connected" with Olson personally—which I am regretting right now. It was the Olson of the 1950s and very early '60s I had learned most from—the Olson of *Mayan Letters*, "Projective Verse," "Human Universe," *The Maximus Poems* I, II and III, *A Bibliography on America for Ed Dorn*. By the time I met him in 1963 he seemed already spacey and impulsive.

He was extending the materially grounded early Maximus books—
those Duncan had said had to be based on "a real occurrence"—
into the speculatively spiritual books IV, V and VI. He was unwisely
chasing younger women who visibly did not want to be chased.
Giving overly long readings that deterioriated into barely compre-
hensible monologues.

February 1970 . . .

Creeley is at Sir George to give a reading. Afterward a bunch of
us go to a pub with him. After a few beers he tells me I should take
more risks. I hope he means in poems. This is the first literary criticism he's given me and I am pissed off and a little bit in agreement.
Maybe it's a short version of what Daphne and Glady have been—
more circumspectly—advising. Or maybe it's what Olson was doing.

. . .

I've applied for a Canadian literature job that's been advertised at
York. It would be complicated to go back to Roads and dispiriting
to return to the cultural claustrophobia of Victoria. Also, Coach
House wants to publish *Weeds*. It seems odd to be applying for a
CanLit job, but then why not, there are hardly any Canadian lit-
erature Ph.D.s around. Meanwhile Warren has written to Robert
Jordan, the new UBC English head, advising him to hire me, even
though there is no advertised job.

. . .

Angela may be having an affair with Stanley Fish, we hear, who is a
visiting prof here. Surprised by sin, Marty giggles. George has been
making fun of her—couldn't you find someone intelligent? he's
been exclaiming. George has finished his tarot poems, and prints
a fifteen-copy "preview edition" and binds it in the kind of folder
students use for handing in essays. The title is *Genève*—which most

readers will think is because he used the Geneva tarot deck, but Linda and I know that it's also because Evelyn is from Geneva. Angela seems to be adding an additional layer of black veils to her widows' weeds. This is a much more serious and complex book than *Gangs of Kosmos* with all its short magazine poems.

. . .

We go to a party at a large Westmount house—it's for the visit of either Atwood or Purdy, who are both here and have been warily sparring. There is a brick of hash as large as a pound of butter in the middle of the table of canapes. F.R. Scott is here too. After four years he is still in a glowering rage at not winning the Governor General's Award for Poetry for his 1966 *Selected Poems*. "I may never have another chance. They gave it to that slip of a girl," he exclaims, gesturing toward Atwood, who is in the adjoining room.

March 1970 . . .

Our son Michael is born. Linda went into labour in the middle of the night but didn't tell me until we were having breakfast. She says the contractions are too far apart for any concern. She phones Angela with the news. That afternoon we spend visiting her and George—with a new baby Linda thinks she will be too busy to visit anyone next week. We go back home and have dinner, and drive to the hospital—Montreal General—around eight o'clock. Linda feels it still may be too early so she brings a deck of cards. We play gin rummy until well after midnight when the nurse tells her she has dilated sufficiently to go to the delivery room. Michael arrives around 2:00 a.m.

I have an adventure when I go to register his birth. There is only one small civil registry office in Montreal, and the non-English-speaking clerk and I are the only ones there. He has difficulty hearing my British-Columbia/Parisian French. *"Vous pourriez passer par l'église,"* he says. But I am very cheerful. I pass by churches every day.

. . .

Daphne seems to feel artistically isolated in Madison. Glady and Cliff are about to leave. I've sent her a *Montreal Star* "spread on Tish" in which George and I are both interviewed. She writes that our comments tell her "how gone all that is. Irrrecoverable." She says that "the most interesting . . . thing . . . about that time was the web of ideas acted on, taken frm so many sources & seen always thru our own limitations (do you remember the hours spent on the essay on Projective Verse?) or particular visions." I'm guessing that she is being diplomatic—that what she probably thinks is that George and I, in our confident assertions to John Richmond, the *Star*'s journalist-interviewer, were revealing that we have mostly abandoned the *Tish* days' "web of ideas" and awareness of "our own limitations." But when I reply I pretend not to have noticed.

. . .

George has won a Governor General's Award for *Gangs of Kosmos* and *Rocky Mountain Foot*. That was a surprise—until I realize Warren was on the jury. George will write better books—has already written better books—but Warren may not be on the jury again. Warren knows how hard it is to win these awards without friends on the jury. Gwendolyn MacEwen has also won.

. . .

York asks to interview me for the job they've posted. Linda and I and our two-week-old son drive to Toronto. She wants to come in case we have to house-hunt. The interview is much like at Royal Roads—a brief discussion in the chair's office, and I am offered the position. We spend the next two days with a real estate agent, often dropping in to whatever vacant house he has access to so Linda can nurse Michael. I suspect that Eli Mandel may have had something to do with my hiring. With York already loaded with poets—besides

Mandel, Irving Layton, Miriam Waddington and Don Coles also teach there—this is unlikely to be a routine job. We also stop by at Coach House. Victor suggests we print some birth announcements, so I provide a small poem. He sets the type on a Linotype machine. The newly cast letters come rattling down, and he prints them on a Vandercook proof press. "The" Vandercook, he says.

April 1970 . . .

Robin Mathews at Carleton has been writing letters of complaint to newspapers and weekly magazines about George's G-G. I've been too busy to pay them much attention. He thinks Milton Acorn should have received it, and that Warren's being on the jury made the process unfair. Also the fact that Warren is still an American. Well, lots of poets should have received it, I think. Jury composition is always unfair—except to the winners.

May 1970 . . .

All leases in Montreal end on April thirtieth. We have to leave our apartment. But we don't have access to our house in Toronto until July first. Bob and Leslie Hogg who live in a small house in Ottawa's "green belt" have offered to rent it to us for those months—they are going be in the U.S. We send most of our stuff to Toronto to be stored, and haul the rest in a U-Haul trailer behind our TR. Linda immediately hates the little house and the clouds of mosquitoes that hover outside. In the mornings I work on poems for my tarot series and in the afternoons read stuff by Earle Birney. In the evenings I go down to the basement and kill mosquitoes.

. . .

I have to rent a suit so we can go to George's G-G Award presentation. I wonder whether Mathews will picket the Rideau Hall gates. He's been stirring up other poets including Layton and Mandel to raise funds to give Acorn a "people's poet" medal. He's been calling George a disloyal Canadian and Warren and *Tish* examples of American "anarchist-individualism." I find all this amusing—experienced poets taking a historically corrupt award so seriously. If Layton or Mandel or Mathews had been on the G-G jury, obviously their good friend Milton would have won. We don't have a babysitter to come to Bob and Leslie's isolated house, so Linda takes Michael along with us to the ceremony and dinner in a car bed, which she puts on an antique table in the dining room. He sleeps throughout the evening, and attracts more attention than George or Gwendolyn. At the ceremony Linda browses the tables for caviar, jesting about how all these uncultured bohemians, like George, Ange and Gwen, are spurning it. At the dinner she expects to get my serving of Atlantic salmon, which I still don't care for after all these years, but I have drunk so much that I eat it and enjoy it. She swears that in revenge she will bake me more every week. I kind of hope she will.

July 1970 . . .

In Toronto, I make the first of many visits to the Coach House Press. Nelson Adams, a lapsed scholar of Greek, has hand-set the text for *Weeds* and Stan Bevington has found some old engravings of various plants that could be printed beneath the text. He experiments with a number of combinations of inks and papers. I want the plants to be almost subliminal, environmental, so that a reader isn't distracted by their particularity. Linda likes Nelson's wry humour, and has agreed to study Greek with him. She was shocked last week to learn that I had never read all the way through *The Odyssey*. You're looking owl-eyed, I say. More salmon for you, she replies.

. . .

I'm working hard on the Birney book, but puzzled about what to say about his recent visual poems. I've never been much interested in such things. I recall bpNichol's indignant defence of the form in *Open Letter*, and so get his phone number from Stan and give him a call. He suggests we meet for lunch at a café on College Street. He's a friendly shambling guy. I learn enough from him over lunch that I'll at least have a vocabulary for talking about Birney's "concrete" stuff, and maybe even for distinguishing among them.

. . .

September 1970 . . .

Weeds is published at Coach House, and my *Four Myths for Sam Perry* by Talonbooks. Overall I like the *Weeds* sequence much better than the poems in *Four Myths*, although for me there are magic passages in each. I hope other people see them. And I have a third book out this month: *Five Readings of Olson's Maximus*, that George has published in his Beaver-Kosmos series.

. . .

At York I am teaching an American poetry course, a creative-writing course, and team-teaching a Canadian-literature survey.

. . .

Daphne sends a small stuffed elephant for our Michael, along with a note. She's back in Madison after spending the summer in Vancouver helping her parents, who were in a serious car accident. While there she managed to finish a new book, "Vancouver Poems," which Coach House is going to publish. I've suggested that I may try to restart *OL* as a mag of letters and theory—she doesn't approve—"you encourage people to make all kinds of statements and counter-statements that lead to theoretical wrangles which ultimately are removed from the WORK and draw energy off from where it shd be employed." She adds, "I don't know why I feel so strongly abt the *OL* thing, about separating statements on poetics from poems not poetics poems. Suspicious of that theoretical area in a perhaps totally superstitious way. But it does seem to me that when people start writing about how they write it's because they're temporarily 'bankrupt,' which makes their statements after the fact and therefore suspect. . . . Figure you'll go ahead and do what you want to do anyhow. & I'll read it too." Hmmm, Daphne knows me too well.

November 1970 . . .

Earle Birney drops by for dinner and to give me an opportunity to clear up some biographical details. Some of them, such as his abandoned doctoral program at Berkeley, trouble me because I have only his story, one in which he matter-of-factly blames almost everyone involved except himself. But there seems to be no publicly accessible documents against which I could double-check things. He doesn't want me to read his files of old letters and papers. I also have doubts about his vague narrating of his annulled first marriage to a teenage Trotskyist—randy Earle having a marriage annulled?

. . .

George has published *George, Vancouver* with Nelson Ball's Weed/ Flower Press. It's another longish poem or poem sequence, which again seems light years better than the short poems he keeps publishing with their cute closed-off endings.

December 1970 . . .

Victor Coleman is urging me to go ahead with relaunching *Open Letter*. He points out that the nine issues already published make *OL* eligible for substantial Canada Council funding. He makes me an offer: Coach House will be the publisher of the magazine, I will be editor, I will use the Canada Council grant to pay for the

printing and to pay contributors, Coach House will do the distribution and bookkeeping in exchange for all subscription revenue
and single-copy sales. Victor doesn't seem to be thinking of the old
OL—he's thinking more of a review journal that would be another
route to finding readers for Coach House titles. Makes sense. But
do I want to become a George Woodcock? Fred has resurfaced,
and has sent Victor a manuscript.

. . .

I've sent Copp Clark my Earle Birney manuscript. Linda has copy-
edited it, but the press's copy-editor has a lot of difficulties understanding my arguments. She would like me to use a Matthew Arnold
vocabulary. I wish I'd used one more like Olson's in *Call Me Ishmael*.
Linda, I've discovered, writes much more graceful prose than I
do—or the copy-editor.

January 1971 . . .

Despite what happened between me and Fred during the first series
of *OL*, I write to him inviting him to be an editor of the relaunch.
Lots has occurred since my last letter to him in '66. "The content
we now project is 60% book reviews, 30% articles, letters, and 10%
poetry. We hope to do things like run 3 reviews of the same book
simultaneously accompanied by a selection of the author's recent
work. We plan to expand to 60 pages, publish 3 times a year, and
seek subscriptions. The Coach House will do the printing (wch
gives us 150 standing orders) with Victor doing design, typography,
& distribution."

February 1971 . . .

George writes that he received "a letter from Daphne yesterday,
unusually long letter for her—she seems happier after leaving her
hubby—along with a poem series about Columbus and D's son."

The poem will be in *Imago* 16. I'd heard something about Daphne being back in Vancouver.

March 1971 . . .

I get a Canada Council travel grant to research the 1904 sinking in the Strait of Juan de Fuca of the American steamship *Clallam*. At Coach House George's *Genève* is being printed. Stan lays the dust jacket out on the upstairs table—he has "secretly" printed on the inside of it all the tarot cards used by George in the order in which George encountered them, where they will be hidden by a double fold. He and artist/cameraman Rick/Simon grin like kids who are pulling a prank. Somewhere else in the book, as in most Coach House titles, there will likely be a minuscule beaver, detectable only under a magnifying glass, with the motto "Printed in Canada by mindless acid freaks."

. . .

bpNichol wins a Governor General's Award for Poetry, sharing the award with Michael Ondaatje's *The Collected Works of Billy the Kid*. bp wins mostly on the basis of visual poems: the sequence *Still Water*, the anthology *The Concrete Chef* and the short text sequence *The true eventual story of Billy the Kid*. Well, visual poems are still not what I understand as poetry for myself, but I like bp. It was probably Warren Tallman's presence on the committee for another year, however, that secured his award. Like George, bp will likely do much better writing later. At least Warren didn't create another scandal by holding out for my *Weeds* and *Four Myths for Sam Perry*, which must have also been in the running. I'll write even better books in the future too.

June 1971

Linda and I and baby Michael fly to Vancouver where we purchase a Datsun sedan and avoid Toronto's higher prices. Linda is pregnant again, and the TR will no longer suffice. We visit her parents in Vancouver—it's the first time I've met them. They only heard about me when Linda called them from Winnipeg in '69 to tell them she'd left Roger and was heading with me to Montreal. We make a brief visit to Abbotsford, which causes my parents to quarrel, and then to abjectly apologize. I spend some time with David Robinson at Talonbooks, which is preparing to publish a new serial poem I've written, *King of Swords*. David is enthusiastic about the book, and about my *Clallam* project. We also visit George and Angela. George has a Canada Council Senior Arts grant, and leave from Sir George, and has come to Vancouver to spend a year writing in familiar surroundings. He jokes, rather seriously, that he didn't use the grant to go to the Greek islands. They are living at the York Street Commune, where Stan Persky is operating New Star Books. Stan would like to publish a selected poems for me. Sounds good to me. Angela is also pregnant, but not as far along as Linda.

. . .

We take the ferry over to Victoria where Roger, who is back from Cambridge but away for the summer, has generously made that lakefront house available to us. As usual, it is impeccably tidy, like a museum. Linda tells me that Roger has always wanted his houses to be like this, and got angry if she left even a hairpin in view to indicate her presence. Even in their bedroom.

But in that bedroom is a surprise. Roger has placed their wedding picture prominently on the night table, making us feel particularly amused and mischievous to be making love in his bed. Linda seems to really get off on it. I doubt that's what Roger had in mind when he put the picture there. Later she says that she might like to sleep with him on their twenty-fifth anniversary—just for laughs, she says. The idea makes her excited all over again.

. . .

I spend a leisurely time in the newspaper archives reading several months' coverage of the *Clallam*'s distress, sinking, the rescue efforts and subsequent inquiry. There was a coroner's inquest, the records of which should be in the provincial archives. They are, still in the court stenographer's impressive nineteenth-century handwriting. In the afternoons while Michael is sleeping, we sometimes take Roger's small sailboat out onto the lake. We drive to some familiar places in Victoria and twice accidentally encounter people we knew at Roads. We also visit Helen, who abandoned her doctoral program shortly after we left and resumed teaching. She seems fine. While we are there our old cat, Smudge, brings in a pheasant.

. . .

When we leave to go back to Vancouver, Linda launders the bed linens. We don't want to give Roger a thrill just yet, she says. From Vancouver the transcontinental train takes us and the Datsun home.

July 1971 . . .

There's a letter from the Canada Council waiting for me—they have awarded me a grant to resume *Open Letter.*

August 1971 . . .

Linda and I have a daughter. We name her Sara Genève. Toronto hospitals are more progressive than those in Montreal, and so I get to watch the birth. Amazingly, baby Sara also watches, her eyes open and focused as she emerges. The obstetrician—who happens to be Lester Pearson's son-in-law—notices and is surprised—he raises a shiney scalpel and moves it from side to side to see if her eyes track it—they do. She doesn't cry, which worries Linda, and so he pokes her foot with a needle and Sara gives a small yelp. "Will that do?" he asks.

I go down to Coach House and borrow the Linotype machine and the Vandercook and literally crank out birth announcements. George writes back quickly—"Does this mean I have to name my kid 'Weeds'?"

September 1971 . . .

I've got George, Fred, Victor, David and Stan Persky on board as "contributing editors" of the revived *OL*. Also Ted Whittaker, who did such a great job for *OL* while I was in LA. I'd have liked to have included Daphne, but she was so emphatically against the idea last September. As she predicted, I'm going ahead and doing what I want to do anyhow. My plan is to take advantage of the new circumstances, the printing expertise at Coach House, the close links between Coach House and the writers in Vancouver. I'm thinking of Olson's field poetics—the first series of *OL*s responded to my isolation in Victoria, this one will respond to what's possible to do in Toronto.

. . .

There are changes too at York. Barbara Godard and Bill Gairdner have been hired, both newly arrived from France where Bill was doing a study year after a Ph.D. at Stanford, and Barbara was completing a doctorate on Québécois fiction, at Bordeaux. Bill has been hired to teach literary criticism and theory—his field seems to be French structuralism. Barbara has studied with Lucien Goldmann and Roland Barthes, and taught at Paris-Vincennes with Hélène Cixous. Both are going to be part of the team in which I teach the Canadian literature survey—we'll be sharing the lecture hours.

. . .

George has published a volume of selected poems, *Touch*, with McClelland and Stewart. I am disappointed that he has gone to a commercial press and associated his work with the mixed "ragbag" of writing that M&S publishes. I had always thought of *Tish* as an end run around establishment CanLit publishing and its careerist ideologies and "star-poet" promotions. From the outside George's book looks like anyone else's M&S selected poems—no news here. There's a few strong poems in an open poetic—"The Descent," "Baseball." Most of the rest are the forgettable one-pagers that get you into magazines and anthologies. I worry that people will forget the open-field poetics and politics that *Tish* stood for. I didn't want George to be just another occasionally perceptive poet alongside D.G. Jones, Newlove, Avison, Souster, Layton, Acorn, Purdy. I wanted his writing to stand for something. I worry that instead he will appear safe and normalized, and the rest of us be forgotten as freaks. Hmmm, I seem to be worrying about George like Daphne and Glady worry for me. What a group. But I don't tell George. I just hope he feels guilty.

October 1971 . . .

I've written almost all of *The Clallam*. I've been working at it slowly since getting back to Toronto, but during two evenings last week I kept having more and more passages come to me, and I would have to leap out of bed and run down to the dining room to write them down. The second night that happened four or five times. George would call this "dictation." I think the poem's very good, maybe even better than *Weeds* and *King of Swords*. It owes a lot to what I've learned from reading Jack Spicer—but again, few Canadian readers will be able to notice.

. . .

George has been in town to give readings, and has been staying with us. bp has been around several times to see George, also Victor and David McFadden. George and bp are trying to persuade Linda to act as their writer's agent, the way Eurithe does for Al Purdy. Al has printed a letterhead in her maiden name, writes letters on it referring to himself in the third person and has Eurithe sign them.

That's how he gets so many readings, George says. You could be my agent, and David's, and Frank's, and Victor's he says to Linda. Linda

finally agrees, but insists that she'll write her own letters. She rents a box at the nearby postal station, and has Stan Bevington print an elegant letterhead and matching envelopes: Linda McCartney, Writer's Agent. I wonder what Robin Mathews would think of that.

Bowering and McFadden select an agent.

November–December 1971 . . .

My Birney book is out, and Earle hates it. My own worry has been that it over-praises his work. But I guess I knew no amount of praise could please him. That's why I was so careful to keep him from seeing the book—or even wanting to see it—before it was printed. He's been sending me vicious and insulting letters—the kind I've sometimes been good at writing—but I'm trying to restrain myself when I write my replies. Somebody may someday see them. He's also threatening to sue—over what, I'm not sure. Friends tell me that he has done this to other people, including Gwen MacEwen, sometimes sending them spurious letters from imaginary lawyers on fake legal letterhead that he's had specially printed, in case he needs it. Everyone's printing imaginary letterhead. I make sure I keep copies of the replies I'm sending him. But I like some of the reviews—particularly those that say that I have used *Tish* poetics to read Birney's poetry. I have. It's something George didn't do in his book on Purdy.

January 1972 . . .

I've got the first new *OL* published. This second series will have nine issues, just like the first did. I want to underline that this is not just another library-friendly literary journal like *Tamarack* or *Cana-*

dian Literature. The issue has a "letter"—on poetry and Marxism—
from Stan Persky. It has an essay connecting it to *Tish*—the "Before
Tish" chapter from the "Oral History of Vancouver" project—a
project that is one of the new radical ventures in Vancouver, and
with which Daphne is also involved. The Persky and an essay by
Vancouver poet George Stanley announce a left-of-centre viewpoint, which readers may not have recognized in *Tish, Open Letter*
or Coach House previously. I contribute a short note on *Genève*—
the kind of poetry writing I wish George would restrict himself to.
And there are reviews of other books most of us want attended to.
Glady reviews Greer's *The Female Eunuch*. Les Mundwiler reviews
Ehrmann's book on structuralism. Victor Coleman reviews books
by Daphne, Gerry Gilbert, David Rosenberg and Brian Fawcett.

. . .

Daphne responds to the *OL* copy I've sent her. It's the first I've
heard from her since she returned to Vancouver. She offers to write
something on Anaïs Nin for the new *OL*. She talks about some of
the old events in Vancouver, but recalls the "Projective Verse" party
as being in March '61—the month we stopped seeing each other,
and a month after my Valentine's Day sonnet.

February 1972 . . .

Quite a surprise. Clara Thomas has asked me to have lunch with
her and Dave Godfrey. She has been writing a guidebook to Canadian literature for New Press, to be titled "Our Nature, Our Voices."
Dave is a co-owner of the press and its literature editor. Clara's
book was projected as a lavish two-volume set, roughly divided
between the canonical and the contemporary, with numerous
photos designed to seduce readers into loving both Canada and
its writing. She has some photos with her, mostly ones that she's
obtained from the National Archives. However, Clara has become
uneasy about undertaking the second volume. The new writing is

so different, she says, from the Ralph Connor to Margaret Laurence works she grew up with, that she is concerned that she may accidentally misrepresent it, or leave out writers who turn out later to have been hugely important. She thinks that I should write the second volume.

Clara's book is openly a celebratory nationalist venture. Dave has been a very public nationalist—a co-founder of both House of Anansi and New Press, author of the short story collection *Death Goes Better with Coca-Cola* and co-author last year with economist Mel Watkins of a New Press book urging a national reclaiming of the Canadian economy, *Gordon to Watkins to You*. Have they got the right Frank Davey?—the Frank Davey who has wanted to be neither a fervent nationalist nor a quiet scholar-critic? In the *Tish* office the latter was Bill New's role—and we didn't publish him.

Dave however is looking a long way forward. He's already aware of computerization, and in touch with Stan at Coach House about the computer-driven laser-typesetting that Stan has been experimenting with. He sees the writing that Clara has difficulty with, and much of that which emanated from *Tish*, as part of a new "networked" array of national utterances, ones that are already coming as strongly from areas outside of Toronto and Montreal as they have been from within. He thinks of many of us as Scottish crofters living uneasily on the margins of a downtown Toronto hegemony. As I talk with them, I also become almost unbearably aware that I am not just here for myself. I am here for those people in Warren's living room in 1961—and especially for Daphne, Fred, George, David, Lionel, even bill bissett and Gerry Gilbert. I'm here for Victor and David McFadden and Clark Blaise and bpNichol. If I don't agree to take this book on, most of these writers may be left out of it.

. . .

I've written a short serial poem based on the seventeenth-century disappearance of the first European ship on the upper Great Lakes, La Salle's *Griffon*. I'm trying to see if I can write history/geography poems in Ontario much like I did in BC. Works for me. But it won't fit into any book I can imagine publishing soon. That's a potential problem when one tends to compose books rather than poems. So I decide to invent my own press and print, bind and publish it myself—so I can at least give it away to my friends. I choose the local Massassauga rattlesnake for the logo—making an obscure connection to the first Tishbook and Rattlesnake Press. I get leftover cover paper from Stan. I copy the design that Nelson Ball used for bp's *True Eventual Story of Billy the Kid.* Massassauga Editions will operate out of Linda's post-office box. The Coutts Library Service in Niagara Falls picks the little book up and manages to distribute about fifty copies.

March 1972 . . .

John Glassco has won this year's Governor General's poetry award. With Tallman off the committee, it has returned to rewarding endurance rather than accomplishment. In the letters to the editor of the *Globe* and the *Star* there are no complaints.

. . .

Stan Persky has sent me a copy of *L'An trentiesme,* my new selected poems, 1961–70. The title is a wry double allusion which probably only one or two readers will get. It comes from Pound's sardonic self-portrayal in the opening passage of "Hugh Selwyn Mauberley," "He passed from men's memory in *l'an trentuniesme / De son eage"*— itself an adaptation of François Villon's fifteenth-century aggressive lament that he was forgotten by his thirtieth year. Pound follows that line with the equally sardonic "the case presents / No adjunct to the muses' diadem." It has the usual New Star proletarian design—typewriter copy offset printed on eight-and-a-half by eleven paper.

. . .

Barbara Godard has been very interested by the new *Open Letter*. She thinks that it should connect with the younger writers in Quebec who are also doing innovative and edgy things. She shows me copies of *La Barre du jour* and *Les Herbes rouge*. She says both communities might benefit. She offers to translate some recently published manifestoes by Jacques Brault, Paul Chamberland, Raoul Duguay and Michèle Lalonde, and obtain clearance to publish them. Barbara's been a welcome colleague. She's a compulsive talker, which has meant that I have learned much more from her than some days I thought I had the patience to learn. Because of her I've read various books I might not have looked at—Bachelard's *The Poetics of Space*, Barthes' *Writing Degree Zero* and *Elements of Semiology*, Poulet's *The Interior Distance*.

May 1972 . . .

Bob Kroetsch has invited me to give a reading in Binghamton. I have to fly all the way to Newark and catch a plane that goes back northward to Binghamton. Bob and Robert Spanos are just getting their postmodernism journal *Boundary 2* off the ground. The first issue, with five of my poems, is scheduled for the fall. Bob's marriage is breaking up. He can't use his house, he says. He drives up to it, gets what he needs, leaving me in the car. We grab dinner in a diner and then begin a driving tour of six or seven local bars. All of the bartenders greet him by name.

June 1972 . . .

My *King of Swords* has been published by Talon. It's another fabulous production—a little book that looks like a deck of cards, with each part of this serial poem on its own page.

. . .

I've started work on my follow-up to Clara's *Our Nature, Our Voices*. With its encyclopedic structure, it's not a difficult book to work on while also doing other things. But New Press is apparently going out of business. Dave Godfrey assures me that he will have his own publishing house in place very soon and be able to take over my contract. But he would still want to publish in September 1974. That doesn't leave a lot of time to get it written and get a Humanities Research Council publishing subvention.

July 1972 . . .

We go to a book-launch garden party at Coach House. Among the new books are Fred's *Among*, bp's *The Martyrology 1 & 2* and Matt Cohen's *Too Bad Galahad*. bp and Matt are both there. It's the first time we've met Matt. Both Linda and I like him immediately. He's nervous and witty and feeling a little out of his element. He doesn't think of himself as a radical or experimental writer. *Korsoniloff*—his first novel—was weird, he says, because he didn't know what he was doing.

. . .

Victor and I have got another *OL* published. Warren has contributed an essay on Olson. bp has contributed one on Gertrude Stein. There's a curious fumetti collectively constructed by Victor, David Young and General Idea. And forty pages of reviews, including Daphne, as promised, reviewing books by Anaïs Nin, George reviewing bp's *Monotones* and Victor reviewing George's newly published *Autobiology* and Bromige's *Threads*. The typesetting is a peculiar process, however. The book is punched into humanly unreadable inch-wide paper tapes, which drive a laser typesetting machine to produce proofs. The tapes are then corrected on a computer from my proofreading instructions. It's a difficult process to have confidence in. Not at all like Letraset.

August 1972 . . .

Daphne writes me about *Griffon*. She says she likes it but is "drawn tho' to closer up kinds of testimony," and then adds "I always have envied your mastery of the satirical edge, distancing tho' it is." She encloses another review for *OL*.

September 1972 . . .

I've got most of this contemporary CanLit survey book done. It's going to mesh unevenly with Clara's book. She wrote on Earle Birney and Miriam Waddington but not Dorothy Livesay or P.K. Page, on Layton but not on Souster or Dudek, on Pratt and Purdy but not Ralph Gustafson, on Richler but not Adele Wiseman or Henry Kreisel, on Laurence but not Munro. So while my subtitle will be Canadian literature since 1960, it's either going to have a lot of curious exclusions and inclusions, or perhaps a lot of overlap with Clara's. Dave is concerned that the coverage issue, which wasn't important to the Humanities Council for Clara's book because a second volume was planned, will now become doubly important to it with mine.

. . .

I ask George whether he has a short manuscript that Massassauga could publish. He sends me the manuscript that will become *The Sensible*.

October 1972 . . .

The new work of *Open Letter* continues. The third issue again links back to *Tish*, with Sister Beverley Mitchell's article "The Genealogy of *Tish*." And thanks to Barbara, it moves for the first time toward francophone Quebec, with her translations of the Brault, Chamberland and Duguay manifestoes. I review Godfrey and Rotstein's newly published *Read Canadian*, and suggest an even more aggressive aesthetic nationalism that would censure Richler for writing "Angry Young Man" novels, Pratt for invoking the heroes of British naval history in *Behind the Log*, the *Dalhousie Review* for trying to resemble *Kenyon Review*, and generations of Canadian poets for being "horizontally" rather than "vertically" influenced— for not seeming to read or allude to the Canadian generations before them. There are also reviews of new books by Purdy, Rosenblatt, Hogg, Coleman, Jacques Ferron and Gaston Bachelard; the reviewers include Bowering, Nichol, Marlatt, Hogg, Godard and Gwendolyn McEwen. I have begun thinking of *OL* as a virtual community, as a site much like the "mail art" image-exchange network that Toronto's General Idea and Vancouver's Western Front gallery have been supporting.

I'm dissatisfied with the editorial board, however. Persky, Dawson and Whittaker have done very little contributing. I think the latter two are probably out of most literary loops, and Persky too engaged with his own publishing efforts in Vancouver. I'm considering asking bp to join in—he's often seemed as much concerned about the mag as I am.

February 1973 . . .

The manuscript that is called "Our Nature, Our Voices, Part 2" is now with Dave Godfrey and on its way for Humanities Council consideration. And my manuscript of *The Clallam* is with David Robinson at Talonbooks. We are already talking about design, and how to make the best use of a faded 1904 newspaper photograph of the unhappy ship.

March 1973 . . .

I'm off to Coach House to pick up copies of *OL* 2:4—the first one with the revised editorial board. The reviews aren't all that interesting, but there are articles by George, Michèle Lalonde, Margaret

Atwood and Matt Cohen—an all-star cast. There's a curious piece on translation by "TRG"—bpNichol and Steve McCaffery's "Toronto Research Group"—and there are two sections from George's new project of poems on contemporary poets—poems in which he responds to each poet as if the poet were one of the tarot cards of *Genève*. I contribute an essay on Gwendolyn MacEwen. And there's a section of photographs of pages from Greg Curnoe's rubber-stamped "Blue Book." It's a knockout issue and I only begin to see that as I carry a dozen copies home. I remember Alan Dawe handing me one of those early issues of *Tamarack*.

April 1973 . . .

Matt Cohen gives me a draft of a new realist novel to read. It's the biggest text he's written. He's thinking of calling it "The Disinherited." Matt has often been stopping by our little bungalow on Elm Road, just a few blocks from Avenue Road and the 401. His marriage to Susan, who still lives on their farm near Trenton, seems troubled. He has a room or rooms in Toronto, but drives to the farm most weekends. On Sunday evenings he will arrive and sometimes sit on our sofa for several hours without speaking more than a couple of words. Decompressing, perhaps. Sometimes he has talked about this novel, which is set near Trenton. It will likely be published by M&S before my new book on CanLit, so I am hoping to squeeze in some discussion of it.

June 1973 . . .

The first Humanities Council reader's report has arrived. It recommends publication, but begins—to my amusement—"I don't know that I would have picked Frank Davey to write a guidebook to contemporary Canadian literature." I don't think I would either. The writer would like to have Northrop Frye and David Helwig added to the book, and Wilfred Watson, saying that "if it came to a choice between a writer like Wilfred Watson, who is out, and Daphne

Marlatt, who is in, I'd say take Watson." Dave barters successfully
with the council by offering to include Frye plus enlarge the list in
the introduction of those who were considered but not included.
I enjoy writing about Frye—I've recently served on a literary jury
with him and found him extremely open. He and I agreed on a
grant to that weirdo Matt Cohen.

. . .

Arcana is now out from Coach House. It's another attractive production, with occult signs printed under the black text in a light
gold. I wanted them to be as subtle and "occulted" as the tarot deck
was behind the *Genève* dust jacket. Both Daphne and David Dawson are said to have been unhappy with the way the images the press
printed behind their texts last year made the poems difficult to
read. Beatrice Warde—she of the "crystal goblet"—would not have
been impressed either. I like this book, and its poems—it's the culmination of my writer-in-residency at Sir George.

July 1973 . . .

It seems Linda and I and the kids spend a lot of time driving together
out to Erin, where Dave's new Press Porcépic is located, and "Uncle
Dave's" farm. With the change in publisher, it's been easy to talk
Dave into a new title for the book—"From There to Here" (with a
nod to Dr. Seuss). "There" can be a bunch of things—Clara's book,
modernism, the *Tamarack Review*s of 1957, commercial publishing's
domination of literary legitimacy. Instead of the romantic photos of
Clara's book, Dave and I agree on documentary ones—photos of
books and magazines that I've collected, plus a few author photos.
But for the first time in quite a while I don't have a new poem series
under way.

September 1973

I've decided to apply for a leave fellowship for next year. York offers a fifty-percent-salaried sabbatical leave after four years' employment, and the Canada Council can grant an academic fellowship that doesn't exceed the other fifty percent. That would pay the mortgage. But I'd have to promise to carry out a scholarly research project. I'd like to apply for a Canada Council arts grant to do more writing, but those grants can't be combined with a sabbatical. I also suspect that my odds of getting one are a lot lower than of getting an academic one. The arts grants go to old guys like Birney and Purdy, and if not go to the G-G lottery winners. I've suggested to Gary Geddes that I could do a Copp Clark monograph on Louis Dudek. He says he'd prefer a combined one on Dudek and Souster, so that's the project I'm proposing to the council. But what I'm doing makes me think back to Glady's anger at my missing the 1963 poetry seminars. Would she think I am "screwing up" my relationship again to poetry?

. . .

Margaret Atwood's second novel, *Surfacing*, has been published. I don't usually read novels eagerly, but the publicity around its launch draws me to it. Almost immediately I'm noticing that she appears to have used George and Angela as models for the narrator's quarrelsome companions David and Anna—George's self-parodying bravado, Ange's amusingly compulsive self-concern. I thought they were all friends. Although she's used no identifiable facts—just mannerisms and speech habits. While having an epiphany in the novel's last pages—where else?—the narrator calls the George character "second-rate, selfish." I'm glad Atwood's not my friend.

. . .

George's new Coach House poetry book is *Curious*. It's that suite of project poems on poets—a poem each, in similar rhythms, on forty-eight contemporary poets, along with twenty-seven photos. The photo of Atwood shows her in the Bowering guest bedroom. On the cover is a 1970 photo of George in a strutting, semi-heroic pose, with Margaret Atwood, in front of her childhood house. Angela is the photographer. Atwood has struck the identical pose, of self-parodying bravado.

October 1973 . . .

Talon has published *The Clallam*. But no one in Toronto is likely to notice—because Anansi has published a criticism book by Atwood—*Survival*. There are big front-page reviews in the Toronto weekend papers. Some combine it with a reprise of *Surfacing*. This is bad news. The book could be deadly—deadly to the decentralization and pluralization of Canadian literature that I thought I was helping bring about. Central Canada strikes back. It's also a book that ignores process and the influence of changing material conditions: Atwood's thesis is a timeless structuralism—Ontario/Quebec literary archetypes of the early nineteenth century that reappear again and again, she argues, in later "Canadian" writing up to the present. Along with a strong implication that they ought to keep reappearing, if new writers want to be non-victimized and "Canadian." It's also a shameless promotion of House of Anansi Press books—themselves mostly central Canadian. Forty-two percent of the book's "recommended" reading—but that's a lesser problem. Is Atwood being malevolent? Probably not. She's merely grown up inside an Ontario-privileging Canada, and likely believes everything she's written. I quickly write an account of it for the next *Open Letter*—which unfortunately is already featuring a small contribution by Atwood.

November 1973 . . .

We get *Open Letter* 2:5 ready. bp creates a satirical cartoon about *Survival*, to accompany my review article. It's another intriguing issue, but again amid the *Survival* hysteria I wonder if anyone will notice. There's a TRG report on narrative, a discussion among Irving Layton, Hugh Hood and Bowering, articles by David McFadden and Fielding Dawson, a section of "letters" from Phyllis Webb to Atwood and reviews of new books by Matt Cohen, Jack Kerouac, Hugh Kenner, Wilfred Watson, Souster and Ondaatje. I should also have thought of republishing George's "Margaret Atwood" from *Curious*—the poem that begins "Peggy has. / I am led to believe I haven't."

January 1974 . . .

I've been granted the Canada Council Leave fellowship to write the Dudek–Souster book. It'll be another risky one. So much easier to write about dead people. But not the kind of risk Creeley was thinking of. Or Glady.

. . .

George has published another collection of magazine verse with McClelland and Stewart—*In the Flesh*. But it's mostly old stuff. From Talonbooks has come his *At War with the U.S.*, dedicated to me. Sure glad the dedication was in it, and not the M&S one. It's a serial poem on the Vietnam War mostly moved forward by wounds and bruises and dreams of death in Vancouver, with many of the bumps and bruises those of his little daughter Thea. Almost all of his recent writing, like *Autobiology* and *Curious*, has been serial work like this, informed not by unrelated occasions but by projects of inquiry, interconnecting events, linguistic constraints.

February 1974 . . .

Barbara comes to me with a request. She's helping organize the first conference of the new Association of Canadian and Quebec Literatures, here in Toronto at the Learneds. She'd like me to give a paper in a session she's putting together on literary criticism. There'll be a big audience, she says. I agree to. I haven't given a paper at the Learneds since that Cohen/Dylan paper in 1969. But if I don't try to offer a perspective that can contextualize Atwood's book, and include the kinds of writing she has shunned, who will?

. . .

Linda has been talking to Atwood. She says that "Peggy" has read my review of *Survival* and thinks that I have "evil-stepmother female-Hitler fantasies" about her. I laugh. So she does believe everything she wrote there.

March 1974 . . .

I hear that *The Clallam* is on the shortlist for the Governor General's Award. Maybe it's *The Clallam* and *Arcana*? There's no official list, and there's a lot of good books this year including George's *Curious*, Eli Mandel's *Crusoe* and Mike Ondaatje's *Rat Jelly*, so I don't lose sleep over whether a win might make me feel pleased or embarrassed. The winner, however, is something of a puzzle. It's Miriam Mandel's *Lions at her Face*, published, people say, as an encouragement to her by Wilfred and Sheila Watson through their White Pelican Press. Miriam has suffered from chronic depression. Sheila Watson is known to be on one or more of the G-G awards committees. Maybe the poetry jurors wanted to please her. Again I don't see any letters of protest in the papers.

April 1974 . . .

Linda has arranged a seven-day, seven-city reading tour for me—Winnipeg, Saskatoon, Regina, Moose Jaw, Calgary, Edmonton and Vancouver. I travel by car through the Qu'appelle Valley from Saskatoon to Regina, by bus to Moose Jaw and Calgary. Each reading is in a library except for in Vancouver, where it's at the Western Front gallery. The Western Front's building is the old east-end Knights of Pythias lodge hall where my father was once "chancellor commander." The gallery has preserved much of the original decor and furnishings of the KP hall. "KP"—my dad's name for the lodge. I give my reading from the lectern from which he once chancellor-commanded.

. . .

I stay a few extra days with George and Angela—it's the first I've seen their large newly purchased Kerrisdale house. It's only three doors or so east on Thirty-seventh Avenue from Warren's house, but much bigger. Very 1920s arts-and-craftsy. As usual I talk more with Angela than I do with George. She tells me that they've been seeing a lot of Fred. He's been suffering severely from agoraphobia, she says, and has been driving two hundred miles or so to Vancouver from Castlegar every couple of weeks for help. For Ange it's a dramatic story, the kind she loves to be privy to and able to indiscreetly tell. He's been driving down regularly even in the recent winter's snows. I'm surprised. Fred has always seemed so matter-of-fact and confident— "together." "Let's start a magazine." What ambitious self-productions we can be. Ange and I reflect, somewhat bemusedly, on Fred's recent poetry books about the pleasures of being rooted in the "nutrient rock" and "creek song" of the Kootenays—*Lardeau, Mountain, Among, Tree, Earth*—books I had read or reread for my Wah discussion in "From There to Here." There's evidently been more at play here than *Tish* poetic theory or Olson's theories of "locus" or advice to Ed Dorn. But I also think back to Fred's cryptic letters from Albuquerque and his silence when in Buffalo, and wonder how painfully unfamiliar those places may have seemed to him. How much of his disappointment in the poems I wrote when first in Victoria was a reflection of his own locus struggles?

May 1974 . . .

At the ACQL meetings I present the paper I have written for Barbara: "Surviving the Paraphrase: Thematic Criticism and its Alternatives." The amphitheatre at U of T is packed. Instead of focusing on Atwood and *Survival*, I link her book to Frye and D.G.Jones. I use most of my time to expose the overgeneralizations in Jones's *Butterfly on Rock*. I note that Atwood and Jones were both Frye's students, but I restrain myself from mentioning that a few years ago they were romantically involved. Just as well—I see Doug and his current wife, Monique, in the audience as I leave, not looking very happy. Miriam Waddington speaks to me from an aisle seat as I pass—"That's good, you don't like structuralism," she says. I also don't like hegemonic nationalisms, and other ideologies that disdain or fear poetics.

June 1974 . . .

Linda and I have been making even more frequent trips to Erin to consult with Dave and his printer, Tim Inkster, about "From There to Here." So many books have been published this past year by the authors I've discussed that at least a third of the entries have had to be updated. I've been collecting more book and magazine covers, and author photos, to use as visuals. The camerawork for these is being done by artist Rick/Simon at Coach House, and shipped up to Erin.

This is probably the biggest printing project Tim has attempted with his own equipment. He's a young poet and a printing protégé of Stan Bevington's. Dave had previously purchased printing equipment similar to that at Coach House and set Tim and his wife, Elke, up as the Press Porcépic printer—"Porcupine's Quill"—in Erin. So far all they seem to have produced is a few elegant hardcover poetry books—Eli Mandel's *Stoney Plain*, Joe Rosenblatt's *Bumblebee Dithyramb* and a book by Tim. I like Tim, but don't see a lot to like yet in his writing.

July 1974 . . .

bp and I are working on a Sheila Watson issue of *OL*—which at 180 pages or more could be the largest *OL* yet. It's mainly bp's idea. He wants *OL* to map "our" connections to Canadian literature by publishing issues that collect obscure work by older writers and artists whom "we" think important because of the priority they gave to matters of language and form. By "we" and "our" he is thinking of an enlarged but rather vague *Tish* community—the older and younger *Tish* generations, the writers who are publishing in *grOnk* and *Iron*, the emerging sound and visual poets, the poets around Coach House. It's another "let's-shift-the-canon" idea. He thinks we should do issues on Warren Tallman and Louis Dudek too. But Sheila, although happy to have the issue assembled, has been very diffident about helping. Some of the material exists only in manuscripts in her possession, but she's reluctant to look for them. Her U of Alberta colleague Doug Barbour, fortunately, has been helping out—going to her house and getting her to open old trunks filled with papers. They've found an unpublished short story from the 1950s—"The Rumble Seat." There could be more. Sheila's not sure.

August 1974 . . .

Victor has resigned as editor of Coach House. He thinks Stan's project to computerize typesetting there—"to fake the past," as Stan puts it—is wrong. That it will be a financial sinkhole and kill the press. bp tells me that Stan hopes his other Toronto authors will be willing to step in and replace Victor with an editorial board. Beep thinks that Victor is totally mistaken about the computer project, but he and I are also worried about the political ramifications. We're not sure what Victor has hoped to achieve—Stan's capitulation? He's insinuated pretty strongly that he'll feel betrayed if any of us bail Stan out.

September 1974 . . .

We now have an editor's board at Coach House—bp, Mike Ondaatje, David Young, Dennis Reid, Linda, me and Martin Kinch—although Martin's not sure how much he can contribute. We're looking for manuscripts for next year. Barbara is suggesting that I bring the press some translations of leading-edge writing from Quebec— that she could help me. Victor's now working in small art galleries— which keeps him away from most of us.

. . .

From There to Here has been published, along with numerous advertisements for it in *Quill & Quire, Books in Canada, Canadian Forum, Tamarack Review*. There are reviews, but no full-page photos or reviews of me in the *Star* or the *Globe* as there were of Atwood. Guess I'm just not photogenic. The reviews most often compare my book to Clara's. "Davey's work is by far the more penetrating and intellectual," writes Dolores Donnelly, the reviewer for the *Bibliographic Society of Canada*. "Poet, critic, academic, and editor— Frank Davey has been, and still is, all of these. . . . His purpose . . . is 'to redress the tendency in recent Canadian criticism toward exclusively thematic interpretation'. In this he succeeds well." I'm pleased she put "poet" first.

"Frank Davey's *From There to Here* . . . is a remarkable improvement on Clara Thomas's first volume . . . the most exciting critical work to come out of English Canada since Atwood's *Survival*," writes the reviewer in the *English Quarterly*. "In many ways it is an answer to *Survival*." "*From There to Here* is the most valuable Canadian critical book to appear in ten years," writes *It Needs to be Said*'s reviewer. "It is for those . . . for whom Margaret Atwood's *Survival* is not enough" says the *Montreal Gazette*. "The best short survey of a comprehensive kind we have had of contemporary Canadian writing," writes George Woodcock in a *Canadian Literature* editorial. Dear George. The comparisons to Clara's book are flattering

but unfair—the two books are emphatically different: hers a celebration of the known and mine mostly an introduction to the
unknown. I prefer the comparisons to *Survival.*

NINE EVER-AFTERWORDS

1. A Toast

An okay spot to stop. "Here." It's best to succeed—or be seen to
succeed—at something. Even if not by a Nobel committee. Even if
not always by Daphne or Glady. I have a photo of myself holding

the reins of a one- or two-ton Shire
horse somewhere in Wales. I did it
well, mainly because of a well-trained
horse. A moment later my Linda, who
once rode quarter horses, wandered
out of the Elizabethan farmhouse's
breakfast room and freaked—like
Jamie Reaney did when he saw the
poems that my typewriter seemed
to have written. The wise horse re-
mained calm. Robin Mathews's thoughts about *From There to Here*
came a couple of years later.

Neither Mathews nor Margaret Atwood ever reviewed *From
There to Here,* although in Box 92 of the Atwood papers at the
Thomas Fisher Rare Book Library there is apparently a five-page
typed draft of a 1973 letter addressed to *Open Letter* "protesting
the bias in Frank Davey's review of *Survival.*" My County Durham
grandmother would have muttered something about the pot calling the kettle black. I presume that draft was never turned into a
letter and mailed. Atwood included two of my poems in her *New
Oxford Anthology of Canadian Poetry* and granted whatever permis-
sions were needed for my 1984 book *Margaret Atwood: A Feminist
Poetics.* In 1982 I wrote a three-page "commendation" of Atwood

for a Welsh Arts Council's award booklet—the council was giving her its International Writers Prize—and included non-evaluative summaries of both *Surfacing* and *Survival.* She didn't put a letter into the mail to me about those either. In 1990 in a New Delhi university bar, she, Graeme Gibson and I had a polite evening together with three or four other people who were attending a Shastri Indo-Canadian Institute anniversary conference. It was like the early part of Gerald Morgan's dinner.

2. God bless 'em, everyone

A lot of people helped bring about that insignificant moment in the New Delhi bar—and the publishing of *From There to Here*, and my going from *Tish* editor to being an editor of Coach House Press. From there to here. During my time in Victoria two of them were probably George Woodcock and Gerald Morgan—Woodcock by invisibly sending me to Charley Morriss and publishing several of my papers, and Gerald by badgering me to write papers for his two conferences and to send one of them to ACUTE, setting off a chain of events in which I travelled to Toronto, encountered Gary Geddes and a contract for a Birney book and became perceived as a "specialist" in Canadian literature. Gerald also contributed unwittingly by delivering Linda and me to each other—Linda who would be my best editor and in time my best lawyer, as well as often my best friend. George [Bowering] helped then and later, not only by persisting in the "unpleasant" exchanges of *Open Letter* but also playing a part, I'm sure, in my being invited as writer-in-residence to Sir George—thus rescuing me from claustrophobic Victoria. And creating the possibility for me to be his editor now and then at Coach House. Warren kept playing an intermittent role—he had a lot of writers he wanted to urge forward. But he kept returning to my life and the lives of my *Tish* companions—with his "Poet in Progress" article in *Canadian Literature,* his alert involvement with *Boundary 2* and the "Wonder Merchants" essay, and in 1979 when he would lament in his essay "Four Ways of Looking at the Canada Council

Literary Section" that he "has pointed out how repeatedly West Coast writers who since 1970 have begun publishing works we consider worthy of consideration for the Governor-General's Award have been passed over. Certainly bill bissett's *sailor* (1978); Frank Davey's *King of Swords* (1972) and *The Clallam* (1973); Gerry Gilbert's *From Next Spring* (1977); Daphne Marlatt's *Steveston* (1974), *Steveston Revisited* (1975), and *Zocalo* (1977); and Fred Wah's *Pictograms from the Interior of BC* (1975) are such culminating volumes . . ." (*In the Midst* 125). Many writers. And the "culmination" of writing largely begun in *Tish*.

All those essays are generous gestures—especially the one in which he sees Frank containing all of *Tish*'s possibilities "in what he has become, hang a sign around his neck, reading, 'this is the

Seizer considers becoming a *Tish* editor.

way *Tish* went'" ("Poets" 206). Blush. However, Warren's preoccupation with the G-Gs—and his collaboration with them—still perplexes me. He knew very well that true poets don't write for prizes, or even for applause. Duncan once wrote that to applaud poetry was like applauding a priest for performing a Mass. "There is no such thing as a first-rate priest, and, . . . I would maintain that there is no such thing as a first-rate poet." Neither poetry nor priestly performance is a competition, except perhaps with oneself. Applause and prizes invite corruption, which in turn subverts the sincerity of the applause and the value of the prize. At dog shows, people who own inferior dogs bring large numbers of friends to the shows to applaud them. Wrote Duncan, "In hell the damnd [sic] clap continuously against the silence in which they fear there is no god" ("Notes" 12–13). With enough applause a dog might make archbishop. The G-Gs won have to an extent cheapened the *Tish* group by normalizing it, by linking its work to the banality and careerism of that of many of the other winners—those dogs that can't "win" without applause—or Duncan's "damnd." The G-Gs and similar awards are also major parts of Central Canada's homogenizing CanLit project—the project in which Atwood and Mathews had remarkably similar essentialist positions. Did Warren want us to be players in that game?

*

Barbara Godard was also a huge help, leading me to read more and more French critical theory, in both English translation and in French, to read Canadian writing for "difference" and to read and learn from Nicole Brossard. And leading me to tip Daphne off about Nicole sometime around 1976, eliciting an earnest reply that Nicole's work was the polar opposite in its language theories to her own. Maybe it was.

There's a lot of close calls here. What if's. If I hadn't wanted to pursue Daphne in 1960 and thrown the "Projective Verse" party. If Duncan hadn't agreed to travel by bus. If my roommate Bill hadn't seen the dark freight train ahead on the highway. If my Ford hadn't skidded past that eighteen-wheeler blocking the highway in the snow south of Bellingham. If I'd declined to write those conference papers for Gerald. If Helen hadn't publicly teased me about Linda at that Christmas ball, god bless her. If Sir George Williams hadn't offered me the writer-in-residency. If Gerald hadn't tried to play peacemaker. If Warren hadn't helped George win that G-G and thus unknowingly goaded Mathews into publicizing the whole bunch of us—hey, there *can* be something good about a G-G (besides the money)! If Victor hadn't been such a principled Luddite. Glady's right that I have been almost unforgiveably lucky. To have had her advice too.

3. The *Tish* PR Guy

I had forgotten about Robin Mathews by 1976—I thought perhaps he'd abandoned literary things after helping make Milton Acorn the best-known loser in CanLit. Another kingly title. Although he was actually a double loser—the award of course had been made not to Bowering alone but jointly to him and Acorn's ex-wife, Gwen MacEwen. She must also have had a friend on the panel. For Milton to lose to her may have been at least as painful as losing to George. But Mathews, Layton and Mandel had rarely mentioned that.

I didn't immediately read Paul Cappon's anthology *In Our Own House* when it came out in 1976, nor Mathews's 1978 book *Canadian Literature: Surrender or Revolution*, in which he implies that the *Tish* writers are pro-American "annexationists." But I did read Diane Bessai and David Jackel's 1978 Festschrift for Sheila Watson, *Figures in a Ground*, which contains a short essay and artwork by my celebrated cousin, the painter Norman Yates. And there right beside Norman's essay was a strangely titled Mathews essay, "The Wacousta Factor." And what was this "Wacousta factor"? Hmmm, part of it was supposed to be me. I was being alleged by Mathews to have argued in *From There to Here* that the sadistic and sexually obsessed "individualist anarchist" title character of John Richardson's 1832 novel *Wacousta* was "the main factor in the Canadian poetic imagination" (Bessai 297, 310). Wacousta?—not once mentioned in *From There to Here*. "Factor"? —maybe Mathews's unconscious, overstimulated by Richardson's lurid narrative, was recalling that old sexist joke about the 1950s cosmetics wars?—"What happened to Helena Rubenstein?" "Max Factor."

Mathews's various over-the-top responses to George's winning of the 1969 G-G were a huge boost to the *Tish* writers. Mathews kept writing about us, with such poor logic and bad prose that by contrast we looked better and better. A student he misled into joining the attack, Keith Richardson, wrote and argued almost as badly. In a sense they had left the high moral ground unoccupied. All any of us had to do to thrive was lower the temperature of the prose in which we responded. Or laugh. I wrote a for-me pretty cool introduction to C.H. Gervais's *Tish* collection, *The Writing Life*, in 1976. George created the Robin-spoofing character "Sparrow" for his novel *A Short Sad Book*, published in 1977, and the satiric essay "Brown Mountain" in 1979. I joined him in 1985 in my poetry

collection *The Louis Riel Organ and Piano Company*, with the poem "Wacouster," a send-up of that "Wacousta Factor" essay and its suggestion that I might be a second-coming of William Kirby's "individualist anarchist" villain. If he'd suggested that about Birney he might have been sued for implying rape and murder.

Mathews has never indicated whether he's read *A Short Sad Book* or "Wacouster." If he has, he probably hasn't understood them. In his 1995 *Treason of the Intellectuals* he commented on Bowering's "Brown Mountain," and read that satiric story about "kindly Americans" coming to BC in 1960 because they "wanted to see poetry get started in Canada" as serious narrative. Poetry was "already 200 years old" in Canada (*Treason* 86), Mathews indignantly expostulated. At another point in *Treason* he quoted Rosemary Sullivan's sardonic remark that in Pinochet's Chile "you knew who the targets were: extremists who somehow deserved it" as proof that Rosemary sympathized with Pinochet and other fascists (106). At another he translated Peter Dale Scott's recommendation that literature should be "more and more grounded in the problematics of global hegemony" as meaning, in less "fancy" language, that literature should be "more and more a part of the modern world in a U.S. imperial system" (174). At yet another he read my accounts in my *Post-National Arguments* of the regrettable spread of globalism in Canadian culture as constituting an endorsement of globalism (50–52).

Robin may not be fully literate, but he has been great for publicity and comic relief. I often see him at conferences, but he has no idea who I am. Once we were both waiting in line to register at a Quebec Learneds, and I had a solemn discussion with him about the sad state of Canadian criticism. He said he couldn't place me. Which of course is true. So I introduced myself as Ed Greengrass. "I know the name," he said.

His central argument in *Treason of the Intellectuals* is that the "blood and will" philosophy of Nazi Germany did not die with Hitler but was carried onward through the work of Heidegger to influence A.J.M. Smith, Northrop Frye, Jacques Derrida and, through Derrida, recent Canadian thinkers such as Linda Hutcheon, Robert Kroetsch, myself and ex-editor of the *Globe and Mail* William Thorsell. In a kind of unconscious reversal of Holocaust denial narrative, Mathews argues that Nazism, with its focus on "earth, blood, Will, and almost mystical bonds with social purpose" (68), has become the ruling ideology of North America and post-modernism. As with the other kind of Holocaust revisionist, it is difficult to tell whether Mathews is deliberately misrepresenting facts, or whether he has simply, in rage and resentment, ventured far out of his intellectual depth. He confuses postmodernism with post-structuralism, and sometimes equates it with pluralism; he ignores national differences among postmodernists and political disagreements among post-structuralists; he bizarrely believes that post-structuralists affirm—rather than deny—"a transcendent Real."

Robin still carries on his vendetta against George—now from a website, vivelecanada.ca. In a 2004 posting in which he attacks a Simon Fraser conference that honoured poet Robin Blaser, he writes that George "is a Canadian taken over by U.S. explanations of being." George is a "cult member"—the cult being those who wish to honour Blaser and "a group of young Canadians devoted to U.S. ideas and personalities and contemptuous of Canadian traditions"—presumably the later *Tish* and Kootenay School of Writing poets. He concludes with a long quotation from George's anti-Vietnam-War book, *At War with the U.S.*, a passage that he amusingly misreads as a pro-American confession:

> 1944 I loved
> the beautiful American army helmet
> Naked, shining, drab, olive green
> Or painted with wide white stripes, maybe MP
> . . .

Or lying alone on the island beach sand in *Life* magazine.

There's no more *Life* magazine.
But the American army helmet lying alone
On the jungle floor is beautiful.

Nevertheless, I have to confess that whenever I think of Mathews I don't do the phonetic trick to the word that created *Tish*.

4. "Mere Anarchy"

The title would have enraged Robin—maybe that's why bp liked it? Throughout the late '70s and '80s Barrie Nichol, aka bp, talked about co-editing a poetry anthology with me, one a bit like the one I had discussed with Daphne in 1968. It would collect poetry by the *Tish* writers and any other Canadian practitioners of "open" or serial poetics. He and I both despised the politics of Yeats's too-often-celebrated poem "The Second Coming"—"Turning and turning in the widening gyre / The falcon cannot hear the falconer; / Things fall apart; the centre cannot hold; / Mere anarchy is loosed upon the world. . . ." Why should the falcon hear—or obey—the falconer?—why should the centre hold? we would ask each other. Yeats's lines sounded to us like an apology for Mathews's or Atwood's monolithic conceptions of CanLit. Barrie was poetically introspective in these years—looking for interconnections between his early books and his *Martyrology*, and for ways to interrelate his visual, sound and text compositions, looking for ways to map his own relationships with what he saw as the multiple strands of Canadian poetry. Like me, he didn't believe in waiting for professional critics and anthologists to do this kind of work through academic presses or some "central" institution such as the Social Sciences and Humanities Research Council of Canada (sshrcc) or the Assistance to Scholarly Publishing (asp) program. We had got the Sheila Watson issue of *OL* published in early 1975—without the intrusion of referees and assessors. We had got Warren Tallman's essays gathered together in 1977, Dudek's uncollected essays in 1981 and Kroetsch's essays in 1983. Because almost all of these essays had been previously published, none of these collections qualified for the ASP funding that academic presses usually required. "Stuff that," said Barrie. To emphasize our views of literary genealogy, Barrie, George, Steve McCaffery and I interviewed Dudek and prefaced the volume with the result.

Consolidate alternativity—sounds like a paradox. A William Blake proverb. But right after *From There to Here* in 1974, I publish the collected *Tish 1–19* with Talonbooks in 1975. In 1976 C.H. Gervais and Black Moss Press in Windsor, Ontario, publishes *The Writing Life: Historical & Critical Views of the Tish Movement*—with Bobby Hogg and the back side of George on the front cover. 1977 brings our Warren Tallman *OL*. 1979 sees Coach House start on-demand printing—the editors are hoping to do the kind of end run around national anthologies that instant printing companies would later do through course packs. And in the same year the press publishes its first academic anthology, Mike Ondaatje's *The Long Poem Anthology*, and at my urging gets George Bowering to begin editing *The Contemporary Canadian Poem Anthology*, which it will publish in 1983 as an alternative to the increasingly conservative Geddes anthology. And *OL* as its spring 1979 issue publishes long interviews by Bowering with Daphne Marlatt, Audrey Thomas and FD. 1981 sees Talon publish volumes of selected poems by *Tish's* Bowering, Wah, Davey and Marlatt, plus bill bissett and bpNichol. In 1982 Bowering publishes with Oberon Press *A Way with Words*, a collection of his essays on Canadian poetry, and in 1983 I publish the essay collection *Surviving the Paraphrase* with Turnstone Press— by publishing these collections with literary presses, both of us are doing yet another end run around the ASP. Bowering dedicates his volume to me, and writes in his introduction that he is "not here trying to rile the scholastic tradesmen of that important nation bounded by Toronto, Montreal and Ottawa. . . . [M]y writing on poetry . . . is . . . a track of a kind of Canadian tradition." Rile away, George.

With George's contemporary poem anthology Coach House
again has to break the rules of the "centre"—plug our ears to that
pesky falconer. The Canada Council gives publishers a fixed amount
of subsidy per title, regardless of the number of pages. Bowering's
anthology is 374 pages. So we do a long press run, bind and release
part of that press run in four small volumes and collect a fourfold
subsidy. Then we bind the remaining pages into a single volume in
time for the Long-liners Conference on the Canadian long poem
that I get Eli Mandel and Ann Munton to help me organize at York
for May of 1984. bp writes his paper for the conference on index
cards and shuffles them into a random order before he reads. He is
still thinking about "Mere Anarchy."

5. Splat!

So all was not particularly "well" when I arrived in Victoria in 1963.
But then all is never entirely well—that's why one keeps working.
There were no readers for my writing there. I don't mean that the
Hudson's Bay customers weren't buying and reading my books—I
mean there was no one who could give me informed feedback about
them. And so what do you do?—you listen to Fred and start a magazine. I don't think I received much useful public feedback there
either, but at least I was in a conversation—one that had implications for what I was writing, even if I was the only one who could
see them. Maybe I was the only one who needed to see them. And
you write to Daphne. You write to Glady. You drive to San Francisco
and LA.

In fact none of the original *Tish* eds were particularly "well" in
the fall of 1963. The *Tish* diaspora was happening, some would
say—I hate the metaphorical ways in which people now use that
word—people who probably know squat about the actual thing.
It should be a reserved term—like "the Holocaust." But maybe
you have to have lived through the Second World War years to see
that. Anyway, David wasn't comfortable being the new leading
editor. Jamie was writing much less; both psychedelia and the

overdetermined politics of the 1960s were beckoning. As George, Fred and I moved into jobs and degree programs at distant universities, Jamie became increasingly disillusioned with the whole *Tish* project—with what he saw as our self-betraying careerism. Fred appeared virtually silenced in Albuquerque. He later told George that he missed the greenery and trees of the BC coast and the Kootenays—there and later in Buffalo. Sick for home—Ruth amid fields of alien corn (that's a double allusion, including one to a displacement that wasn't diasporic, but if you haven't studied the Old Testament in college you may not recognize it). I didn't begin to see again the adventurous Fred I had known in the *Tish* days until he published *Pictograms from the Interior of B.C.* with Talonbooks in 1975. Welcome back, I thought. I think part of the problem for both Fred and me was the huge importance of place—*locus*—in *Tish* poetics—the understanding that a writer works within an environmental context, with that "work" informed and qualified—and thus partly written—by the historic cultural social and personal environmental forces that he or she lives "among." In a new place you are a changed person.

In Calgary George was working harder and more successfully than both Fred and I to understand his new "location"—and to remain plugged in to the old projects and network. Even as he is publishing all those cute short closed-off poems, anathema to *Tish* poetics, he is publishing *Imago*, a magazine of the long extended series, or serial poem. In her letters to me, Glady wasn't always convinced by the latter, sometimes seeing it merely as another George attempt to be hip. I heard some Vancouver writers call it "I'm a go." I once joked that George often seemed more interested in the "cereal poem"—a reference to one of George's "cute" poems in which one of Ange's really cute breasts accidentally dips into a bowl of milk-covered Cheerios—than the serial poem. But we were wrong. In the early 2000s after Angela died I could not teach his extended poem "Winter Solstice" without being on the edge of weeping. (Now I'm consciously avoiding an allusion to the quiet madman Irving Layton.) George didn't stay long in Calgary, or Lon-

don, or Montreal, and returned to Vancouver in 1971—"for good"—
or perhaps "for love."

The most insistent of us all on holding to the theoretical
grounds that our 1961–63 poetry newsletter had proclaimed were
not George or Fred or David or myself, but Gladys and Daphne. It
was they who kept urging a writing that was "in close," attentive
to the details of the ongoing moment, that avoided fashionable
rhetoric, that re-examined and questioned what had been written as
it was written, that was suspicious of comfortable or self-satisfying
pronouncements. It was they who questioned whether some life
decisions might be short-sighted betrayals of ideological commitments. Daphne has kept writing in close—her work overall is the
closest to what in those early years we could vaguely envision.
Gladys—Glady, who now prefers her middle name, Maria—has
written much less, possibly because the standards to which she holds
herself—and others—are so demanding.

But here in late 1975 where I've stopped my narrative we are, at
least in terms of productivity and audience, as close as we may get
to a golden age of *Tish*—or, as I would have exuberantly written in
1961, the age of the slippery golden *Tish*. That smudged newsletter
has now produced seven Coach House Press poets—Cull, Dawson,
Hogg, Wah and Marlatt as well as George and me. Wah has published three books since returning to the Kootenays, and Marlatt
also three, including the widely admired *Steveston*, since returning
to Vancouver. *Tish* hasn't exactly exploded the texts of Canadian
culture—the rearguard efforts of Anansi apologists Atwood and
Dennis Lee have seen to that—but it has inserted numbers of
problematizing and destabilizing lines. And it will write a few more,
including *SwiftCurrent*, the world's first online literary magazine.
Better however that it had seriously diminished the power of
Ontario-based commercial poetry anthologies such as the Geddes,
Bennett and Brown, and Newlove to protect the "official" Canadian poetry canon as a marketplace of individual career accomplishment. Fred and I thought in the late 1980s that we might accomplish
that with *SwiftCurrent*, by shifting much of the "legitimation"

process away from professional editors and toward curious readers. But it was clear that professionally ambitious writers themselves would resist—by declining to participate, by welcoming new prizes that increased the power of institutions and their jurors and by encouraging the founding of new institutions such as the Public Lending Right (PLR) and Access Copyright that valorized both commercialism and the official "book." Few of the early books of the *Tish* writers, or KSW (Kootenay School of Writing) writers, have sufficient pages to qualify as "books" under the new 1980s–90s rules of both the Canada Council and the PLR. But we all eventually learned to add epigraphs and blank space, and to count pages.

6. Ideology!

"Ideology, the word is out!", Barbara Godard begins the third part of her commentary on our 1984 Long-liners Conference on the Canadian Long Poem ("Epi(pro)logue" 307). She is referring to Eli Mandel's speculation toward the end of his keynote address to the conference that Terry Eagleton's assertion that literary questions are ideological may explain and support Mandel's own Bloomian view of literary history as "what really matters is the replacement of one establishment by another, sons eating fathers, who's in, who's out" ("Death" 22). Even George, the most ambitious of us Tishers to be "established" as well as "radical," would have been uneasy about a goal of merely replacing one establishment with another and reinstalling along with it another charade of "common-sense" objectivity and rectitude.

Ideology however was/is a loaded word—in common usage a pejorative—and it's indeed instructive how quickly Mandel moved in that keynote to defuse and normalize it by reducing it to the familiar shifts of fashion and generational power. Even in 2011 few of those with power and authority want to admit that their views, like yours and mine, are necessarily ideological—that there is no "outside" to being ideological. In *From There to Here* I had deliberately substituted "political" for "ideological" in making such declarations as "Every poem, film or novel carries in its form political implications. The tightly controlled, formalistic and elegant poem shares formal assumptions with a company directorship . . ." (14). My (ideological) arguments there were for viewing culture not as a field to be dominated but as "an environment in which no one element fully controls any other" (20). Robert Duncan's announced "end of masterworks" ("Ideas" 61) had meant for me also the end of masters, cultural centralization, canonical authority.

What *Tish* had worked for in 1961–63 had been alternativity such as Duncan's—to occupy space in a decentralized cultural field without necessarily displacing even the work we argued against or scorned. It turned out that we were the leading edge of numbers of alternative magazines and presses that were self-consciously ideological in various communal, regional, gender, racial or sexual-orientation ways. Legitimacy could be local. Poetry could be a process of construction even alongside poems that celebrated the genius of the imperial subject. Canons could be other than national and academic. "Tradition" was a context, not an obligation. The academy and industrial publishing were potential, but not necessarily necessary, partners. Sequence and history could be chance operations. But you had to intervene and take your lumps and chances.

7. "Loose" Ends

In the middle 1970s when I was coordinating the creative writing program at York, I hired Alice Munro to teach a writing course. She was no longer behind a cash register.

. . .

Evelyn Meyer, the beautiful blonde brownie-baking English-department receptionist at Sir George, returned to Europe and eventually obtained a doctorate in Tamil literature at the University of Heidelberg.

. . .

I later discovered that I had met "Binky" Marks, the Duthie's bookstore paperback manager who used to buy copies of *Tish* from me
and then give them away to interested young people, years before I
arrived at UBC. He was a founder and first manager of the Peoples
Cooperative Bookstore from which I had once bought those handsome Soviet editions of Pushkin, Turgenev and Chekov. He and the
store had also cheered up my mother by co-sponsoring that first
Paul Robeson cross-border concert in 1952 in Peace Arch Park.

. . .

My wife Linda became a lawyer in 1978, and did art law and other
work for various clients including Clark Blaise and Bharati Muk-
herjee, Matt Cohen, bpNichol, Phyllis Grosskurth, Mike Ondaatje,
Christopher Dewdney, Paul Quarrington and Robert Priest. She
wrote the chapter on copyright for Milrad and Agnew's *The Art
World*, and copy-edited the other chapters. She edited books by Paul
Quarrington, David McFadden, Andrew Birrell and Bowering at
Coach House.

. . .

Eli Mandel probably had nothing to do with my hiring by York in
1970. He had fled the English Department for the Humanities
Department a year or two earlier. Other faculty members there
told me that Clara Thomas had opposed my hiring, arguing that
I would return to BC as soon as there was an opportunity. A reasonable assumption. Now I live a few blocks from her in her old
Ontario hometown of Strathroy. She published a moving review
of my memoir *How Linda Died*.

. . .

George did not name his kid "Weeds."

. . .

The 1972 note from Daphne about my *Griffon*, saying that she was "drawn to closer up kinds of testimony," was the last from either her or Glady urging me to be less "controlled," more risk-taking, less ironic and superficial. To stop "sliding through." Maybe they gave up on me. Maybe they stopped reading. Maybe they stopped theorizing. Maybe they thought Linda was telling me. I am of course concealing my conflicted feelings here under a few parallel statements. You know what I mean.

. . .

Roger did complete his Ph.D. at Cambridge, and accepted a tenure-stream position in computer linguistics later that year at UBC. Within two years the job bored him, he resigned, bought a very large sailing yacht, and for a few years operated a charter service out of the British Virgin Islands. In the late 1970s he returned to Victoria and remarried. For one year he taught again at Roads. One summer, 1978 I think, he crewed as navigator on our navy's ancient 102-foot ketch HMCS *Oriole* (built 1921), helped overload it with cases of beer and a grand piano and then guided it through unexpected storms to victory in the semi-annual Victoria–Maui race. He visited Linda and me only one more time, in the early 1970s. Just for a day. Linda sent him off with me to see Harbourfront—grinning afterward that she was sure this wasn't what he had come for.

. . .

After the Governor General's Award given to her first book, Miriam Mandel published two further collections before dying by suicide in 1982. Sheila Watson edited a posthumous *Collected Poems of Miriam Mandel* (1984).

. . .

Because of changes in the ownership of the Copp Clark series—
sold first to McGill-Queen's and then to Douglas & McIntyre—
my book on Dudek and Souster wasn't published until 1980,
although I had finished it in the summer of 1975. Dudek liked the
book; Souster was disappointed and—somewhat like Birney—felt
betrayed. But he kept his cool.

. . .

In the late 1960s Jamie and his wife, Carol, joined the Maoist-lean-
ing CPC (ML), led by Hardial Bains—undertaking whatever jobs the
party assigned. He would occasionally visit old friends like Warren,
or myself and Linda, warning—without rancour—that when the
revolution occurred compradors like us would be likely among the
first to be executed. On one visit my five-year-old son asked him
how he had hurt his bandaged arm, and Jamie replied that exploita-
tive capitalist owners of his factory decreed that production be done
at excessive speed thus endangering the welfare of the workers, and
Michael responded, "But Jamie, what happened to your arm?" He
left the party when Albania's "Hoxhaist" government collapsed in
early 1990, and resumed writing. Of the various writers associated
with *Tish*, he contributed the most to organizing the October 2001
Tish reunion, "Tish Happens."

. . .

Angela in the late 1980s had decorators emboss several stanzas
from George's poem "The House" in eight-inch letters around the
top of the living room walls at their spacious Kerrisdale house—as a
"gift" to George.

. . .

My editorial work with Coach House was not entirely a happy extension of the *Tish* years. Owner Stan Bevington and several of the other editors saw the press as a "farm team" for commercial publishers—they expected their writers to "mature," or "graduate." Except for George, the *Tish* editors had seen commercial publishers of poetry as regressive, and publication with alternative presses as a means of discrediting the commercials' editorial choices and the canons those choices protected. Despite the disruptive alternative publishing the Coach House editors were doing, bpNichol and I and my partner Linda were the only editors who believed that it was a mistake for writers who wished to disrupt conservative author-centred canons to give credibility to commercial publishers by publishing with them. After bp's death in 1988 George and Mike Ondaatje co-edited a bpNichol selected poems, *An H in the Heart*, for McClelland & Stewart, an act I and others saw as a betrayal of the beliefs that had informed bp's publishing practices. But it was consistent with the Coach House Press "farm team" self-image. They meant well. Dying can be very maturing. Die and the big leagues might want you.

. . .

Tiger Mountain is now more difficult to see—there are numerous high buildings in twenty-first-century Abbotsford—and so it is even less clear whether the tiger is a lamb or the lamb a tiger. If I had asked Ginsberg in that Montreal taxi, he would have told me—correctly—that they were both. If I had asked Ted Whittaker in 1967 he would have said that either is a kingly title. That's why one can have conflicted feelings and still continue, still love. My Linda could sure burn bright.

. . .

When I invited Ray Souster to my home for an interview, he brought his wife with him, who lengthily answered each of my questions before he did. She cared about him. A really conscientious *Tish* writer would have included some of this in his book.

. . .

Retired from teaching, Helen was leading physical conditioning classes in Victoria as late as March 2008, the last time she's written. She had attached to her e-mail a recent photo of herself still easily wearing the forty-year-old blue lamé dress. When Linda had died in 2000, the only "Victoria" dress in her closet was the one she had worn to that snowy New Year's party.

. . .

The history of *Tish* and its multi-nefarious presence in Canadian lit can be tracked after the death of bp through the strangely coherent accumulation of issues and guest editors and contributors of my journal *Open Letter*. You think I'm kidding. "Canada's most intriguing literary journal," poet-blogger Sina Queyras will call it in 2006. Intrigue. That would worry our friend Robin. No, I'm not kidding, I'm scheming. Openly?

8. Just the Beginning

It was a wild, disciplined and impulsive run of nineteen months and nineteen newsletters—and they are not the main event. This is only the beginning of the *Tish* group. In a short time it will be multiplied by four—a "second wave" *Tish* in Vancouver edited by younger writers who have been a part of the newsletter's general community, *SUM* edited from the U.S. by Fred, *Imago* edited by George from Calgary and then London and Montreal, and *Open Letter*, which I will edit from Victoria, Toronto, London and now Clara's Strathroy. In terms of years and issues and numbers of pages there are even larger multiples. It is this multiplying that Tallman will try to emphasize during the 1985 discussion published in *Beyond Tish* as

"A Tishstory," when he says "the subsequent story beyond *Tish* gets even more interesting because, as a group, their communal sense was extraordinarily powerful. [. . .] *Tish* wound down . . . the summer of 1963. And it seemed as though it was over, but actually it was just beginning. A number of the main movers of *Tish* . . . went off to other places. . . . But they continued the activity of the newsletter in its most effective sense. . . ." Maybe that's why I've been writing this book.

There has been a lot of ink spilled over just what years and events should be called "Tish," or who should be considered part of the "Tish group." For me, and for Warren, *Tish* 1–19 was just an extended lift-off and launch. There were booster rockets still to be fired, multiple vehicles to be separated and long journeys to be taken. "*Tish*" for me includes the subsequent 1963–69 issues of the newsletter and the subsequent work of editors such as Daphne Buckle (Marlatt), Gladys (Maria) Hindmarch and Dan McLeod; it includes McLeod's hippie newspaper *The Georgia Straight* and its ten "writing supplements," it includes newsletters and periodicals such as *Motion*, SUM, *Scree*, *Imago*, *Open Letter* and Daphne Marlatt and Paul de Barros's *Periodics*, it includes George's Beaver-Kosmos books, Fred's SUM Books, Daphne's and John Marshall's Island Writing Series. It includes later books by its editors such as Bowering's *Errata*, Marlatt's *Touch to My Tongue* and *Ana Historic*, Wah's *Waiting for Saskatchewan*, my *Abbotsford Guide to India* and *How Linda Died*. Agreed—these books reflect considerable and disparate evolutionary paths. But the kind of argument Polish scholar Eugenia Sojka has made about Marlatt—that her "openness to the Black Mountain projective poetics . . . was the basis of her shift into *écriture feminine*"—can be made in slightly different ways for every one of them. That is, the *Tish* emphases on process and provisionality, on attending to language before "content" and on ascertaining one's locus in a variety of dimensions, on the self as a consciousness in process rather than a stable persona, on language that is multi-discursive, on forms that are dialogical and self-interrogative, on writing that is thinking rather than thought, are the grounds of them all.

However, there have been tactical reasons for both critics and participants to claim otherwise. For antagonists, it has been useful to attempt to confine *Tish* to this 1961–63 period, and regard the subsequent careers of Bowering, Wah, Marlatt and myself as separate, "individualist" phenomena. Such a containment tactic minimizes the powerful and complex collectivity of the *Tish* happening, and transforms its writers into the independent entrepreneurial careerist model that traditional literary criticism in Canada has seen as normal. For critics who are attempting to stake out later territory, it can also be useful to declare *Tish* over and some of its writers moved on to new—and possibly "better"—things. Roy Miki seems to have moved in that direction in 1985 when he exclaimed, "The original *Tish* collective, I should point out, abandoned the project [in 1963] as they went to all those various places" (Niechoda 93). What project, Roy? Susan Rudy and Pauline Butling try this tactic in their book *Writing in Our Time*, when they argue that Marlatt and Wah became in the 1980s part of a new less subtle but more assertive social radicality that superseded the linguistic, philosophical and formal radicalities of *Tish*. For *Tish* writers themselves, a seeming split from *Tish* can make their careers seem "new and improved," as when Fred became perceived as Chinese or Daphne as lesbian feminist. Sojka's article suggests, however, that while writers might sometimes want to take themselves out of *Tish*, the radical poetics of *Tish* can still remain in the writer. Or, as I might have written in *Tish* 1, we're all still full of it.

9. What *Tish* Will Leave Behind

My parents and I are packing up to leave a campsite. "Did you leave anything behind, Bill?" my mother asks—it's her ritual question. "Yes, Doris," my father replies. "Would you like to go back and pick it up?" Not the most promising start for a conversation. However, the group that began talking and theorizing in 1960–61 has kept—intermittently at least—talking among themselves and publicly theorizing. Picking up on each other. Reviewing and cribbing from each other's books. Reproving each other. Teaching others. Several universities as well as the National Archives have bundles or mul-

tiple file boxes of the letters they have exchanged in some decades. Marlatt and Bower-ing have produced volumes of poetics—Wah too has pro-duced a volume, although of course he had to fake it. Wah's work in the 1970s at Selkirk College and David Thomp-son University Centre in the Kootenays led—both directly

George Bowering, Fred Wah, and me, April 2010. Photo by Jean Baird.

and indirectly—to the also continuing phenomenon of KSW/The Kootenay School of Writing—poets for the most part even more upfront about poetics-as-ideology than us Tishers.

Although George would write a history of British Columbia (*Bowering's BC*, 1996) and a portrait—*Egotists and Autocrats* (1999)—of the prime ministers of Canada, Daphne edit books on the histo-ries of Steveston and Vancouver's East End and I write skeptical self-reflexive studies of Prime Minister Kim Campbell (*Reading "KIM" Right*, 1993) and Governor-General Adrienne Clarkson and her consort (*Mr. & Mrs G-G*, 2003), none of us, apart from Jamie and his Marxist-Leninist service, would attempt to intervene more directly in political processes. None of us conferred with the others about political change. Some of us did believe, however, and as I continue to believe, that if we could change the language of litera-ture, we might change how readers viewed and lived in language. We might democratize reading by producing "readerly" poems and fictions that were "open" to reader participation in the produc-tion of their meaning, or by producing critical essays that—rather than asserting "correct" or "authoritative" readings—enacted the process of producing meaning through reading. As I wrote in *From There to Here*, the goal was "the decentralization of human power, whether literary, political, or economic," to enable a citizen to be "a *participant*, the normal and desirable human condition" (21). To offer texts that were dialogic rather than univocal—texts in which the writer was visibly produced by discourse rather than only its clever producer. But to reach the most readers, these texts would have to enter at least local canons and schools. Do you join the canon makers, as George and Mike had the maturely dead bpNichol do, or do you seek some other, most likely subversive, way of dissemination? George often went the national/multinational route, publishing some of his most tradition-challenging books—*Egotists and Autocrats*, his novel *Caprice*—with multinational publishers such as Viking/Penguin. Daphne published books that have indeed changed many readers' understandings of the ideologies of articulation mostly with non-commercial presses—Coach House, Talon, NeWest, Turnstone, Longspoon, Gynergy—presses on which feminist reader-communities have tended to rely. Fred also in the last few decades has found audiences, including unestablished editors and critics, through such publishers. Text spreaders. An unmeasurable something *is* being left behind.

The most important writings that *Tish* will leave on the literary records will be those published by alternative presses, writings that exceed the bounds of individual performance and demonstrate what is possible when texts are conceived as fields of competing languages and desires. There's an ideological opinion. Another remainder will be the possibilities that *Tish* and its writings opened for subsequent writers as its writers moved from the serial poem, as in *Baseball* and *Rings*, through conceptual poems such my *Abbotsford Guide to India* to procedural poems such as Wah's "Music at the Heart of Thinking" or George's *My Darling Nellie Grey* or my *Bardy Google*. Barbara Godard would have noted how these last two books extend the long-standing *Tish* movement from idiolect to sociolect, from the privacy of the lyric to the public discursive field once associated mostly with the epic. I miss Barbara. I'd expected she would live to read this. She would have teased me about once again mischievously putting "Tish" beside "movement."

Paradoxically some of *Tish*'s most distinctive—and ultimately characteristic?—writing has to date received the least attention—mostly because Canadian literature's focus moved in the 1980s and '90s away from writing and toward social representation. The shift didn't affect Fred and Daphne all that much—apart from obscuring her achievement in *Steveston*—but it meant that the work of the KSW poets was less visible than it might have been, and that books such as George's *Kerrisdale Elegies* and *The Moustache* and my *Popular Narratives, The Louis Riel Organ and Piano Co.* and *Abbotsford Guide to India* could be published almost without notice. When someday the *Tish* anthology is published, it will probably include large portions of *Steveston* as well as parts of texts such as *Touch to my Tongue* and *Ana Historic*, perhaps all of *Mountain* as well as parts of *Waiting for Saskatchewan* and *Diamond Grill*, and one or more of Hindmarch's stories from her *The Watery Part of the World* and a Carol Bolt play—maybe *Red Emma* or *One Night Stand*. And a section from Lionel's *Convergences*. I'd probably take the Reid and Dawson pieces from *Tish* itself—pissing off Jamie, I know. Maybe also his much more recent but as elegantly cadenced "Homage to Paul Eluard." Among the numerous Bowering selections I wouldn't want to see "Grandfather," but it would be great to have "Brown Mountain," "Winter Solstice" and a chapter from *Caprice*. My part is probably stuck with my magazine poems "The Piano" and "She Said." But I hope there will be parts of the much longer *Weeds* or *The Clallam*, or maybe one or two of "The Arches," "Riel," "Sarnath," "Dead in Canada," "In Love with Cindy Jones," "Agnes Bernauer," "Postcard Translations" and the "Johnny Hazard" sequence from *Capitalistic Affection!*. That one makes me weep. Too close up. Seriously. And hmmm, I've just reread *The Louis Riel Organ and Piano Co.*—I still like everything in it. Especially that "Wacouster." I wouldn't want to be the poem-cutting editor. Might have to be a fat brown and loose anthology.

SELECTED BIBLIOGRAPHY

Allen, Donald M., ed. *The New American Poetry 1945–1960*. New York: Grove Press, 1960.

Barbour, Douglas, ed. *Beyond Tish*. Edmonton: NeWest Press, 1991. Also published as *West Coast Line* 25:1 (1991).

Bayard, Caroline, and Jack David. Interview with George Bowering. In Bayard and David, eds., *Outposts/Avant-Postes*. Erin, Ontario: Press Porcépic, 1976. 77–99.

Bergé, Carol. *The Vancouver Report*. New York: Fuck You Press, 1964.

Bessai, Diane, and David Jackel. *Figures in a Ground: Canadian Essays on Modern Literature Collected in Honour of Sheila Watson*. Saskatoon: Western Producer Prairie Books, 1978.

Birney, Earle. "On Proletarian Literature." *The Link* 1:3 (1937).

Boughm, Michael. "Olson's Buffalo." http://individual.utoronto.ca/amlit/ olson2.htm. Accessed: 24 December, 2009.

Bowering, George. *Curious*. Toronto: Coach House Press, 1973.

_____. *A Magpie Life: Growing a Writer*. Toronto: Key Porter, 2001.

_____. "Given this Body: An interview with Daphne Marlatt." *Open Letter*, Series 4, Number 3 (Spring 1979): 32–88.

Butling, Pauline. "'Hall of Fame Blocks Women' Re / Righting Literary History." *Open Letter* Series 7, Number 8 (Summer 1990): 60–76.

_____. "Robert Duncan in Vancouver." http://www.kswnet.org/editables/ pdfsAND-scans-WMAG/w10.pdf. Accessed: 22 September, 2009.

Butling, Pauline, and Susan Rudy. *Writing in Our Time.* Waterloo: Wilfrid Laurier University Press, 2005.

Cameron, Elspeth. *Earle Birney: A Life.* Toronto: Viking, 1994.

Carr, Brenda. "Between Continuity and Difference: An Interview with Daphne Marlatt." In Barbour, 99–107.

Cooley, Dennis. "Three Recent Tish Items." *Canadian Poetry* 3 (Fall/Winter 1978): 98.

Creeley, Robert. Vancouver Lectures, August 26, 28, and 29, 1962. Tape-recordings in my private possession.

Davey, Frank. *From There to Here: A Guide to English-Canadian Literature Since 1960.* Erin, Ontario: Press Porcépic, 1974.

_____. "The Beginnings of an End to Coach House Press." *Open Letter,* Series 9, Number 8 (Fall 1994): 40–77.

Davey, Frank, ed. *Tish 1–19.* Vancouver: Talonbooks, 1975.

Djwa, Sandra. *Professing English: A Life of Roy Daniells.* Toronto: University of Toronto Press, 2002.

Duncan, Robert. "Ideas of the Meaning of Form." *Kulchur* 1:4 (1961): 60–74.

_____. *Letters.* Highlands, NC: Jargon, 1958.

_____. "Notes from a Reading at The Poetry Center, San Francisco, March 1, 1964," *The Floating Bear* 31 (1965): [12–13].

_____. Vancouver Lectures, July 23, 24, and 25, 1961. Tape-recordings in my private possession.

Fee, Margery, and Sneja Gunew. "An Interview with Fred Wah." http://www.canlit.ca/interviews.php?interview=1 Accessed 10 October, 2009.

Frye, Northrop. *The Bush Garden: Essays on the Canadian Imagination.* Toronto: House of Anansi, 1971.

Gervais, C.H., ed. *The Writing Life: Historical & Critical Views of the Tish Movement.* Windsor: Black Moss Press, 1976.

Godard, Barbara. "Epi(pro)logue: In Pursuit of the Long Poem." *Open Letter,* Series 6, Numbers 2–3 (Summer–Fall 1985): 301–335.

Mandel, Eli. "The Death of the Long Poem." *Open Letter,* Series 6, Numbers 2–3 (Summer–Fall 1985): 11–30.

Mathews, Robin. "Poetics: The Struggle for Voice in Canada," *CVII* 2:4 (December 1976): 6–7.